HOW
TRUST
WORKS

HOW
TRUST
WORKS

The Science of
How Relationships Are
Built, Broken, and Repaired

PETER H. KIM, PH.D.

FLATIRON
BOOKS
NEW YORK

HOW TRUST WORKS. Copyright © 2023 by Peter H. Kim. All rights reserved. Printed in the United States of America. For information, address Flatiron Books, 120 Broadway, New York, NY 10271.

www.flatironbooks.com

The Library of Congress Cataloging-in-Publication Data is available upon request.

ISBN 978-1-250-83815-5 (hardcover)
ISBN 978-1-250-83816-2 (ebook)

Our books may be purchased in bulk for promotional, educational, or business use. Please contact your local bookseller or the Macmillan Corporate and Premium Sales Department at 1-800-221-7945, extension 5442, or by email at MacmillanSpecialMarkets@macmillan.com.

First Edition: 2023

10 9 8 7 6 5 4 3 2 1

To Augustine, Julia, and Beth—
you are my purpose and my inspiration

CONTENTS

HOW
TRUST
WORKS

A NOTE FROM THE AUTHOR

My father was a dreamer. He had to be. How else could someone nearing middle age, with only moderate fluency in English, decide to take his wife and two infants on a two-year journey from South Korea through South America to arrive in the U.S., where his education would be meaningless and where he would have few prospects for work? Like countless other immigrants, he believed the U.S. was filled with promise and worth the risk.

But my family's attempts to find a better life in this country did not follow a simple path. My nondrinking father became a bartender. My mother waited tables. Eventually, they saved enough to start a small business. But as they ran that little shop, they were robbed and assaulted on multiple occasions by members of the same community their business served. My family moved every few years in search of safer neighborhoods and better schools and eventually managed to buy a modest house. But my parents lost that house to foreclosure a few years later, when their small business ultimately failed, and they were forced to return to the kind of life they had worked so hard to escape. In that wake, my mother kept my family afloat by getting her Realtor's license and selling houses she could never afford, while my father gained temporary work as a driver. Then one day, my father's work forced him to lift something far too heavy. It severely injured his spine and left him unable to walk without crippling pain for the remaining decades of his life.

Yet my father always managed to repair his trust in the American dream, despite how often that trust was bruised or shattered. Even though he could no longer work and was forced to lie in bed with a body that refused to mend. And even when, in time, he could only live most of that dream through me.

But this isn't just my father's story. Regardless of who we are or where we were born, we all know what it means to have our trust broken. Maybe, like my father, you believed that hard work would bring you a better life, but now struggle to make ends meet due to circumstances beyond your control. Perhaps you witnessed the brutality of a police officer, the abuse of a supervisor, or the dishonesty of a government official. You may have discovered too late that your health insurance ultimately means little due to loopholes in the fine print or getting your claim rejected. Or maybe you were betrayed by a close friend, colleague, or life partner you thought was on your side.

You probably also know the sting of having your own trustworthiness called into question—of how your relationships, reputation, and prospects for the future can be damaged by things you may have done, failed to do, or were falsely accused of doing. To experience guilt and struggle to achieve redemption, that is part of our life journey too. Regardless of the part we play in these stories, we all need to cope with the sense of loss and betrayal and somehow find a way to move forward. Because the truth is that we are all vulnerable to these experiences. That is what it means to trust.

It is hard to overstate the importance of trust in society. Trust plays a central role in how we navigate almost every aspect of our social world. Yet despite that importance, it has become clear both in my own life and as a research scientist studying this topic that we generally assess the trustworthiness of others quite poorly. I had glimpses of this shortcoming very early as a child, as we moved frequently from one new community to another in our search for a better life. This made the need to trust (and gain the trust of) strangers an ongoing challenge. It also made me aware of how seemingly insignificant details, such as where I lived, the jobs my parents held, or what they thought I represented, could make such an important difference in the trust others placed in me—who chose me as a friend, whether I was offered a part-time job, or whether I was welcomed into someone's home.

As an outsider struggling to navigate unfamiliar waters without social or economic safety nets, those experiences instilled hard-learned lessons. And they eventually established some enduring questions in my life. How do we come to trust and mistrust one another, and why are the beliefs that underlie those decisions so often wrong? How do those beliefs ultimately affect the way we relate, strive, and navigate through the world? And if those beliefs are wrong, what, if anything, can we do to correct them?

These questions spurred my interest in the social sciences and my fascination with both fictional and real-life accounts of these journeys, from the story of Caleb in John Steinbeck's *East of Eden,* who struggled to believe he could become a good person, to the tumultuous journey of Rodrigo Mendoza, the slave trader turned priest from the movie *The Mission,* and the enigmatic duality of Alfred Nobel, the pacifist who founded the Nobel Prize but who also built his fortune by inventing and manufacturing the explosives used to kill so many in war. Regardless of their form, I have always been gripped by stories of guilt and redemption.

Yet as I began my career as a social scientist, I was also struck by how little we really knew about this topic. The scientific literature on trust, its violation, and its repair was at its infancy when I started. And even today, public discourse in this domain is largely dominated by anecdotes and conjecture. That is why I have devoted over two decades of my life to these questions. And though we still don't have the complete picture (since that will probably take at least another lifetime of study), the seemingly endless breaches of trust that afflict our world, and so many of us in it, have ultimately underscored the need to report what I have found thus far.

For those who have struggled with trust or mistrust and glimpsed how the beliefs that affect those sentiments can be biased or entirely mistaken. For those who have faced the violation of trust as either offender or victim and seek to understand how one might repair those relationships. For those who seek to understand how trust can be established with new people or groups and ultimately strengthened. And for those who seek some way to reconcile our increasingly polarized sociopolitical divides and understand how we can all better manage trust in society. I hope this book makes a positive difference.

INTRODUCTION

I f I asked you how important trust is in your life, I have no doubt you would say it is essential. We intuitively understand that trust is a critical foundation that allows us to form new friendships; find a partner, job, or home; start and run a business; and engage in any number of transactions, especially in the internet economy. But even though we are all acutely aware of the importance of trust, a growing body of evidence reveals that we consistently misjudge the trustworthiness of other people—and we are even worse at defending our own trustworthiness when it comes under fire. The really bad news is that this problem seems to be getting worse, not better.

A 2019 report by the Pew Research Center found that 64 percent of respondents in the United States felt that their trust in one another has diminished, and 75 percent indicated that their trust in the federal government has diminished. A large majority also indicated that this diminished trust has made it harder to solve many of the nation's problems and that it was very important for the country to improve these plummeting trust levels.[1] A 2021 report by the United Nations Department of Economic and Social Affairs likewise concludes that although people's trust in institutions varies significantly across countries, there has been a broad decline in that trust worldwide since 2000.[2] The percentage of the population across three broad parts of the globe (which the authors referred to as Afro, Euro, and Latino regions) who expressed confidence in their national government or parliament dropped from a peak of 46 percent in 2006 to just 36 percent by 2019. Moreover, trust in financial institutions across these countries has dropped from 55 percent to 46 percent over the same period.

It might therefore be surprising to hear that the fundamental problem with trust in society is not our failure to establish it. We actually tend to exhibit quite high levels of trust in those we don't know, and that is a good thing. This high initial trust makes it easier to make friends, change jobs, and venture outside our homes without wearing a bulletproof vest. Instead, our problems with trust arise because that high initial trust is also exceedingly fragile. It can take just one questionable incident, unsubstantiated allegation, or quietly whispered rumor for trust to be damaged. And despite how easily and often trust can be violated, we know surprisingly little about how to respond effectively when that happens. Even worse, our natural reactions to such incidents quite often fail to help and can even make the repair of trust less likely, as an ineffectual apology or defense can reinforce the notion that mistrust was warranted in the first place.

When I began my career as a social scientist, I was surprised at how little substantive research had been conducted on these issues. Research on trust up to that point had been limited to rudimentary economic games, where participants would simply choose whether or not to cooperate with an unknown counterpart based on the incentives. These games offered a useful starting point for understanding how people might behave in interpersonal situations. However, they ultimately failed to capture the broad scope of social, psychological, institutional, and cultural considerations that underlie the richness and dynamic complexity of trust as it is experienced in the real world.[3]

Even worse, discussions of trust, its violation, and its repair by both social scientists and practitioners still relied quite heavily on case studies and other anecdotes. Such stories could certainly provide vivid and compelling accounts of these experiences. However, they ultimately fail to dig below the surface to consider the underlying psychological mechanisms that might explain why even the exact same attempts to repair trust may succeed in some cases but not others. I have devoted most of my career to addressing these unanswered—and mostly unasked—questions. And it is that more than twenty-year scientific effort—with its wide range of surprising, and sometimes disturbing, insights—that forms the foundation of this book.

In the years since I started sharing some of my initial findings with other research scientists, students, executives, journalists, family, and friends, I have been constantly reminded of the extraordinary resonance these issues have with people. No matter the audience, this work triggers animated conversations and heartfelt questions, and it often leads people to share their own deeply personal stories of their struggles to build and maintain trust with others. It is, thus, clear to me that people yearn for this kind of knowledge.

In this book, I will explain the intricacies of my research through the lens of the two most powerful determinants of trust. The first is *competence*, or the belief that someone possesses the technical and interpersonal skills that are required for a task. And the second is *integrity*, or the belief that someone will adhere to a set of principles one finds acceptable. Both are important, but the evidence makes clear that we also interpret these two factors quite differently when we perceive others.

Competence enjoys a positive bias. We tend to take a single successful performance as a reliable signal of competence, based on the assumption that those without competence would not be able to perform well in any circumstance. But we're also willing to discount a single poor performance as a signal of incompetence, based on the assumption that even highly competent people can occasionally fall short of what they would normally be able to achieve. Thus, if a trust violation is perceived to be a matter of competence, it can often be overcome.

In the case of integrity, however, the bias is reversed. We intuitively believe that those with high integrity would refrain from dishonest behavior in *any* situation, whereas those with low integrity will act either honestly or dishonestly depending on the incentives. For this reason, people won't take a single honest behavior as a signal of high integrity, since we generally assume that anyone can behave honestly at least some of the time. But we see a single dishonest behavior as a reliable signal of low integrity, based on the assumption that only those with low integrity would ever act in dishonest ways. Thus, it is much harder to overcome a trust violation if it is perceived to be a matter of integrity.

There may be no better illustration of these tendencies than the public's perceptions of Donald Trump, a man who has routinely engaged in strategically nonsensical acts, like admitting that Russia helped him win the presidency, only to deny it twenty minutes later.[4] His followers seem willing to filter his shortcomings through the lens of competence. He doesn't have the skills (low competence) because he's "not a politician," which his supporters see as a good thing, compared to career politicians, who are practiced at lying (low integrity) for a living. In contrast, those on the other side perceive Mr. Trump's actions to be the result of profound selfishness, the pursuit of power, and a complete disregard for right and wrong—unforgivable violations of integrity.

Note that the important factor is how the behavior is perceived, not the behavior itself. In this book, I will illustrate the implications of my research by describing the unexpected and often-disastrous outcomes of such perceptions, as well as our often erroneous assumptions about how trust is developed and how trust violations should be handled. We will review the sex scandals of several well-known public figures (to explore why, for example, the public might have forgiven Arnold Schwarzenegger, but not Bill Clinton, when those incidents were first reported). We will consider the refusal of Linda Fairstein, the Central Park Five's lead prosecutor, to apologize for pursuing those convictions, which were later vacated (and why it might not have helped even if she had apologized). We will examine the Italian fashion company Dolce & Gabbana's struggle to overcome a racial controversy in China, as well as the Sackler family's efforts to evade culpability for their role in the opioid crisis. And we'll also look at experiences with infidelity and domestic abuse that don't often make headlines.

The book will, furthermore, build on these insights to confront the challenges of mistrust at a societal level. I'll introduce you to Father Greg, who founded Homeboy Industries in the most dangerous part of Los Angeles, to rehabilitate gang members, and then draw on his astounding success to discuss how poorly we deal with matters of justice and redemption in general. We will revisit the violent clashes at the 2017 Unite the Right rally in Charlottesville, Virginia, the divergent reactions to the police killings of Breonna Taylor and George Floyd, and the bloody legacy of the Great Partition of India, to consider how our responses can be shaped by our group memberships. We will consider how different cultures, both between countries and within the same country, can develop very different views about what constitutes an irredeemable transgression. And we will also compare the attempts in the Nuremberg trials in West Germany, the Truth and

Reconciliation Commission in South Africa, and the Gacaca courts in Rwanda to address gross human rights abuses and heal those divided nations.

As I reflect on where things stand, at the time of this writing, examples of how trust has been threatened around the world seem endless. A 2021 report by a Brazilian senate committee accused the country's president, Jair Bolsonaro, of committing crimes against humanity for letting the COVID-19 virus rip through the country and kill hundreds of thousands of people in a failed bid to achieve herd immunity.[5] The United Kingdom's government has been riddled by a host of scandals, including the 2009 disclosure of widespread thefts by members of Parliament through fraudulent expense claims,[6] the April 2022 resignation of member of Parliament Neil Parish after being caught watching pornography on his phone, twice, in the House of Commons,[7] and the forced resignation of Prime Minister Boris Johnson on July 7, 2022, after a historic revolt within his government over a series of ethics scandals.[8] A 2021 Social Weather Stations (SWS) survey in the Philippines found that 51 percent of that country's adults have difficulty spotting fake news on television, radio, or social media.[9] Moreover, most major economies have witnessed growing levels of income inequality over the past three decades,[10] a condition that is negatively related to trust.[11]

But the decline in trust seems particularly acute in the United States. A 2021 poll by the Impact Genome Project and the Associated Press–NORC Center for Public Affairs Research found that 18 percent of U.S. adults, or about forty-six million people, say they have just one person or no one they can trust for help in their personal lives.[12] Twenty percent, or forty-nine million people, say they have just one person or nobody they can trust to help draft a résumé, connect to an employer, or navigate workplace challenges. Moreover, 36 percent of those below the federal poverty level report having no one to turn to for help.

The U.S. has struggled with myriad failures, rampant misinformation, and persistent vaccine hesitancy during the COVID-19 pandemic. We have confronted one another over the teaching of critical race theory and the role of affirmative action in our schools. We have reeled from countless stories of sexual harassment at the workplace and witnessed the ravages of drug addiction, homelessness, and mass shootings in our neighborhoods. And many have found it increasingly difficult to discuss social, environmental, and political differences with friends or family at their own dining tables.

Some have suggested that the January 6, 2021, assault on the U.S. Capitol was the point where this country hit rock bottom. And though the realist in me worries that things can still get worse, it certainly seems clear that trust in this country has never been damaged to this degree in recent times. Yet a silver lining from our reaching this semblance of a bottom can be found in the extent to which that horrific event has spurred a growing recognition by at least some political leaders, and certainly by the broader public, of the need to change course. Of the need to move beyond cynical partisanship, conspiracy thinking, and self-serving attacks on the truth. Of the need to reestablish our faith and *trust* in the democratic principles of our country, in our institutions, in facts, and in one another—the neighbors, coworkers, acquaintances, friends, and family members with whom our trust can be established, violated, and repaired day-to-day. We have never been in more need of a serious conversation about how to repair trust, a conversation based on rigorous scientific research on this topic rather than mere conjecture, a conversation that can help us make sense of these dark times and chart a path forward.

My goal for this book is to give you a better understanding of how trust can arise, how it is damaged, and what it means to repair it, as well as practical insights into how to rebuild your own social connections in the face of the turmoil, disappointments, betrayals, and tragedies we so frequently experience. However, this book is *not* intended to be a superficial step-by-step guide for those who are only interested in crude quick fixes. It deliberately avoids that approach, not only because too much of what this research has uncovered is ripe for abuse but also because efforts to apply the book's findings without taking the time to understand their nuances first can easily backfire. Yet the practical lessons are certainly there for those who take the time to discern them. And my hope is that, by the end, you will have ultimately acquired a substantive tool kit that will help you better evaluate how to build, maintain, and repair trust not only in your personal relationships but also with society.

Overall, this book represents the culmination of my efforts to address a glaring gap in our understanding of how to address some of the most important experiences in our lives. I have devoted more than two decades of my life to developing a rigorous body of scientific knowledge where very little had previously existed. The insights I will share with you span what has too often been an enormous gulf between fundamental knowledge and real-world relevance. And my hope, given how often trust, its violation, and its repair remain central concerns in so many of our lives, is that this work gives readers a broader, deeper, and more substantive basis from which they might better address these challenges. In these extraordinarily turbulent times, it is clear we need this help more than ever.

1

YOU'RE NOT AS
CYNICAL AS YOU THINK

Dale's first question when meeting Sam is whether Sam is in any way associated with either the government or Dale's former employer. He doesn't seem reassured when Sam answers no. Then why is Sam talking to him for free? It must all be part of an intricate scheme to "subdue" him and place him "under firm control."

Sam asks, "Why would they want to do that?" Dale explains it's because he knows too much about the fraud, lies, and deceit in the highest places. Sam questions how he could know this as a sanitation worker for the municipality. The question visibly offends Dale, and he exclaims, "There are more secrets in people's trash than in the CIA!" His phones are tapped, his mail intercepted and inspected, and there was a mysterious fire in his apartment only days after he filed a complaint against a police officer.

When Sam inquires how long it has been since Dale last went out with friends, Dale has to think hard before answering, "Four years ago." Why so long? Is he a recluse by nature? Dale responds, "Not at all"; he is quite gregarious. But you never know when something you have said in company will be used against you, and those so-called friends had been asking too many intrusive questions lately.

When Sam asks, "So what do you do all alone at home?" Dale laughs bitterly and exclaims, "Won't they love to know my next moves!" At the end of the conversation, Dale insists on inspecting Sam's phone jacks and the undersurfaces of his desk. He explains, "You can never be too careful."

Dale is not an ordinary person. He was diagnosed with paranoid personality disorder, as Sam Vaknin, a writer and professor of psychology, detailed in a book about Dale and hundreds of others diagnosed with narcissistic and antisocial personality disorders.[1] And my guess is that, just from reading this text, you could tell that Dale could use some help.

But this depiction of Dale's outlook on the world is not far from how most of us assume trust works. We generally believe that trust starts at zero and only builds gradually over time as we learn more about one another. We also believe this approach is prudent and rational. Why would we ever trust someone we don't know, especially when that puts us at risk?

The wisdom of such caution not only makes intuitive sense but also has been underscored by traditional scientific thinking. Research on trust has typically been based on the notion that people are selfish and exploitive. And this has led social scientists to underscore the need for us to *not* trust others unless it is clearly warranted.

This view is perhaps most starkly articulated in the work of Oliver E. Williamson, one of two recipients of the 2009 Nobel Prize in economics. Economists care about trust because it is closely connected to economic activity, with the lack of trust, for example, typically leading to lower wages, profits, and employment. However, Williamson's work differed from that of other economists, who focused on the independent decisions of rational actors in a free market, by considering how such actors might agree to cooperate with one another in more enduring relationships. He, furthermore, explored the challenges people can face in those relationships by grounding his work on a central assumption about human nature—that people are opportunistic.

This assumption takes a step beyond the premise that people are self-interested.[2] Being self-interested, as the entire field of economics presumes us to be, means that each of us will continuously seek to satisfy our own preferences and act in ways that will maximize our self-benefit (such as by striving to increase our earnings). But as Williamson observed, that assumption also presumes that we will candidly disclose all pertinent information when asked and that we will reliably honor our agreements. Being opportunistic, in contrast, means that we will not only seek to satisfy our own preferences but that we will also do so with guile—with deceitful cunning.

Williamson draws on this darker portrayal of human nature to underscore the notion that people won't necessarily tell the truth, behave responsibly, or fulfill their promises if doing so interferes with getting what they want. And he combined this assumption with the notion that we are also limited in our ability to anticipate and address all the ways in which that might happen, to highlight the risks of making ourselves vulnerable to others' actions.

Given these concerns, the dominant focus of this area of research, known as "transaction cost economics" (due to its focus on how to organize transactions in ways that would minimize economic losses), has thus been on how individuals might mitigate these hazards.* It has explored how people might reduce their vulnerability and risk in the face of others' fundamentally opportunistic nature. And it is for that reason that transaction cost economists' general stance toward trust has been that we should ultimately avoid exhibiting it when possible.

Social scientists have defined *trust* as "a psychological state comprising the intention to accept vulnerability based on positive expectations of the intentions or behavior of another."[3] This definition may seem like a lot to digest. However, we only need to unpack its three major elements to develop a better sense of what trust really means—1) trust as a psychological state, 2) trust as a willingness to be vulnerable, and 3) trust as a function of the positive expectations one might have about another.

Let's start with the last element of this definition, the notion that trust is based on positive expectations about the intentions or behavior of another. This is an obvious problem for trust from the perspective of transaction cost economics, given its assumption that people would pursue their own interests in ways that are sly, cunning, and deceitful. If that's the case, then what might provide the basis for us to hold positive expectations about others despite their inherently opportunistic nature? If people are bound to take

---

* Although this field has typically concerned how economic actors might use contracts as formal legal instruments to achieve these ends in the context of business relationships, it is important to note that contracts have a much broader meaning as well. A contract can concern any form of agreement. It can either be written or simply spoken. A contract can be explicit, but it can also take the form of implicit assumptions by those involved. These kinds of agreements are, furthermore, not limited to formal business relationships but can also arise among any two or more parties, including family members, friends, neighbors, and complete strangers.

advantage of you to serve their own interests, as these economists suggest, then how would anyone trust anyone else?

The answer, according to this perspective, is to find ways to discourage them from acting upon those opportunistic inclinations. This recommendation has direct implications for the second condition for trust I noted earlier, the intention to accept vulnerability. For example, if Susan and Mark are thinking about starting a business together, and Susan is worried that Mark may not uphold his part of the bargain, then Susan can try to include clauses in their contract that articulate what the consequences would be if her expectations are not met. Doing so can make it less desirable for Mark to cheat, and thus lower Susan's vulnerability to those kinds of problems.

Of course, those kinds of preventative measures probably won't eliminate all risk. None of us can ever foresee all the ways in which agreements can be violated, and we often don't really know whether the kinds of clauses we might add to protect ourselves would be adequate. Mark could fulfill the letter of his contract with Susan, for example, but he may still find countless ways of violating that agreement's spirit, such as by compromising the quality of what he has agreed to deliver in ways that are harder to notice and measure until well after the enforcement period has ended. Thus, Susan may still need to accept some level of risk, despite her efforts to mitigate it. Nevertheless, the core message from transaction cost economists regarding the second condition for trust—namely, the acceptance of vulnerability—remains that we should *not* accept vulnerability to the extent that we can avoid it. It suggests that we should exhibit as little trust as reasonably possible and ultimately as a last resort.

Finally, the very first element of how social scientists have defined trust, the depiction of trust as a psychological state, seeks to address the notion that we can sometimes *appear* as if we trust another person, even when we don't trust that person at all. We may not possess positive expectations about that individual or wish to make ourselves vulnerable to their actions. But we may still act as if we trust that person if there are other reasons to behave that way. In the case of Susan and Mark's new business venture, for example, Susan may not think well of Mark or want to risk running a business with him. But she may still start that venture with Mark if the potential upsides of the business are attractive enough, she has no other options for getting that business started, and she believes she can find ways to prevent Mark from doing too much damage.

From the standpoint of economists, Susan's ultimate decision to start the business with Mark is what really matters. She has acted as if she trusted Mark, and that is what will allow each of them (as well as the broader economy) to reap the benefits of their collective endeavor. But from an interpersonal standpoint, my sense is that few of us are likely to believe that Susan really trusts Mark at all.

There is a big difference between whether people make themselves vulnerable despite the risk it would entail or exhibit the same behavior because its associated risk and vulnerability have been removed. Efforts to achieve cooperation by reducing risk, as transaction cost economics has explored, are ultimately about taking steps to eliminate the need for trust. Letting your teenage daughter go on a date so long as you can come along, for example, doesn't mean you trust her would-be Romeo. Real trust, in contrast, requires a willingness to make yourself vulnerable based on the belief that others won't let you down, even though they could. From the standpoint of traditional thinking about trust, the latter wouldn't really make sense. Why would we ever not want to protect ourselves from that kind of danger?

Now, let's keep these points in mind as I recount the following example. Not too long ago, I ordered dinner for my family and friends from a new restaurant to be delivered to my home. This involved giving my credit card number and security code to a stranger for processing and started a sequence of steps through which several other strangers with unknown personal histories and motivations prepared and assembled ingredients that were purchased from a wide range of unknown farmers, distributors, and resellers. These meals were then picked up by yet another stranger, who wasn't even affiliated with the restaurant, for transport through a delivery service to my address. And those in my home then proceeded to consume the meals without drawing straws to see who would taste them first to make sure they hadn't been poisoned.

I am sure people like Dale from the start of this chapter would consider this foolish. He could easily refer me to the famous case of Typhoid Mary, whose cooking infected fifty-three people with typhoid fever and killed three of them. He could also refer me to the fact that more than half of the estimated seventy-three thousand cases of potentially deadly *E. coli* infection that occur in the U.S. each year are transmitted through food.[4] I would have to acknowledge the truth of those statements, as well as the fact that, by giving my credit card information to a complete stranger, I could have easily become a victim of fraud. Moreover, I would likewise have to admit that when I interact with new people in other aspects of my life, my general expectation has been that they won't cause me harm, that they will follow through on their promises, and that they will ultimately deserve the trust I place in them.

Maybe this makes me seem naive and idealistic. But maybe it also makes me sound just like you. In fact, a growing body of scientific evidence reveals that people can exhibit surprisingly high levels of trust in those they don't know. This can be illustrated by one of the earliest experiments on trust I conducted with researchers Donald Ferrin, Cecily Cooper, and Kurt Dirks.[5] In this experiment, we asked participants to watch a videotaped job interview for a position in the tax department of an accounting firm, called McNeale and Associates, and then provide their own evaluation of the job candidate. Let's review this exchange so you can form your own opinions about this applicant.

During the video, the interviewer notes, "So I see here that you have had your CPA [Certified Public Accountant certification] for a few years."

The applicant responds, "Yes, that's right. I have quite a bit of experience in that area, and I feel that I would be suited for the type of position that you advertised."

The interviewer then asks why the applicant would like to work at this company. And the candidate responds, "Well, there are actually quite a few reasons. First of all, McNeale is known for its training and development programs. I would like the chance to be able to take advantage of that. Then, there's the fact that McNeale has a generally good reputation as a place to work and is thought highly of in the area of public accounting. [*pause*] And I also have a few people I know who work here, in various departments, and they all seem to really enjoy working here and just generally speak highly of the firm. I get the impression that it would be a good fit for me."

Finally, when the interviewer asks the candidate what skill sets the candidate would bring to the company, the candidate responds, "Well, let's see. Besides being competent in all the areas of individual and corporate tax, I've worked really hard to become an expert in estate tax planning—I took extra classes and professional development courses, plus in my last job, I was able to get assigned to several clients where I could work on estate tax planning. Also, I am easy to get along with, and people tell me I'm a very good team member. And finally, I've learned to be well organized, which I think is critical during tax season when you have to juggle so many clients and returns and deadlines."

What would your opinion be of this candidate? To what extent would you trust and be willing to hire this person? Hiring anyone for a job can pose a real risk for employers, especially when it involves major responsibilities, such as the kind of work a tax accountant would be expected to perform. Trust can, therefore, play a major role in those decisions. We also know that it is quite easy for job applicants to falsify details on their résumé. Though the data on this phenomenon varies, recent reports suggest that anywhere from 30 percent to 78 percent of job applicants admit to lying on their résumés, with the majority of those never getting caught.[6] Moreover, it is just as possible that the candidate's verbal claims during the video were made-up; those claims certainly weren't verified by the interviewer in any way during the conversation. All we have are the candidate's assertions and the need to decide how much to trust her.

The logical answer, from the perspective of traditional scientific thinking about trust, is straightforward. The candidate is a stranger who could have easily fabricated any or even all the claims that were made in the interview to get hired. None of those claims were verified, so we can only rely on this person's word. Moreover, hiring the wrong person could easily expose the accounting firm to significant legal and financial risk. Thus, the rational thing to do from this traditional perspective would be not to trust the candidate at all, at least until the candidate's claims could be independently verified.

Yet this was not what our study found. We gauged trust in this candidate with several multi-item scales that had been validated by prior trust research, which asked participants to respond to statements like "I would give the candidate a task or problem that was critical to me, even if I could not monitor her actions" (on a range of 1–7, where 1 means "strongly agree" and 7 means "strongly disagree"). The results revealed that trust was never close to the bottom, as traditional depictions of trust would lead us to assume. Instead, participants' initial levels of trust were remarkably high in both this and other experiments we had conducted, typically around or even above the midpoint of these scales.

How should we respond to these findings? If you are anything like me, someone who has admitted to being a bit idealistic and naive, you are likely to find these results rather obvious. In fact, they were so obvious to my entire research team that we did not at first even run this experiment. We simply expected people to exhibit some initial trust in this candidate based on the interview, and this led us instead to focus on addressing what we considered to be more interesting questions of how that trust might be violated and subsequently repaired. However, the initial reviewers of our work did not share our sentiment. Their minds had already been committed to the traditional premise that trust starts at zero and would only increase gradually over time. That is why we decided to conduct this additional experiment to challenge those assumptions with clear evidence.

Even so, one might still question whether these findings represent actual trust, or at least the kind of trust we typically think about with our closest friends and family. It is certainly true that trust in close relationships is different from the trust we might initially exhibit in a stranger. Trust in close relationships is often stronger than trust in strangers, at least in part because it is based on more information about the trusted party. Trust in close relationships can also be based on different types of considerations and motivations, due to the different stakes involved, as I will describe a bit later in this chapter. However, it would be hard to say that these results don't represent trust, given that they are based on the same widely accepted measures of trust that have been used in other trust studies.

Finally, a third concern one might raise is that even if these results do provide evidence that people can exhibit high initial trust in those they do not know, this kind of trust is ultimately less important than trust in close relationships. That probably seems quite intuitive. Matters of trust in our closest relationships (with our spouse, parents, siblings, and lifelong friends) are likely to be particularly salient to most of us, and this is the kind of trust that we may be keenest to nurture. Yet trust in non-close relationships can often be just as important as trust in close relationships, and there is little doubt that it is also far more common.

We can make ourselves just as vulnerable to risk by relocating to another part of the country to accept a job offer with a new company, for example, as we would by relocating to the same location to be with a romantic partner we have known for years. Trust should, therefore, play an important role in either case. Moreover, whereas the U.S. Census Bureau reports that the average family consisted of just 3.15 persons in 2020 and the Survey Center on American Life reported in 2021 that 87 percent of us have ten or fewer close friends,[7,8] there is little doubt that our circle of non-close relationships is comparatively much larger. This numerical difference is also the reason why we are much likelier to find jobs not through those with whom our relationships are strong but rather through those with whom our relationships are weak, as sociologist Mark Granovetter has discovered through his seminal work on this topic.[9]

Even further, the study of non-close relationships also provides important advantages for our understanding of trust. It is ultimately essential for us to understand how trust works across a broader swath of society, such as with leaders, public figures, organizations, and government institutions. Moreover, because trust in newly formed relationships tends to be much more fragile than in relationships where we have much more invested, trust in non-close relationships can be more sensitive to and more revealing of influences that are often obscured in stronger relationships. It's like a canary in a coal mine, whose very delicateness is precisely what provides the basis for keener insight—an understanding of how, when, whom, and why we trust or distrust that would be far less apparent if we focused on trust in a more robust form.

It would, therefore, be a mistake to discount evidence of high initial trust in those one does not really know as invalid or unimportant. This point is something my field has now come to recognize and embrace, not only with several awards for the research that helped establish this new way of thinking but also through the growing body of research that has sought to build on these ideas. Instead, the more prudent way to respond to these findings would be to do two things. First, we should devote more careful attention to how this high initial trust might arise. And second, we should seek better insight into the ways in which that high initial trust might and might not differ from trust in closer relationships.

Trust researchers have begun to address the first part of this agenda by identifying three broad categories of influences that can affect people's initial trust in those they do not know. First, at the broadest level, social scientists have recognized that people's initial trust in others can depend on considerations that have less to do with the specific people involved than the context in which that trust might be displayed. This is underscored by the early studies on trust I briefly mentioned in the introduction, which devoted the bulk of their attention to how people would behave in mixed-motive situations (that is, circumstances where participants would be collectively better off if they cooperated but also possessed individual incentives not to do so). This type of situation is quite common in the world, as one might observe in societal debates about environmental conservation, military arms races, and both personal and corporate taxation. Substantial research in this domain has, furthermore, made clear how changes to the incentives each party faces for acting cooperatively, versus in a more individualistic manner, can affect the trust they are likely to exhibit.

These incentives can depend on a host of considerations. This includes immediate economic payoffs, reputational considerations, the potential for legal prosecution, and the threat of social disapproval or ostracism. Each of these considerations can meaningfully affect people's willingness to exhibit trust in others. For example, most of us are presumably less likely to be concerned about others harming us when those specific actions would result in their getting fired, sued, or arrested. Likewise, in the job interview study described earlier, participants may have been more inclined to trust the candidate's own retelling of their qualifications because they knew lying

could backfire if those qualifications were checked. However, these effects ar(
not based on knowing anything about the people involved, beyond the bas:
assumption that those individuals are not so irrational that they would wa
to make themselves worse off. Instead, this kind of trust is based on our be
that society's laws, regulations, norms, and institutions will keep other pe(
in check, even when we don't know them well or at all. And though t}
technically more about reducing risk than increasing trust, these con:
ations can still be of interest to social scientists who are primarily inte
in trusting behaviors (that is, whether people act as if they trust ot}
in how trust may be affected by incentives that don't mitigate risk er

The second factor that can affect people's initial trust in those
not know can be found in each one of us. Studies have found t}
of us are fundamentally predisposed to trust others due to our p
traits.[10] This predisposition may seem foolhardy to those who
inclined. However, the scientific evidence generally suggests tha:
naive at all. Psychologist Julian Rotter has found, for example
trustors" are less likely to be unhappy, conflicted, or maladjus:
over, his work suggests that if gullibility means being naive or
trustors are *not* more gullible than those who are predispose(
based on how they are subsequently treated.

These findings are also consistent with other research o
outlooks on the world can affect their well-being. The bas:
those studies is that we are generally better off when we ha:
perceptions of ourselves, the world, and the future than w
tions are accurate. In one classic set of experiments, for e)
Lauren Alloy and Lyn Abramson tested participants fo1
psychological instrument called the Beck Depression '
asked them to press a button that could trigger a gre(
pants were asked to estimate the degree to which their
the button caused the light to flash.[12] The results reve
of depressed participants were surprisingly accurate.
mates of nondepressed participants. In short, havir
of the world was not related to being happier; if :
accuracy were negatively correlated. A similar cor

other side of the same coin, was also underscored by psychologists Shelley Taylor and Jonathan Brown, who found that people in general not only tend to hold unrealistically positive views of themselves, their control over events, and their future but that such positive illusions generally improved well-being.[13] These results suggest that even overly optimistic views of what will happen, such as when we err on the side of trusting others, can generally be a good thing for our mental health and functioning.

Of course, positive illusions can also be detrimental when they become too unrealistic. It doesn't help if people believe they can control the rotation of the earth with their minds, for example, or if positive illusions prevent people from taking sensible preventive actions for medical risks.[14] However, the evidence indicates that we are generally better off erring on the side of positive outlooks for a host of reasons. Those illusions not only make us happier but also help us engage in productive and creative work, because they help empower healthy actions (such as investing in oneself or applying for a better job). Likewise, similar implications can arise when people possess positive beliefs about the trustworthiness of others. Rotter's research, for example, found that high trustors were not only less likely to be unhappy, conflicted, or maladjusted but were also likelier to be sought out as a friend by both low-trusting and high-trusting people. And other evidence suggests that trusting others can even encourage the trusted to become more trustworthy, and thus reciprocate those positive expectations through their behavior, as I will discuss a bit later in this chapter.

Finally, the third reason why people can exhibit high initial trust gets closer to what most of us probably think about when it comes to how trust is formed. This can be found in a host of characteristics we can try to gauge about another person when deciding whether trust would be warranted. One set of studies, for example, has found that we can consider as many as ten characteristics when evaluating a person's trustworthiness.[15] These are: availability (Are they present when needed?), competence (Do they have the knowledge and skills for a specific task?), consistency (Are they reliable and predictable?), discreetness (Can they keep a secret?), fairness (Do they treat others impartially and justly?), integrity (Do they have an honest and moral character?), loyalty (Will they stand by you?), openness (Will they

share ideas and information freely?), promise fulfillment (Will they keep their word?), and receptivity (Will they accept your ideas?).

The relative importance of each of these characteristics for trust may, of course, differ depending on the type of relationship we have with the trustee. For example, we might care more about loyalty than competence from our spouse, we may become more concerned with promise fulfillment than openness from a delivery service, or we may prioritize competence over receptivity when choosing a heart surgeon. Thus, both the type and closeness of the relationship are likely to affect the kinds of characteristics we consider important when evaluating the trustworthiness of others. However, the main point for now is simply to recognize how the breadth of this list supports the notion that a person's characteristics can certainly affect our trust in that individual. The more information we have about that person, as might be the case in closer and long-lasting relationships, the more accurate our assessment of that person's trustworthiness can be.

What complicates this basic premise, however, is that we often make these judgments before enough information is available. Trust researchers have observed that we tend to make these judgments immediately, based on a host of rapid cognitive cues that can often tell us little about the actual trustworthiness of the individual in question.[16] As we will consider more thoroughly later in this book, we often make quick inferences about others based on the groups to which they belong, such as their political affiliation, what they do for a living, where they live, and the schools they attended. We rely quite readily on hearsay or that person's deliberate efforts to construct their own public image. And we frequently make a host of assumptions based on demographic and physical characteristics, such as a person's age, gender, ethnicity, height, weight, and attractiveness.

All these cues can be encountered within the first few minutes of, or even prior to, meeting a stranger, and they are likely to be noisy and unreliable indicators of how trustworthy that stranger really is. Thus, it can be easy to infer that the wiser course of action would be to withhold trust in that individual, at least until more robust information about that person can be gathered. But this is not how trust works. Participants in the job interview study I previously mentioned, for example, were quite willing to exhibit high trust in a job candidate they did not really know, based on their first impressions about the candidate and information the candidate could have easily falsified. This finding is, furthermore, consistent with the results of countless other studies, which have shown that short, unstructured interviews are basically worthless as an evaluation tool because they are so easily influenced by the interviewer's biased and subjective judgments.[17]

This approach to gauging the trustworthiness of others can undoubtedly create problems in certain cases. Of particular concern is the potential for people to make unfair distinctions in whom to trust based on largely irrelevant considerations—such as one's race, gender, weight, or other physical characteristics—that might exclude those who might be deserving. But the broader lesson we should draw from considering all three bases of initial trust (people's incentives, our underlying dispositions, and the rapid cognitive cues we acquire about others) is that our tendency to evaluate the trustworthiness of others quickly is ultimately a double-edged sword. The clear downside can be found in its potential to distort our trust judgments based on considerations that can have very little to do with the actual trustworthiness of the person we are evaluating. And in so doing, we can not only withhold trust from those who are trustworthy but also make ourselves quite vulnerable to those who are not.

But this tendency to make trust judgments so quickly can create major benefits as well. One broad implication of the fact that people's trust in others can be influenced by incentives, our underlying dispositions, and the rapid impressions we can form about others is that these influences can generally encourage us to place greater faith in others than we would have otherwise. Most societal laws, rules, and norms are generally designed to promote ethical principles and can thus facilitate higher levels of initial trust. Likewise, the fact that some of us have personality traits that predispose us to trust others means that, even if others are less trusting, the average level of initial trust in society will still be above zero. And even if our reliance on rapid cognitive cues about others (based on group memberships, reputations, and stereotypes) can sometimes produce flawed and even unfair inferences, it's still better than exhibiting zero initial trust in everyone.

In short, the net effect of these three broad influences is to encourage us to place greater faith in those we don't know. And the evidence thus far suggests that we generally profit from that bet. In the absence of any trust, cooperation becomes almost impossible. We would spend our time monitoring and trying to protect ourselves from others at the expense of everything else. Thus, even though people's willingness to trust others so quickly can be flawed and at times even unfairly biased, my sense is that it would be better to focus on addressing this problem by improving initial trust in those who are more deserving, by giving more people a chance, than to achieve a level playing field by exhibiting zero trust all the time.

The merits of being more, rather than less, willing to trust are also supported by several other research studies. Consider, for example, one of the results from an experiment I conducted with organizational psychologists Tina Diekmann and Ann Tenbrunsel on the effects of providing feedback in negotiations.[18] Negotiations raise major concerns about trust because they are inherently mixed-motive in nature. Negotiators can collectively benefit by acting cooperatively, sharing information, and seeking mutually beneficial solutions. But each party also faces personal incentives to withhold and misrepresent information, mislead their counterpart, and pursue individual rather than collective interests. My collaborators and I were, therefore, interested in understanding how a negotiator might respond to feedback about how they had been viewed in a prior negotiation when they were preparing to negotiate with the same person again.

We, therefore, asked participants to complete two different negotiations with a feedback phase in between. This study randomly assigned one of the participants to the role of feedback provider and the other participant to the role of feedback recipient. However, what we didn't tell the participants at the start of the study was that the specific feedback the provider would share with the recipient had been randomly determined in advance. It was only during the feedback phase, when participants were temporarily placed in separate rooms, that we privately instructed the feedback providers to make an exact and legible copy of feedback text we had provided (to help make the process of providing the feedback seem more realistic) and then make every effort to appear as if they had produced this feedback on their own. Feedback recipients, in contrast, were not made aware that their feedback had been prefabricated so we could test how people would respond to very specific types of perceptions that they believed to be real.

Now please try to put yourself in the role of the feedback recipient who had just completed the first negotiation. And imagine that during the feedback phase, your counterpart wrote the following: "I feel a little weird saying this kind of stuff. I only had one reaction to you in the first negotiation. You seem to be an ethical negotiator in the sense that I didn't get the impression that you were trying to lie and take advantage of me."

How would this affect your approach to the subsequent negotiation with that feedback provider? The feedback provider believes you are trustworthy. Moreover, traditional depictions of how trust should be managed suggest that this creates an opportunity for you to exploit that person's trust, to exhibit "opportunism with guile." Yet even though this can certainly happen in many negotiations, this is not how most participants who received that feedback responded. Instead, they intended to be more cooperative (rather than self-serving) in the subsequent negotiation to maintain the belief that their counterpart's trust in them was deserved. For most of us, when someone trusts us, we want to prove them right.

Likewise, consider the seemingly questionable practice of gauging the trustworthiness of others based on their faces. Evidence suggests that even this seemingly arbitrary reason to trust other people can sometimes have predictive value. Organizational psychologists Michael Slepian and Daniel Ames, for example, demonstrated this point by having independent judges rate the facial trustworthiness of each study participant and then having the participants play a simple economic game where players had to decide whether to tell the truth or not about their subsequent actions. They found that people tend to be aware of how trustworthy their own faces make them appear. But rather than exploit that awareness for personal monetary gain, those with more trustworthy faces were instead likelier to be honest because they wanted to live up to that expectation.[19] Furthermore, in a longitudinal study conducted in China, developmental psychologists Qinggong Li, Gail Heyman, Jing Mei, and Kang Lee revealed that the more trustworthy children's faces looked, in a sample of eight-to-twelve-year-olds, the more they were accepted by peers, expected to be kind, and kindly treated. This ultimately predicted their real-world trustworthiness in class both initially, when the photographs were taken, as well as one year later.[20]

These findings suggest that even when our initial trust in others seems unwarranted or arbitrary, that trust can ultimately create conditions in which it would be justified. We tend to treat those we trust better, and this encourages them to reciprocate that behavior. The trusted also tend to view that trust not as an opportunity for exploitation but rather as a precious resource to preserve for the future. In effect, what may seem like irrational displays of high initial trust can ultimately become rational, as what may initially be overly positive beliefs about the trustworthiness of others lead people to behave in ways that create a self-fulfilling prophecy.

The bottom line is that there is a big difference between how we might think trust operates and how most of us choose to trust in real life. Our willingness to trust based on very little information is the norm, not the exception. And that is a good thing, because this kind of initial trust has been found to be essential for virtually every collective endeavor in society, from ad hoc groups to formal organizations to virtually every transaction in the economy. This high initial trust makes it easier to make friends, change jobs, start new businesses, and visit places without wearing a bulletproof vest. And such benefits can ultimately affect the success of nations, where very strong positive relationships have been found between a country's level of trust and its prosperity.[21]

The problem, however, is that this high initial trust can also be difficult to maintain. Although there are many cases in which this initial presumption of trustworthiness will be fulfilled, at any point along the way, and even after very strong bonds have been nurtured, there remains a very real risk that this trust will be violated. Thus, we need to understand what trust violations mean, the different ways they can occur and may be experienced, and what this can entail for overall levels of trust in society before we can begin to explore how one might address them.

2

WHEN TRUST IS BROKEN

Ava was twenty-seven when she married her Prince Charming. Before then, she had been doing perfectly fine on her own. She managed a gift shop, owned a car, and maintained an active social life. But she was swept away by the man she met from a neighboring town. He was smart, attentive, and generous, and he often surprised her with gifts and visits at work to take her out to lunch. So, when he asked her to marry him a few months into their relationship, she enthusiastically agreed. She had ignored signs that her suitor might have a dark side.

As time passed, however, that dark side became harder to ignore. He belittled her, called her names, and cursed at her in ways that made Ava cringe. Then six years into the marriage, Ava's husband escalated to physical violence by pinning her down and choking her. Her five-year-old son ran to the phone, dialed the operator, and cried, "My dad's killing my mom. Please help!" The operator traced the call and sent a county sheriff's deputy to the house. But even though the attack left Ava with bruises and visible marks, the deputy eventually left without doing anything.

Three months later, Ava's husband again became violent. He pushed her into a wall and began choking her during an argument. She managed to break free and tried to call 911. But her husband knocked the phone out of her hand, smashed it with his foot, and then beat her so severely she had to go to the emergency room. "My children watched me get stitches that night," Ava said. "I thought about the example I was setting for them if I stayed." But when she left home with her children the next day to search for a shelter, each one she found was full. She had nowhere else to turn because, over the years, she had become alienated from her friends and family. Thus, lacking any options, she ultimately returned home to her husband.

Later that week, after another early-morning rage by her husband, Ava found her three-year-old daughter hiding under blankets, shivering and crying because she was so frightened of her father. Desperate, Ava renewed her search for options and found the number for a domestic abuse hotline. Through tears, she told one of its advocates how embarrassed and ashamed she was that she hadn't been able to protect herself or her children. Ava had never wanted them to see how he treated her behind closed doors. The advocate told her to pack what she could in her car and drive with her children to the nearest city. The hotline then helped find Ava and her children housing, childcare, counseling, and legal advice so they could begin rebuilding their lives.

But almost eight years after she left, Ava said, "I still deal with my after." There are still days that she apologizes incessantly, cries at the drop of a hat, and feels completely worthless. "To this day, I don't like scarves . . . or really anything touching my neck. And I worry that no matter how many times I say I am a *survivor* of domestic violence, I will have nightmares for the rest of my life."

This story is a compilation of real experiences of survivors who have contacted the National Domestic Violence Hotline.[1] The name and details have been changed to protect the survivors' identities. The main themes in these survivors' stories, however, remain the same because their experiences with domestic abuse, and this pattern of escalation, are so common.

At the core of this story, there are a central violator and a victim—in this case, an abusive husband and an abused spouse. But, as is so often the case, the ramifications of that abuse can radiate out from those central figures to create a larger tapestry of harm and responsibility that involves many others. This tapestry includes direct witnesses, like Ava's children, who can be psychologically scarred by such events even when they are not the direct targets of the violence. It includes third parties, such as the county sheriff's deputy who was called to the home or the social services Ava first contacted, each of whom might have helped but did not and could thus share part of the blame through their inaction. We can also add to the mix Ava's own sense of responsibility and shame for not having done more to protect herself and her children by pressing charges against her husband, leaving earlier, or somehow being more resourceful, no matter how far-fetched those options may have been. So too might we include people who had nothing to do with what happened but bear some superficial resemblance to her husband. Like the scarves Ava can no longer wear around her neck, relationships with other men might become a source of fear for Ava, just as her children may have learned similarly damaging lessons about what it means to be a spouse and parent.[2] And by the end, the repercussions of these events can also expand to include each one of us who bears witness to these stories as we try to make sense of these incidents and learn vicariously from what happened.

At each stage, what might have otherwise appeared to be very specific and targeted instances of harm can grow to ensnare a broader swath of society. In so doing, this contagion can damage the positive expectations those affected might have otherwise held about the world—the people around them, their communities, the institutions on which they might rely, and the broader society. Regardless of whether they were directly harmed by those incidents or not, those damaged expectations ultimately represent a violation of trust.

Research on trust has made clear how easily this kind of damage can occur. Let's go back to the job interview study I mentioned in chapter 1, which began by documenting the high levels of initial trust people exhibited in a job candidate. That study then asked the same participants to watch a second short video in which the recruiter brought up an unsubstantiated allegation about that job candidate by unknown third parties. The recruiter mentioned that some of the candidate's references had said the candidate had been involved in an accounting-related transgression in her previous job. Then, after playing this second video, we asked the participants to assess their trust in that candidate again. Thus, by comparing trust levels before and after the allegation, we were able to demonstrate that the allegation dramatically lowered participants' trust in that candidate.

The strength and consistency of these findings shouldn't be a surprise for most of us. Without a willingness to trust early and often, our social spheres would become incredibly small and our efforts to navigate the larger world would be enormously burdened. Yet without a keen sensitivity to signals that someone should not be trusted, we can also subject ourselves to unnecessary risk. Indeed, this sensitivity is so high that the allegation raised by our study sharply lowered trust in the job candidate (by roughly

1.5 to almost 3 points on these 7-point scales), even though the participants had not been personally harmed by the alleged incident, the accusers
had not been identified, and the alleged incident remained vague and unsubstantiated. This finding, furthermore, is consistent with evidence from
many other studies that have also found that people are quite willing to
believe unsubstantiated allegations about others, despite the difficulties of
determining whether those allegations are accurate.[*,3]

These results underscore the notion that even if trust is generally beneficial for society, it is also quite fragile. And one reason why can be found
in the fact that we don't equally weigh the potential gains and losses from
trusting others. A substantial body of scientific evidence first introduced by
psychologists Amos Tversky and Daniel Kahneman, the latter of whom won
the 2002 Nobel Prize in economics for his work with Tversky after Tversky's
death,[**] makes clear that people tend to consider losses far more important
than gains.[4] It doesn't really matter, for example, if most men Ava, whom
we met at the beginning of this chapter, encounters are not abusive or if
Ava's own husband did not harm her on most days. What matters are the
occasions in which her husband did commit those abuses, the ramifications
of which overshadowed everything else and ultimately lingered well beyond
her decision to leave that marriage. Our experiences with trust violations can
leave long-lasting marks that can impede our future interactions, even when
those violations are unlikely to be repeated, and even when our subsequent
lack of trust is likely to set us back in the long run. For Ava, distrust can
be a reasonable response that will keep her and her family safe. However,
that stance can also come with a serious price if it prevents her from taking
the risk of entering new relationships and finding a partner who would be
loving and supportive.

I don't make these observations lightly. I know full well how vulnerable we
can feel when our trust has been broken. I also know how the vulnerable are
typically the first to be targeted. Predators often hunt those they perceive to

---

* For example, research on eyewitness testimony has found that more detailed witness accounts
could affect judgments of guilt, even when the detail was unrelated to the culprit.

** The Nobel Prize is not awarded posthumously.

be weak, those who can't fight back, and those whose victimization is likely to go unnoticed. There are real monsters in the world. However, we sometimes also fight phantoms of our own making. And tragedies can arise when we can't distinguish between the two.

A case in point can be found in the fallout from the notorious Tuskegee experiment, which began in 1932.[5] The purpose of this study was to investigate the full progression of syphilis in adults. The researchers, therefore, recruited 600 African American men from Macon County, Alabama—399 with latent syphilis and a control group of 201 others who did not have the sexually transmitted infection—by promising them free medical care. These participants, however, were not offered treatment for the disease, even when penicillin became the treatment of choice for syphilis by 1943, and despite the severe health problems the afflicted participants subsequently experienced, including blindness, mental impairment, and an increasing number of deaths either from syphilis or disease-related complications. It was only after public outrage, when the Associated Press published a story about this experiment in 1972, that an ad hoc advisory panel was appointed to review it, that panel deemed the study to be "ethically unjustified," and the assistant secretary for health and scientific affairs finally announced the decision to stop it.

References to the Tuskegee experiment continue to this day to explain why the African American community remains mistrustful of the medical establishment. This mistrust is understandable, given the fact that the experiment lasted for almost four decades, it was recent enough to have occurred during many of their own lifetimes, and it was only stopped after the Associated Press story led to a public outcry. Moreover, as the health reporter Kristen Brown notes in a 2021 article for Bloomberg, the Tuskegee experiment has ultimately become a shorthand in the African American community for a broader history of racial injustices that have stoked concerns about how much the medical establishment, and other institutions, can be trusted.[6]

The significance of this mistrust has been particularly important during the COVID 19 crisis that began in 2020, as some members of the African American community resisted taking newly developed coronavirus vaccines, even though the pandemic has had an outsized impact on people of color. In one poll conducted by the survey website FiveThirtyEight shortly before the Food and Drug Administration issued emergency use authorization for the Pfizer vaccine, for example, 61 percent of white adults polled in the U.S. indicated that they would either definitely or probably get the vaccine, whereas only 42 percent of Black adults expressed those sentiments.[7] Likewise, a survey conducted that same fall by the National Association for the Advancement of Colored People (NAACP) in conjunction with two other organizations found that just 14 percent of the African Americans surveyed indicated that they "mostly or completely trust" the vaccine's safety.[8]

Black Americans resisted the COVID-19 vaccine despite the fact that they were dying at twice the rate of white Americans from this virus, according to data from the Centers for Disease Control and Prevention (CDC).[9] They also resisted despite substantial data supporting the efficacy of these vaccines[10] and many efforts to persuade Black Americans to get vaccinated. The Kaiser Family Foundation, for example, reported that the percent of white people who received at least one COVID-19 vaccine dose (49 percent) was 1.3 times higher than the rate for Black people (38 percent) eight months after emergency use authorization for the vaccines had been issued.[11] And the consequences of that vaccine reluctance have been tragic, with the APM Research Lab reporting that over seventy-three thousand Black Americans lost their lives to COVID-19 between December 8, 2020, and March 2, 2021, even as the deadlier Delta variant of that virus was just beginning to take hold.[12]

Of course, we can't be certain how many of these lives would have been saved if trust had been higher. The vaccines were not yet widely available for much of this period, and even when they did become available, their distribution became a significant hurdle. Yet racial disparities in vaccination rates were reported as early as mid-January 2021, with a Kaiser Health News report showing that Black Americans were being vaccinated at rates 2–3 times below that of white Americans.[13] It is also not difficult to see how a tiny increase in those vaccination rates, even just 1 percent of the 73,000 who lost their lives in that early December through early March time period, could have saved several times more Black lives than the 128 participants who died from syphilis and disease-related complications through the almost forty-year duration of the Tuskegee experiment.[14]

This kind of result illustrates how our reactions to trust violations can take on a life of their own and grow well beyond the scope of the instigating transgression. In the eyes of the mistrustful, it probably does not matter if they were not personally harmed by the Tuskegee experiment. It is enough to know that others like them had that experience. They are also likely to discount the significance of new guidelines that were issued shortly after the Tuskegee experiment was ended to protect human subjects in other U.S. government–funded research projects, as well as the $10 million out-of-court settlement that was paid to study participants and their heirs, both of which should deter this kind of incident from ever happening again. It likely also doesn't matter that Peter Buxtun, the epidemiologist and whistleblower who initially expressed ethical concerns about the study despite fears that this would cost him his job and ultimately chose to make it public through the Associated Press, was white. "You bet I thought about having to find another job, perhaps in another city and probably outside of government," Buxtun said.[15] Few are aware of his actions, and his courageous role often serves as little more than a footnote in this story.

Moreover, it can be easy for the mistrustful to ignore a fundamental difference between the goals of the Tuskegee experiment and the effort to promote the adoption of COVID-19 vaccines. As journalist Melba Newsome observed in an article for *Scientific American*,[16] the harm caused by the Tuskegee experiment involved the *withholding* of a treatment (penicillin) that would have healed participants already infected with syphilis. That study did not involve the injection of syphilis to make otherwise healthy participants sick. Thus, rather than use the Tuskegee experiment as a reason to avoid getting a coronavirus vaccine, the lesson that should be drawn from that disgraceful episode in U.S. history should be for Black Americans to clamor for treatments white Americans are also getting. The same lesson likewise applies if we consider references to the Tuskegee experiment shorthand for the injustices within health care African Americans still face today, as these too generally concern barriers that limit their access to equal medical treatment. The natural response should be to demand more. The problem, however, is that our reactions to trust violations can often seem less than rational when they are considered on purely objective terms, and those reactions can often compound the harm we have already experienced.

One way to understand some of the longer-term implications of trust violations is by looking at psychophysiological research on the effects of trauma. This research provides insight into post-traumatic stress disorder (PTSD) by studying the interrelationships between the mind and body. Of course, trust violations don't necessarily cause PTSD. Likewise, even though many causes of PTSD (such as the experience of war, childhood abuse, rape, or a horrific accident) can violate trust on some level, that isn't always the case. War veterans, for example, can maintain their trust in the military, the government, and the purpose of military intervention even as they struggle to manage the effects of their own battlefield trauma after they return home, just as victims of freak accidents may exhibit PTSD symptoms even though their trust in others has not really changed.

Yet both trust violations and cases of trauma can ultimately be understood from the standpoint of how people respond to perceived harm. The most serious instances of harm can certainly create both mistrust and trauma. Each of these experiences can shatter our positive beliefs about the world that both nurture our well-being and help us engage with others more effectively. Moreover, both traumatic experiences and trust violations can create patterns of behavior that can affect all sorts of future interactions. We can be imprinted by those experiences, the lasting harmful effects of which can be seen even decades later.

As psychiatrist Bessel van der Kolk detailed so powerfully in his bestselling book *The Body Keeps the Score: Brain, Mind, and Body in the Healing of Trauma*,[17] based on his research on post-traumatic stress disorder, the experience of trauma can lead people to exhibit a host of symptoms. We can develop hair-trigger reactions to external stimuli that bear only a superficial resemblance to the traumatic events, such as when war veterans struggle with incidental loud noises that overwhelm their rational thought and activate automatic fight-or-flight symptoms years after their military service has ended. We can develop dysfunctional habits to find some semblance of control over traumatic experiences, such as when victims of child sexual abuse engage in subsequent self-destructive tendencies, self-harm ideation, suicide ideation, and suicide attempts as young adults.[18] The trauma can even affect how victims see themselves in ways that increase the chances of facing similar traumatic experiences in the future, as they develop negative self-views that make them gravitate toward those who are likelier to hurt them.[19]

These consequences of traumatic events echo the kinds of effects that can arise from trust violations we discussed earlier. We often overgeneralize from those specific experiences to include situations and people that have only a superficial resemblance to what happened. This can lead us to behave in ways that can exacerbate the harm from the instigating incident by exhibiting mistrust in cases where that isn't warranted. The experiences can also fundamentally affect how we see ourselves and others in ways that can prove detrimental to all of us.

Consider, for example, the results of the 2019 Pew Research Center report on trust that I mentioned in this book's introduction. That report found that 64 percent of American respondents felt that their trust in one another has diminished and that 75 percent indicated that their trust in the federal government has diminished. Those results can make it easy to infer that people have become less willing to exhibit the kind of initial trust that my own and other studies have previously documented.

However, it is just as possible that, rather than represent a fundamental decline in our willingness to exhibit initial trust, those findings reflect a growth in perceived trust violations and our difficulty repairing trust after such incidents. Indeed, when asked why trust levels have declined, the Pew survey respondents had no trouble identifying a laundry list of societal and political causes, including experiences with people being less reliable, lazier, greedier, and more dishonest than they used to be; political gridlock; and divisive and sensational coverage by the news media. Yet 86 percent still thought that the confidence people have in one another could be improved, and 84 percent believed it was possible to improve the levels of confidence people have in the government.[20]

All of this suggests that we need to develop better insight into how trust violations can occur so we can begin exploring how to address them. And this requires that we dig more deeply to consider how the exact same incident may violate trust in some cases but not others. Earlier in this chapter, I defined trust violations as incidents that damage the positive expectations we might have otherwise held about our world. However, I did not specify what those expectations might have been or how such expectations might change based on the situation. Thus, we will need to draw from research on trust and from across the social sciences to start answering those questions.

At the broadest level, we should note that both qualitative and quantitative considerations can play a role in how people view potential violations. On the qualitative front, the type of relationship in which such incidents occurred can make an important difference in how they are viewed (as we noted in chapter 1). People can consider a range of characteristics when gauging their trust in others, and they can regard some of these characteristics to be more important for trust in some relationships than others. We might expect a spouse to be loyal in a marriage, for example, but not necessarily competent at providing medical advice, whereas the opposite may be true with a physician. Thus, we would probably be much less inclined to hold a spouse accountable for violating trust if they dismissed health symptoms that turned out to be quite serious than we would the doctor for doing the same thing.

I have a dear friend, for example, who once noticed a bump on his arm and told his normally warm and supportive wife he thought it might be arm cancer. She looked at it and promptly dismissed his concern as ridiculous. He went to his doctor anyway, and it was indeed diagnosed as a (thankfully treatable) cancerous tumor in his arm—an inflammatory fibrosarcoma growing out of the bone near his elbow that was almost the size of a golf ball. He and his wife remain happily married many years later and find humor in the experience.

Moreover, evidence suggests that situational cues can affect the expectations people hold, even when the type of relationship remains the same. A case in point can be found in a field study of ten private day care centers that was conducted by economists Uri Gneezy and Aldo Rustichini.[21] The day care centers were facing a problem where teachers kept having to stay after closing time to wait for parents who arrived late to collect their children. The researchers, therefore, sought to address this issue by imposing a monetary fine on the tardy parents. Yet rather resolve this problem, the results revealed that the fine caused more than twice as many parents to show up late, because the monetary fine changed how parents viewed that behavior. In their minds, their late arrivals were no longer an embarrassing violation of social norms that made the lives of day care teachers more difficult but instead an accepted activity with a reasonable price tag.

Researchers in my field (an interdisciplinary domain called *organizational behavior,* which builds on the disciplines of psychology, sociology, and economics) have described this kind of change as a shift in how the decision has been framed, in this case, from matters of ethics to business. Studies of this phenomenon have not only investigated how situational cues, such as the presence of fees and fines, can prompt this shift but also demonstrated how people can become less cooperative and honest when that shift occurs.

This kind of shift can often make perfect sense. Norms of interaction naturally differ depending on whether we are at work or at home, or whether we are addressing a serious medical issue or playing a party game with friends. The problem, however, is that people don't always share the same expectations for how we should behave in these different situations. And when that is the case, those involved can have very different sentiments about whether trust has been violated. We will devote more attention to these kinds of problems later in this book when we explore the ways in which people can differ in their moral judgments. The main goal for now is simply to recognize that there can be important qualitative differences in what people believe to be a transgression based on the expectations they hold.

Moreover, when it comes to *quantitative* differences, we need to consider how, even when the behavior is considered wrong and the actor is completely at fault, there can be important differences in how seriously such incidents may be treated. This is where the strength of the relationship can really matter. In the case of domestic abuse that was introduced at the start of this chapter, for example, Ava ignored the signs of her husband's dark side for years and only tried to leave after his second violent attack sent her to the emergency room. This is a common pattern in accounts of domestic abuse, as well as in people's reactions to other transgressions by those with whom they are close. And a straightforward reason why can be found in the fact that people are generally motivated to preserve those close relationships.[22] As with Ava, they can try to ignore or forget the offenses. They can try to give the offender the benefit of the doubt or make excuses for their actions, such as by blaming themselves or other victims. They can, furthermore, even try to rationalize the offenses in ways that allow them to see those faults in more positive terms.

Psychologists Sandra Murray and John Holmes raised the latter possibility with their research on romantic partners.[23] They first asked participants to describe their partners' conflict-avoidant tendencies and then had them write open-ended narratives about that shortcoming in their partner. Murray and Holmes found that participants exhibited considerable flexibility in their thinking to transform the meaning of those faults into virtues, such as by reinterpreting their partner's conflict-avoidant tendencies to view them as signs of the partner "being receptive to my needs" and being "willing to adapt if necessary."

These findings can explain how we might rationalize a close other's upsetting emotional outburst, for example, by interpreting it not as a character flaw but rather as evidence of overwhelming passion and caring, and remain committed to the relationship as a result. However, we would have little reason to rationalize similar outbursts in this way when they are instigated by a mere acquaintance or stranger. We are simply less motivated to do so when the relationship is not close, because we have less invested in those relationships and thus have less to lose by ending them. This is how the strength of the relationship can serve as a buffer that can mute the effects of a potential trust violation, by leading those who have strong relationships with the offender to consider the incident less serious than those whose relationship with the offender is weak.

Yet other considerations may work in the opposite direction, by making us more sensitive to potential trust violations. It is possible, for example, that just as certain differences in our psychological makeup can make some of us more inclined to trust than others, there may be other individual differences that make some people likelier to believe their trust has been violated (such as those like Dale, from chapter 1, who are diagnosed with paranoid personality disorder). However, we are ultimately better served by focusing on another category of influences that is not only more broadly relevant but also more specific in its implications for how people might respond to potential trust violations—research on our ability to learn through association.

Research on associative learning concerns the connections humans and animals can make between two unrelated elements (such as objects, sights, sounds, ideas, and behaviors) through a process known as *conditioning*. Perhaps the most well-known example of this effect can be found in the Russian scientist Ivan Pavlov's studies in which he would ring a bell and then give dogs food soon afterward, so the dogs would learn to salivate when they heard the bell even without the food being delivered. To this, we might also add a less well-known and rather dubious invention called Project Pigeon, by psychologist B. F. Skinner, which sought to solve the problem of bombing inaccuracy during World War II. The proposed solution involved inserting three street pigeons into the nose of a bomb, with each pigeon trained to peck whenever it saw the pattern of a target so their combined efforts would guide the explosive.[24] The military granted Skinner $25,000 to pursue the idea, but ultimately rejected it, despite Skinner's successful demonstration of his trained birds.

Oddities aside, this fundamental capacity to learn by association is important for people as well. As with Ava's reaction to scarves after her experience with domestic abuse and war veterans who continue to struggle with incidental loud noises long after they have left the battlefield, these experiences can make us hypervigilant against similar harms and prompt hair-trigger reactions against stimuli associated with those experiences. These stimuli can include sensory memories that involve a similar sound, touch, or smell; similar places or situations; or even superficial similarities to those who committed the transgression based on appearance, gender, ethnicity, or other characteristics. And though these kinds of reactions are certainly evident after many traumatic episodes, they can also arise with incidents that violate trust but might not necessarily be considered traumatic.

We are all conditioned to learn through our experiences, to make inferences about what will bring rewards and what will inflict harm. And the million-dollar question when this occurs is whether those inferences are ultimately warranted or not, particularly when each of our own experiences can so drastically differ. Anyone who has experienced workplace harassment, for example, will likely be far more attuned to the prospect of its recurrence than those who haven't and therefore react to questionable incidents in ways that are likely to differ. Those reactions may also differ depending on whether they were the direct targets of that harassment, were third-party witnesses of such incidents, or had only heard accounts of what happened after the fact.

In each case, the associations people in that workplace might learn to make can be at odds. This, in turn, can create repercussions for how people relate to one another in that context that can persist long after the harassment has ended. For those who have not borne the brunt of that harm, the harassment may be something they condemn but quickly relegate to the past. They might reason that the culprit was ultimately reprimanded or fired for those actions and thus consider the matter resolved. However, for those most directly victimized by what happened, the dangers may still be lurking. All it takes is one more person willing to step over the line. What remains salient is the harm that was inflicted. And just as easy to recall is how long it took and how difficult it might have been to put a halt to those transgressions in the first place. They remain wary and hypervigilant because they have learned too well from their experience the cost of letting those kinds of questionable actions slide.

Similar differences can likewise be found across many other spheres. This includes people's responses to claims of systemic racism, impingements on civil rights, efforts to pass gun rights legislation, the repeal of abortion rights, and perceptions of media bias. In these and other domains, there are some who may exhibit hair-trigger reactions to what they perceive to be real threats to their well-being, whereas others may dismiss those reactions as overblown. Where each of us falls along this divide ultimately depends on the specific issue in question and our own past experiences. We all learn through association, and the ways in which we are conditioned to respond based on our experience can generally help us navigate the world. But this underlying associative learning process can sometimes also make us scarcely different from Skinner's street pigeons, trained to peck away in a bomb toward our doom.

More broadly, each of the qualitative and quantitative influences I have reviewed helps underscore how difficult it can be to reach consensus on whether a trust violation has occurred. This problem, furthermore, becomes even more significant when this lack of agreement occurs not just among those whose trust might have been violated but also between those potential victims and the purported violator. This can create situations where potential victims conclude that trust has been violated, but the violator is unaware that this has happened. The victims, in such cases, may experience long-lasting mistrust because the violator hasn't recognized the need to address it, and the onus may therefore fall on those victims to bring this matter to that person's attention before any progress can be made.

Furthermore, even if violators recognize that others believe trust has been violated, they may not necessarily believe that sentiment is warranted or agree they shouldn't be trusted. This can sometimes also be for good reasons. As we have seen, the research evidence makes clear that people are quite willing to believe false accusations about others. This makes it easy to blame the innocent. Our need to find someone at fault when bad things happen can often prompt the search for convenient scapegoats. Moreover, even when those blamed bear some responsibility, those pointing the finger may not have a full understanding of why the violation happened and thus make inferences that can distort both the nature of the incident and the violator's role. Thus, even though those perceiving the incident may be in the best position to gauge their own experience of whether they have been harmed and whether their trust has been violated, they may not necessarily be correct in their assumptions about who is at fault, the purported violator's level of accountability, or how best to address that kind of incident.

Additionally, while we are considering how potential victims can be wrong, we also need to account for how those accused of trust violations may not necessarily get things right either. They can fail to take the perspective of potential victims and thereby overlook the harm their actions may have caused. They can engage in self-serving rationalizations that allow them to believe the actions were justified or diminish their own responsibility for what happened. Moreover, even if they accept the premise that their behavior was wrong and that they are responsible, they may nevertheless disagree about how much punishment, restitution, and other forms of remedial intervention would be appropriate. And we must also confront the fact that repairing trust in the violator sometimes *isn't* warranted, that the violator may be likely to commit similar offenses in the future, and that potential victims may simply be better off walking away.

These complications are also compounded by the fact that reestablishing trust after it has been violated is not only much more difficult than exhibiting trust from the beginning (since one must now overcome salient reasons *not* to trust) but also more difficult than forgiveness or preventing future violations. The American Psychological Association has defined *forgiveness* as "willfully putting aside feelings of resentment toward an individual who has committed a wrong, been unfair or hurtful, or otherwise harmed one in some way." There is also growing evidence that forgiveness can improve the mental and physical health of those who have been victimized, by reducing stress, anxiety, and depression.[25] However, forgiveness does not necessarily entail reconciliation, continued interactions with the offender, or the offender even acknowledging the harm. It is simply a process through which victims can reach a place of empathy and understanding that can allow them to move forward on their own. Ava, whom we met at the beginning of this chapter, for example, may someday find it in herself to forgive her abusive husband and feel better as a result, even if she has no intention of ever making herself or her children vulnerable to him again. Her forgiveness does not require reestablishing trust or the relationship.

Likewise, although preventive measures like new regulations or monitoring systems may allow violators and victims to engage with one another again, this largely does not repair trust; it just reduces risk. In chapter 1, we considered how the reduction of risk ultimately reduces the need to trust. Hence, the main goal of preventive measures is to allow people to act as if they trust one another even when they may not trust one another at all. Moreover, even if preventive measures may be sufficient in some cases, they can typically account for only a limited number of possible infractions. This leaves the question of how to address the broad set of circumstances where risk has not been eliminated. Additionally, evidence suggests that preventive measures may sometimes even backfire because they can foster the belief that others would only act in a trustworthy manner when they are compelled to do so and that they would reveal their true untrustworthy selves when given a chance.[26] If two people in a business venture, for example, each fulfilled their part of the bargain despite weaknesses in the contract that made it easy for them to cheat, it would be easy to infer this was because they were trustworthy. However, if the contract was strong enough to make cheating impossible, there would remain a question of what would have happened if their cooperation hadn't been forced.

The bottom line is that even though forgiveness and the implementation of preventive measures can offer important benefits, they ultimately do little to resolve the harder and more fundamental problem of how to reestablish, or repair, trust after it has been violated. To address it, we need to understand what may allow us to make ourselves vulnerable to those violators *despite* the risk that would entail. And that, in turn, requires that we obtain deeper insight into how people might reconcile their often-disparate beliefs about the violation and why it occurred, as well as the violator's guilt, responsibility, and likelihood of redemption.

3

THE PROBLEM WITH APOLOGIES

t was a Saturday afternoon, August 15, 1998, in the Northern Ireland town of Omagh, when a red Vauxhall drove into the center of town. With just two weeks before the start of school, many parents were out with their children to purchase school uniforms. The red Vauxhall parked about four hundred yards from the courthouse, and the two men in the car armed the five-hundred-pound bomb hidden inside, with the timer set to detonate in forty minutes, before walking away.[1] The bombing killed 29 people, including a woman pregnant with twins, and injured 220 others, making this the single deadliest bombing atrocity of the Troubles in Northern Ireland.

This bombing caused local and international outrage and dealt a severe blow to the dissident Irish republican campaign that was held responsible for the tragedy, the Real Irish Republican Army (Real IRA). Shortly after this incident, that group declared a cease-fire in its efforts to oppose a resolution to the political conflict in Northern Ireland, known as the Good Friday Agreement. Then, in an August 18 statement, the Real IRA offered an apology to the victims, which underscored their regret for the tragedy, by explaining that civilians had not been the targets. Indeed, the goal of the Real IRA's bombings in Northern Ireland had historically been to cause economic harm and disruption rather than the loss of civilian life. Thus, to avoid that at Omagh, the group had issued three warnings to the police and made clear that the bomb was located three to four hundred yards from the courthouse.

The Real IRA, furthermore, did not try to lessen its responsibility for the tragedy at the time, despite their belief that they had only been minimally involved. As one of its spokesmen explained almost a decade later, "Our code word was used; nothing more. To have stated this at the time would have been lost in an understandable wave of emotion," and "Omagh was an absolute tragedy. Any loss of civilian life is regrettable."[2] Thus, this group implemented what has widely been considered the gold standard for effective crisis management, as well as the repair of trust more generally. They accepted full responsibility for the bombing and conveyed complete remorse for its devastation.

This approach echoes the lessons from a classic case study of Johnson & Johnson's efforts sixteen years earlier when poisoned Tylenol pills started to appear in stores. On September 29, 1982, three people in the Chicago area died after taking cyanide-laced Tylenol at the outset of a poisoning spree that would eventually claim seven victims. The case was never solved, and without a suspect to revile, the public outrage could have fallen squarely on Tylenol. However, Johnson & Johnson took full ownership for what happened by recalling its Tylenol from store shelves and issuing national warnings urging the public not to take those pills. These moves cost the company millions of dollars but quickly reestablished the Tylenol brand and allowed the company to recover the entire market it lost during the cyanide scare. Hence, this notion of taking full responsibility for a tragedy, as the Real IRA sought to do, has since become the model for how to manage crises taught by business schools, crisis management consultants, and even the U.S. Department of Defense.[3,4]

The field of crisis management is concerned with how organizations deal with disruptive events that can harm an organization and its stakeholders. Its purpose is, therefore, tightly linked to the question of how one might repair trust after a transgression, with the primary difference stemming from its narrower focus. Crisis management is typically concerned with how organizations might address these kinds of incidents through public relations, as opposed to how one might repair trust at the interpersonal, group, or societal level. Hence, researchers in this field tend to use high-profile case studies of organizational crisis management efforts to uncover broadly applicable insights into how to address these kinds of trust breaches.

In the Tylenol pill-tampering case, the lesson was straightforward. Johnson & Johnson did not try to avoid responsibility for the cyanide poisoning. Instead, the company took concrete corrective actions. This sent a clear signal that it regretted the incident and that it would strive to keep this kind of tampering from being repeated. From the standpoint of crisis management, the straightforward takeaway was that these kinds of efforts to assume responsibility for what happened should help repair trust, because they will convey positive information about the organization's intentions and behavior that should allay the public's concerns about similar harmful events occurring in the future.

Yet the Real IRA's effort to apologize and accept responsibility for the bombing provoked very different reactions. Conservatives and Liberal Democrats in Ireland condemned the apology by the Real IRA as a "cynical and outrageous insult" to the dead and wounded. The Tory deputy chairman, Michael Ancram, described the apology as a pathetic attempt by evil men "to extricate themselves from the worldwide opprobrium which their murderous action on Saturday has brought down on their heads." He declared, "No weasel words can disguise their murderous culpability, no belated and grudging apology can repair the terrible human damage they have wrought." Likewise, the deputy leader of the Democratic Unionist Party, Peter Robinson, said it was clear to him that the Real IRA had set out to murder, whatever its intended target.[5]

Why were the reactions to the Omagh bombing and Tylenol pill-tampering cases so different? Could this discrepancy be explained by some deficiency in the Real IRA's apology? Psychologists have investigated what might make an apology more effective, and their work does raise the possibility that some efforts to tweak the Real IRA's apology could have helped. Researchers Roy Lewicki, Beth Polin, and Robert Lount Jr., for example, identified six underlying structural components of apologies based on previous studies.[6] These were:

1. an **expression of regret** conveying how sorry they are for the offense
2. an **explanation** that provides reasons why the offense occurred
3. an **acknowledgment of responsibility** to demonstrate that the violator understands their part in the offense

4. a **declaration of repentance** that expresses a promise not to repeat the offense

5. an **offer of repair** that proposes a way to work toward rebuilding trust; and

6. a **request for forgiveness** to pardon the violator's actions.

Lewicki and his collaborators then conducted two experiments using the job interview paradigm that my own research team had developed (as described in the prior chapters). They asked their study participants to imagine that a job candidate they were asked to evaluate had been accused of committing a transgression and that the candidate offered an apology that contained one or more of these six apology components. Their findings revealed that the more components the apology contained, the more effective participants perceived it to be. Moreover, some of these components appeared to be more important to include in an apology than others. Across the two studies, participants considered the acknowledgment of responsibility and the offer of repair most important, and the request for forgiveness least important. Thus, their results support the notion that the type of apology offered can matter.

However, if we were to compare the Real IRA's apology for the Omagh bombing with Johnson & Johnson's response to the tampering of its Tylenol pills, we would see that J&J did not actually apologize at all. J&J took full ownership of that incident through their actions, as did the Real IRA with Omagh at the time. However, if the question is who offered the better apology, you would think that some formal apology would be better than none.

Can the difference instead be traced to the fact that Johnson & Johnson addressed its Tylenol crisis by introducing new tamperproof bottles, whereas the Real IRA resumed its bombing operations two years later? The problem with this explanation is that the public would not have known about the eventual decision to resume bombing at the time the Real IRA issued their apology. Moreover, the notion that Johnson & Johnson resolved its pill-tampering problems is also challenged by several copycat poisonings involving Tylenol that subsequently occurred in the 1980s and early 1990s, underscoring how these over-the-counter medications are still not entirely safe.[7]

Thus, we are still missing important pieces of the puzzle. These were the kinds of issues that my research team sought to address with some of our early studies on this topic. Those studies began with the observation that apologies and associated attempts to accept full blame are ultimately double-edged in nature, because they communicate competing signals. They are beneficial in the sense that they convey remorse, a sentiment that expresses regret for the wrong that was committed and at least an implicit signal that the apologizer intends to avoid similar violations in the future. This can alleviate concerns about being vulnerable to that party's subsequent actions and thus encourage others to trust that person again. However, apologies are also harmful because they confirm guilt. This can underscore the notion that the apologizer had been untrustworthy and would likely remain untrustworthy thereafter.

These competing signals ultimately raised the question of how people would weigh the positive signals of remorse and negative signals of guilt when gauging whether, and how much, trust should be repaired. This led my team to propose that one factor that might affect this weighting could be the type of violation. More specifically, we predicted that our tendency to focus on the positive or negative signals the same apology might convey would depend on whether the offense concerned matters of competence or integrity.

Matters of competence and integrity deserve particular attention when considering how trust might be repaired for two reasons. First, although I have previously noted (in chapter 1) that people can consider as many as ten characteristics when evaluating a person's trustworthiness, many of those characteristics tend to be less critical for trust than others. Characteristics like discreetness or consistency, for example, are certainly relevant in some situations. However, the empirical evidence suggests that perceptions of competence (the belief that someone "possesses the technical and interpersonal skills that are required for a task") and integrity (the belief that someone "adheres to a set of principles one finds acceptable") are almost always the most important.[8] Thus, we considered it likely that these two considerations would be especially important for the repair of trust as well.

Second, on a theoretical level, we had reasons to think that people would weigh positive and negative information about these characteristics quite differently.[9] For example, as I mentioned at the very start of this book, people tend to weigh positive information about competence more heavily than negative information about competence. This is because we intuitively believe that those with high competence can perform at many levels, depending on their motivation and task demands, whereas those with low competence can only perform at levels that are in line with or lower than their level of competence. For this reason, we tend to consider a single successful performance a reliable signal of competence, based on the belief that those without competence would not be able to achieve that performance level. However, we also tend to discount a single poor performance as a signal of incompetence, based on the belief that even the highly competent can perform poorly in certain situations (such as when there is little motivation or opportunity to perform well).

Yet for matters of integrity, this relationship is reversed. People tend to weigh negative information about integrity much more heavily than positive information. This is because we intuitively believe that those with high integrity would refrain from unethical behavior in any situation, whereas those with low integrity may behave either ethically or unethically depending on their incentives and opportunities. For this reason, we typically discount a single honest behavior as a signal of integrity since those with high or low integrity can each behave honestly in certain situations (such as when there are benefits for behaving honestly or enough surveillance to prevent dishonest acts). However, we also tend to consider a single dishonest behavior a reliable signal of low integrity, based on the belief that only those with low integrity would act in dishonest ways.

Thus, hitting a home run once can make us home run hitters in the eyes of others, even if we strike out afterward. However, if you get caught cheating on your spouse and respond by saying, "But I didn't cheat on you yesterday!" that probably won't work out so well.

These differences in how people weigh information about competence and integrity can offer critical insight into why apologies, and similar efforts to take full ownership for a transgression, may not always help. They suggest that apologies can be helpful for competence-based violations because, in such cases, people will pay less attention to the response's confirmation of guilt (negative information about competence) than its signal that the offender regrets the offense and will strive to avoid similar offenses in the future (positive information about competence). But for integrity-based violations, an apology may do little good and even make things worse because, in such cases, people will instead focus on the response's confirmation of the offender's guilt (negative information about integrity) and largely dismiss its accompanying signals of repentance and redemption (positive information about integrity).

My research team tested this reasoning through a series of experiments and found strong and consistent support for these patterns. In some of those studies, for example, we asked participants to watch different versions of the videotaped job interview for a tax accountant position I mentioned testing earlier.[10] As that interview progressed, the interviewer would disclose that someone at the candidate's previous job mentioned that the candidate had been involved in an accounting-related violation. The applicant was either accused of filing the incorrect return due to inadequate knowledge of the relevant tax codes (a competence-based violation) or of filing the incorrect return intentionally to satisfy an important client (an integrity-based violation). The applicant would then respond to the accusation with either an apology or a denial.

Every other aspect of the interview was kept the same. Yet people evaluated this same candidate in dramatically different ways. When the violation concerned matters of competence, participants were more inclined to trust and hire the candidate when she responded with an apology than a denial. However, when the violation concerned matters of integrity, this pattern was completely reversed. People were far more inclined to trust and hire the candidate when she denied, rather than apologized for, the violation.

This doesn't mean that trust was ever repaired completely. Even when the candidate's response significantly improved trust from the levels that were observed immediately after the allegation, participants' trust in the candidate still fell short of the high initial trust they exhibited before the allegation was raised. This shortfall is common after trust-repair attempts, and it is a testament to how difficult the challenge of trust repair can be in general.

Nevertheless, the fact that the relative efficacy of these responses was found to depend so markedly on the type of violation can help explain the different public reactions to the Omagh bombing and Tylenol pill-tampering incidents. What was clear in the Tylenol case is that it involved a problem that few people at the time would have anticipated—a scenario in which one or more people would go out of their way to lace Tylenol pills with cyanide, return those pills to their bottles, and then furtively place those bottles on store shelves for public purchase and consumption. Johnson & Johnson's role in the poisonings was, thus, interpreted as a failure to foresee those bizarre actions as a possibility; their failure was considered a matter of competence. Moreover, because people tend to weigh negative information about competence less heavily than positive information about competence, Johnson & Johnson was able to overcome the negative implications of that failure through its prompt recall and national warnings, which conveyed positive signals of competence.

The Omagh bombing, in contrast, was interpreted quite differently. In the public's view, those associated with the Real IRA chose to plant a bomb in the center of town and set it off at a time when parents would be out with their children. They knew they would be putting innocent lives in danger but chose to detonate the bomb anyway. That conscious decision is what made this incident a matter of integrity, by indicating that those involved did not share the public's values regarding the needless endangerment of human life. It is also for this reason that, when the Real IRA apologized for the deaths the bombing caused, the public was far more inclined to focus on the apology's confirmation of guilt (negative information about integrity) rather than the apology's signals of regret (positive information about integrity).

These considerations also suggest a relatively straightforward way to distinguish between these two types of offenses. The difference between competence- and integrity-based violations seems to hinge on whether the violator intended to do something wrong or not. This observation ultimately led me to conduct a different set of experiments, specifically on the implications of contract breaches, to investigate the role intentionality can play in how transgressions are viewed.[11]

As I noted in chapter 1, when we reach agreements with others, we can certainly try to add explicit clauses and provisions to those contracts to ensure that our expectations are fulfilled. However, we are also limited in our ability to anticipate and account for every way in which those expectations might be violated. We can't predict the future or foresee every devious way in which someone might get around those explicit contract terms. Moreover, even if all our expectations have been documented, this still doesn't guarantee that those expectations will be met. I, therefore, wondered how people would interpret violations that concerned the letter of the law (i.e., the documented expectations), as opposed to its spirit (i.e., the undocumented expectations), as well as how they would respond if an apology was offered for such incidents. This was important because the contracting literature provided the basis for two contradictory predictions about what would happen.

Some of this research suggests that if someone wanted to take advantage of a contracting counterpart, it would make more sense to do that by violating expectations that had not been documented (the spirit of the law) rather than by violating expectations that had been documented (the letter of the law). This is because violations of undocumented expectations may be less easily noticed and would also be harder to enforce (e.g., through the legal system). In short, it's easier to get away with a contract breach if the contract doesn't explicitly ban it. Hence, violating the letter of the law is likely to be *less* intentional than violating the spirit of the law, because if that person did want to violate the contract, that person would have sought to do so by violating the spirit of the law instead. However, other research suggests that if an expectation has been explicitly documented, people are likelier to know if they are about to violate it than if the expectation had not been explicitly documented. Thus, if they were to violate that documented expectation anyway (the letter of the law), this would be *more* intentional than if they violated an undocumented expectation (the spirit of the law).

I designed an elaborate experiment to test these competing possibilities.

The study informed participants that its purpose was to investigate interactions between contractors and subcontractors, because those two types of parties often have different financial motivations in the real world. Thus, one participant would play the role of contractor, whereas the other would play the role of subcontractor. And their task was to first reach an agreement about the details of a home and then have the subcontractor build it using materials the study provided.

The study also informed participants that each role would have different financial incentives to reflect the different motivations contractors and subcontractors can possess in the real world. The contractor would either earn twenty-five dollars cash if no major flaw requiring reconstruction of the house was found, or ten lottery tickets offering just a chance to win one of three twenty-five-dollar gift cards if a major flaw was found. In either case, contractors would also have the option at the end of the study to allocate some of those earnings (i.e., either cash or lottery tickets) to their subcontractor for their involvement. This gave subcontractors an incentive to build the house properly, because their contractor might allocate a portion of the twenty-five dollars cash to them if major flaws were avoided. However, each subcontractor could also personally earn up to ten dollars cash by using as few materials as possible to save on building costs. This gave subcontractors an additional ulterior motive.

Now, let's imagine that you were a participant in this study and had been assigned to the contractor role. You would start by receiving a picture of the house that was required. This was a two-story home with a garage that had roughly fifteen unique specifications that could be documented, including the house color, the number and location of windows, and the building's physical dimensions. You would be asked to write a contract for the subcontractor, who would need to build the house without the benefit of seeing the picture (to simulate the challenge of not having a full understanding of what a client might want in the real world). Then, after writing this contract, you would be asked to email it to the research assistant in another room, who would print it out for the subcontractor to evaluate, request clarifications, and (if necessary) ask to be revised.

Next, let's say that about fifteen minutes after sending your contract proposal, the research assistant in your room received a call from the assistant in the subcontractor room stating that your subcontractor had fully agreed to all the contract terms and would take the next fifteen minutes to build the house. Then, after that time had elapsed, your own room's assistant received another call indicating that the house had been finished, that the assistant at the subcontractor site was inspecting and taking a picture of the house, and that this assistant would email the picture and assessment of the house directly to you. You were also informed that your subcontractor had been asked to provide a handwritten comment about the assessment that would be delivered to you as well. The assistant in your room would then step out for a few minutes to obtain the report and message, give this information to you once they returned, and then gauge your responses based on what happened.

So, how would you feel if the inspection report you received concluded that the house your subcontractor constructed was inadequate due to a major flaw, in this case because the home was ridiculously narrow, not even as deep as the garage? This major flaw meant that you would not receive the twenty-five dollars cash you were hoping to earn and instead earn a few lottery tickets. But this flaw also meant that the subcontractor was personally able to earn seven dollars cash by using fewer building materials. How would you view what happened and the subcontractor's accompanying offer of an apology? How many, if any, of your measly lottery tickets would you share with that person? And would that depend on whether you had previously documented what the minimum house depth needed to be in the contract?

As you ponder these questions, I should let you in on a little secret. The subcontractor never existed. The study simply led participants to believe that they, as contractors, were interacting with another participant who had been assigned to that subcontractor role through communications that appeared to be relayed by the research assistants at each of their locations. These steps, along with another subtle nudge, which affected whether participants documented the minimum house depth in the contract (as detailed below), are what allowed this experiment to create the conditions it sought to investigate.

We have already noted that violations of the letter versus the spirit of the law can be distinguished by whether the violated expectation has been documented. This led me to alter the type of violation, in this study, by focusing on an expectation that virtually everyone would have about a home—namely, that it should be at least as deep as its garage—but wouldn't necessarily state in a contract because that requirement would seem obvious. Moreover, when participants at the start of the study were given the picture of the required home and a short, inexhaustive list of details to consider including in the contract for their subcontractor, the study either did or did not include the minimum house depth requirement as one of the details.

Participants were far likelier to include the house depth requirement in their contract when it was included as an option in that short inexhaustive list than when it was not included. Additionally, both the photo and the inspection of the home each subcontractor ostensibly built always reported that this was the requirement that had been violated. Thus, each contractor was presented with the same objective violation, a ridiculously narrow house that caused the participant to lose the twenty-five-dollar cash reward but allowed their subcontractor to earn seven dollars cash by using fewer materials. However, contractors could still interpret that violation as either a letter or spirit violation depending on whether they had documented that requirement in the contract. And the question was how that difference would affect the perceived intentionality of the violation and participants' reactions to the subcontractors' subsequent apology.

The evidence from this study revealed that even if people seeking to violate a contract are inclined to do so by breaking the spirit rather than the letter of the law (by skirting, rather than directly breaching, the documented contract terms), participants nevertheless considered letter violations to be more intentional than spirit violations. This, in turn, led participants to exhibit less trust in, and become more willing to punish, the subcontractor (by allocating fewer earnings to that party) when the subcontractor apologized for violating the letter than the spirit of the contract. In fact, the more intentional participants perceived the violation to be, the less willing they were to trust, and the more inclined they were to punish the subcontractor after that party offered an apology.

These findings support the notion that the perception of intent is what leads people to view a violation as a matter of integrity (rather than competence) and, thus, respond less positively to an apology. The more intentional the violation seemed, the less effective the apology became, just like when an apology was offered for matters of integrity rather than competence. But now that we have simplified the difference between matters of competence and integrity to the perception of intent, we also need to expand our understanding of what intent really means.

In criminal law, the intention to commit a crime is known as *mens rea,* a term whose literal translation from Latin is "guilty mind." This state of mind is required to convict a defendant of many crimes, by distinguishing between cases in which a person intends to commit a crime (or knows that their action or inaction would cause a crime to be committed) from cases in which the person commits a crime without intending to do so. The latter situation might occur, for example, if the defendant could not have known the victim would be harmed (such as with accidents), if the defendant was unable to understand the harm a crime might cause (such as in cases of mental deficiency), or if the defendant had somehow been forced to commit that crime by circumstances beyond that person's control (such as at gunpoint). Each of those cases may more aptly be attributed to the defendant's lack of ability (i.e., the ability to know, understand, or control what would happen). Thus, we can again see how the intentionality of an offense can be used to distinguish between matters of competence and integrity.

Yet even though mens rea has been used as the standard test of criminal liability in much of the world, the application of that standard has differed across those jurisdictions. This is because the determination of intent can become quite complicated in practice. In the United States, for example, this standard was widely acknowledged by the late 1950s to be a slippery, vague, and confused mess.[12] That is one of the reasons why the American Law Institute adopted the Model Penal Code in 1962, which differentiated mens rea into five distinct levels of culpability.

At the lowest level, there is *strict liability,* in which the defendant engaged in conduct for which that person's mental state is considered irrelevant.

Strict liability is often applied in criminal law to vehicular traffic offenses where in the case of speeding, for example, it doesn't matter whether the defendant knew the posted speed limit was being exceeded. Next comes *negligence,* which concerns cases in which a reasonable person "should be aware" of a substantial and unjustifiable risk that the conduct would lead to the prohibited result. The third is *recklessness,* which concerns cases in which a defendant "consciously disregards" a substantial and unjustifiable risk that the prohibited result would arise from that conduct. Fourth, the defendant could have committed the crime *knowingly,* by being aware of the conduct and being "practically certain" that the conduct would cause the prohibited result. And finally, the defendant could have committed the crime *purposefully,* by consciously engaging in conduct that this person "believes or hopes" will produce the prohibited result.

The problem, however, is that this elaboration of intent still falls short of providing clear guidance in many cases. Consider, for example, the criminal case that began on August 31, 2021, against Elizabeth Anne Holmes, the founder and chief executive of Theranos, a now-defunct health technology company that claimed to have revolutionized blood testing by developing methods to analyze small volumes of blood from a finger prick. When those claims were revealed to be false, the U.S. Securities and Exchange Commission first charged Theranos and Holmes in 2018 with "massive fraud" through false or exaggerated claims about the accuracy of the company's blood-testing technology. Holmes settled those charges by paying a $500,000 fine, returning 18.9 million shares to the company, relinquishing her voting control of Theranos, and being barred from serving as an officer or director of a public company for ten years.[13] However, she was also indicted in June 2018 by a federal grand jury on nine counts of wire fraud and two counts of conspiracy to commit wire fraud for distributing blood tests with falsified results to consumers,[14] charges for which she faced up to twenty years in federal prison and potentially millions in restitution and fines.

It can be easy to see why Holmes would be guilty of those charges. Indeed, Holmes was ultimately convicted on four of the eleven charges of fraud for which she had been indicted,[15] and her former partner and former Theranos chief operating officer, Ramesh "Sunny" Balwani, was convicted on all twelve counts of fraud that he faced.[16] Holmes's investor presentations claimed that Theranos's blood-testing technology provided "the highest levels of accuracy and precision," despite clear evidence that company insiders knew the technology was plagued by issues and repeatedly failed quality control standards. She falsely suggested that Theranos's miniature blood-testing lab had been vetted by Pfizer, that its technology was being used by the U.S. military, and that it would achieve more than $140 million in revenue by the end of 2014, which prosecutor Robert Leach observed Theranos was "nowhere near achieving."[17] Moreover, despite claims that its machine could perform more than 240 different blood tests with just a finger prick, only 10 percent of the blood tests performed by the company used Theranos's technology, with the rest requiring more traditional testing methods.

Yet Holmes is far from alone in this kind of dishonesty. Start-ups in Silicon Valley have long embraced the notion that founders should pursue their ideas with almost reckless determination, as expressed by the well-known credo "Fake it till you make it." Alex Gibney's 2019 documentary about Theranos, *The Inventor: Out for Blood in Silicon Valley*, underscored this point with the example of Thomas Edison, who falsely proclaimed his success at inventing the incandescent bulb in 1878 and then faked demonstrations to investors and journalists until he finally found a solution four years later, after ten thousand failures. Walter Isaacson's biography *Steve Jobs* referred to employees at Apple commenting on Jobs's use of a figurative "reality distortion field," with which Jobs was able to convince himself, and others around him, that the impossible tasks they confronted were possible.[18] Moreover, Eric Berger reports in his book, *Liftoff,* that when Elon Musk unveiled SpaceX's Falcon rocket in Washington, D.C., on December 4, 2003, that rocket was merely a clever fake.[19] It wasn't until almost five years later, on September 28, 2008, that the Falcon rocket was able to launch successfully into orbit.

These comparative examples raise a natural question. Why indict Holmes but not these other entrepreneurs? How would it make sense to infer that Holmes intentionally engaged in criminal conduct, while also believing that countless others who likewise adopted the "Fake it till you make it" credo should not?

For some, Holmes's case is clearly different. One Silicon Valley venture capitalist, for example, tweeted that it was "silly" to suggest that Silicon Valley's culture was on trial with the Holmes case. "(Alleged) fraud is not the same as willful suspension of disbelief when you have full access to the data and teams required to perform diligence."[20] Yet that claim doesn't really explain how (alleged) fraud and the "willful suspension of disbelief" should be distinguished. Indeed, it is precisely that kind of question that lies at the heart of the Holmes trial.

As legal journalist Jody Godoy reported in an article for Reuters,[21] the prosecution's opening statement asserted, "This is a case about fraud—about lying and cheating to get money." The prosecutor, Robert Leach, claimed that "the scheme brought [Holmes] fame, it brought her honor, and it brought her adoration," which also made her a billionaire at the expense of investors and patients. The defense, however, challenged that view by telling jurors, "Elizabeth Holmes did not go to work every day intending to lie, cheat and steal. The government would have you believe her company, her entire life, is a fraud. That is wrong." Instead, her defense lawyer, Lance Wade, claimed, "She was all in on Theranos, motivated by its mission, not money, committed to that mission until that very last day."

Moreover, rather than simply oppose the prosecution's claims, the defense also presented the jurors a different narrative. One difference between Holmes and the other entrepreneurs mentioned earlier is that Holmes ultimately failed, whereas the others did not. Yet "failure is not a crime," Wade said. "Trying your hardest and coming up short is not a crime." Wade, thus, asked jurors to consider whether Theranos failed because its technology was a fraud or "because a young CEO and her company confronted and could not overcome business obstacles that others saw but she naively underestimated."

The defense, furthermore, underscored this portrayal of Holmes having failed despite having every intention to make Theranos's technology work with an additional strategy. It claimed that Sunny Balwani, Holmes's onetime boyfriend and the former president and chief operating officer of Theranos, had deceived Holmes about the company's financial models and subjected her to intimate partner abuse. Holmes claimed that Balwani abused her emotionally and psychologically, which Balwani denied, and that this abuse caused Holmes to believe whatever he told her about the company's financial models.

My goal is not to advocate for Holmes. The actions she took with Theranos clearly stepped well over the line, the most troubling of which from my perspective concerned the decision to use the public as unsuspecting guinea pigs by pushing its technology to market even though it was not working. Rather, my goal is simply to underscore how, even with the Model Penal Code's attempt to elaborate what mens rea means, the determination of intent can still be subject to serious debate. Even when people agree on what might have happened, when there was clear harm, and when everyone has the same information about the incident, it can be easy to construct alternative narratives about why the transgression occurred. Reasonable people can often disagree about which narrative is correct because we rarely have direct access to what the offender had really been thinking.

That is why our criminal justice system relies on a jury of six to twelve to make this subjective judgment. This is based on the recognition that each juror will form their own opinion by drawing on not just the facts but also their own background, experiences, biases, and intuitions. In Holmes's case, each juror may have held different views about whether the indictment stemmed at least partly from the fact that she was a woman in a Silicon Valley culture dominated by men. The extent to which they believed claims by the defense that Holmes's actions were due to her former boyfriend's emotional and psychological abuse may depend on whether they have experienced relationship abuse themselves. Moreover, their views about the acceptability of Holmes's lies and deceptions may depend on whether they are more inclined to identify with Silicon Valley entrepreneurs trying to "change the world" or with Theranos's investors or patients.

The system is, therefore, designed so that even if one or more jurors' inferences are flawed, their attempts to form a collective judgment may still allow the jury to converge on the appropriate interpretation. Yet the criminal justice system also recognizes that this elaborate and time-consuming approach to gauging the intentionality of a defendant can still fail. Entire juries can be wrong, even after lengthy discussions. That is why the justice system has made a deliberate decision to reduce the chances of making one type of error (convicting the innocent) in favor of another (letting the guilty go free) by using the standard of "beyond a reasonable doubt" as a high threshold for guilt in criminal cases.

Now, let's compare this highly involved approach by the justice system with how we make intentionality judgments in our own lives. Are we even close to being as systematic and careful? Do we try to give equal consideration to alternative explanations for what might have happened? Do we account for how our own past experiences might shape how we view the incident? Do we try to engage in discussions with others to reconcile those idiosyncratic differences of opinion and converge on more robust and defensible judgments? And do we accept the possibility that, even after all those efforts, our inferences might still be wrong?

These questions are not meant to suggest that we need to treat every offense like a criminal trial or that the criminal justice system is perfect. Performing that kind of systematic assessment of every possible infraction may simply not be practical. Moreover, the determination of criminal guilt is quite different from being guilty of a trust violation. Guilt in criminal cases needs to satisfy two simultaneous questions—whether the defendant was responsible for the crime (actus reus) and whether the defendant had intended for that to happen (mens rea). However, research on the repair of trust treats guilt simply as a matter of whether one is responsible for the transgression and treats the matter of intent as an entirely different matter of why the transgression might have happened (to gauge the extent to which the violator should be trusted in the future). This is one of the reasons why, as chapter 6 will detail, the criminal justice system is not well suited to determining how trust might be repaired and, in many cases, can even prevent that from happening.

Nevertheless, the fact that matters of intent are scrutinized so much more carefully in the criminal justice system than in our own lives raises the need to consider the implications of our often automatic inferences about intent in the broader context of trust violations. Because the perception of intentionality differentiates how those violations are viewed (as a matter of competence or integrity), and this can make such a marked difference in how people respond when violators apologize and assume responsibility for what occurred, we will also need to devote more careful attention to what this might entail for a broader array of efforts to repair trust after such incidents. Moreover, as we do so, we will likewise need to consider how those whose trust has been violated may often bear as much responsibility for what happens after a transgression as the violators themselves.

4

SOWING THE SEEDS OF
OUR FRUSTRATION

On the night of April 19, 1989, a jogger was brutally beaten and raped in New York City's Central Park. Five boys, all between the ages of fourteen and sixteen, who had been in the park were arrested and interrogated for hours until they confessed to the rape. The boys all later recanted those confessions, which were inconsistent not only with one another but also with other aspects of the crime. What's more, the DNA evidence did not match any of the five boys'. But the prosecutors proceeded to trial anyway and convicted all of them based on those initial statements. Four of the boys were charged as juveniles and served six to seven years each, while the sixteen-year-old was charged as an adult and served thirteen years in an adult prison, before a man named Matias Reyes confessed to the crime in 2002. Reyes's confession was subsequently confirmed by the DNA evidence, so the boys' convictions had to be vacated.[1]

The lead prosecutor, Linda Fairstein, has never apologized for her role in these convictions. Instead, she told *The New Yorker* in 2002 that her office's handling of the case was solid and remained adamant that, even if their convictions have to be vacated, such a finding shouldn't be taken as proof of their innocence.[2] Moreover, in response to a dramatized portrayal of the case in the 2019 Netflix miniseries *When They See Us*, she wrote, "None of this is true," adding that the woman known as the "Central Park Jogger," Trisha Meili, was not the only one in the park that night. "Eight others were attacked, including two men who were beaten so savagely that they required hospitalizations for head injuries. Nothing Mr. Reyes said exonerated these five of those attacks. And there was certainly more than enough evidence to support those convictions of first-degree assault, robbery, riot, and other charges."[3]

The strength of the claims by both Fairstein and her detractors has long been a matter of dispute, given the complex nature of this case.[4] However, public furor over the incident reached an entirely new level when the Netflix miniseries threw a metaphorical hand grenade into the complex racial politics surrounding these events, by offering an interpretation that was sure to resonate in these hypersensitive times. It claimed that the boys were convicted because white people in positions of power could only see them as violent criminals and portrayed Fairstein as a bigot and unethical villain.

The series' portrayal has created enormous backlash for Fairstein.[5] Online petitions and a hashtag, #CancelLindaFairstein, have called for a boycott of her books and her removal from prominent board positions, she was dropped from her publisher,[6] and she was forced to take down her own Twitter account after receiving a barrage of criticism. Though there were many other parties that participated in arresting, interrogating, and convicting the boys, much of the backlash centered on her. As Ken Burns, the famed documentary maker who offered his own account of this incident in his 2012 film, *The Central Park Five,* observed, "A lot of the anger [that] has been directed toward Fairstein also makes some sense . . . because Fairstein has repeatedly defended the work of the police and her office."[7]

Fairstein responded to this backlash by filing a defamation suit against Netflix, the series' director, Ava DuVernay, and the series' writer and producer, Attica Locke, for the show's alleged falsehoods—a suit that a U.S. district judge allowed to move forward in an August 9, 2021, judgment[8] but, at the time of this writing, has yet to reach a conclusion. However, that backlash has also led others, such as the Vox journalist Alissa Wilkinson, to pose a question: "Would things have been different for Fairstein in the court of public opinion if she'd offered an apology for the wrongful convictions and become an advocate for change in the system in the years following the exonerations?"[9]

Based on the research evidence from chapter 3, my guess is no. I take no pleasure in this response, given that so many who believed the allegations of racism that have been made against Fairstein, as well as others involved in the case, have wanted her to apologize. In fact, most of us would probably say that a sincere apology would be particularly important if someone has committed this kind of integrity-based violation. Yet if we consider the public's reactions to the Real IRA's apology after the Omagh bombing and scientific research on this issue, the evidence suggests that when those who commit such transgressions do apologize, we tend to hate them even more. And this can ultimately discourage violators from apologizing.

Consider, for example, the fashion company Dolce & Gabbana's attempt to apologize for a controversy it caused in mainland China in 2018. At the time, the company had posted a series of promotional videos ahead of the Shanghai fashion show, which were widely criticized as racist and disrespectful of Chinese culture. The videos depicted a Chinese model struggling to eat pizza, cannoli, and pasta with chopsticks, set to a soundtrack of stereotypical Chinese music, while a patronizing Mandarin voiceover instructed her on how to eat Italian dishes. Fuel was then added to the fire when screenshots of private messages on Instagram were released, which allegedly showed the brand's cofounder and designer Stefano Gabbana responding to the ad controversy with a series of derogatory remarks about China and Chinese people. They included a description of China as "the country of . . ." followed by a string of excrement emojis and another message with the phrase "China Ignorant Dirty Smelling Mafia."[10]

The fallout was immediate. Mentions of the brand surged by 2,512 percent on Weibo, the Chinese version of Twitter, with many social media users filming themselves destroying D&G products. The brand's Shanghai fashion show had to be canceled just days later. Its products were pulled from almost all major Chinese e-commerce platforms, including Alibaba's Tmall and JD.com. Moreover, Chinese models and celebrities terminated their contracts with D&G en masse, with one famous actress stating that she would never buy or wear the brand again.

Anxious to quell the backlash, Gabbana and cofounder Domenico Dolce posted a one-and-a-half-minute apology video on social media. It began with them sitting side by side at a table saying directly to the camera, "Over the past few days, we have thought long and hard with great sadness about everything that has happened and what we have caused in your country, and we are very sorry." Then after underscoring their respect for cultures around the world and their love for China in particular, they concluded by stating, "We will never forget this experience, and it will certainly never happen again. In fact, we will work to do things better. We will respect the Chinese culture in every way possible. From the bottom of our hearts, we ask for forgiveness. Sorry."[11]

As far as apologies go, this one wasn't terrible. From the standpoint of research on the components of an apology, described in chapter 3, this video seems to touch either implicitly or explicitly on most of the components that people might look for in this kind of response. Yet D&G's apology didn't sway Chinese public sentiment at all.[12] The company's Beijing and Shanghai stores remained almost empty. The label remained entirely frozen out of major Chinese e-retailers. By June 2021, almost three years after the scandal, Chinese consumers had still not forgiven or forgotten what happened. This was underscored when the Hong Kong pop singer Karen Mok came under fire on social media that summer for wearing a D&G cloak in the music video for her new song, "A Woman for All Seasons." As journalist Megan Hills reported for CNN, many criticized Mok for insulting China with that choice, with one calling her a "two-faced person who comes to the mainland to make money."[13]

These reactions seem to reflect a genuine dissatisfaction with how this scandal has been handled, a sentiment the Chinese public certainly had a right to express. But a growing body of scientific evidence suggests that such reactions can encourage offenders to address their transgressions in ways that many of us are likely to think would be even worse. Let's return, for example, to the job interview experiments in chapter 3, which found that even though we may want an apology from those who commit an integrity-based violation, we ultimately evaluate them less favorably if they offer that apology rather than a denial. This finding suggests that we not only punish those who apologize for these kinds of incidents but also unwittingly encourage them to deny culpability instead.

A case in point can be found in the Facebook initiative, code-named Project Amplify, that Mark Zuckerberg approved in August 2021. This initiative represented a broad shift in strategy for the company, which for years had confronted crisis after crisis over concerns about privacy, misinformation, and hate speech on its platform by publicly apologizing. Mr. Zuckerberg personally apologized in 2018, for example, after the company extracted personal data from approximately fifty million people and allowed a data firm working for the 2016 Trump campaign to exploit it.[14] However, these apologies did little to quell criticism of the company on a host of issues, including the site's tolerance for racist speech and vaccine misinformation, or win Facebook any supporters.

The company, therefore, decided to change course by going on the offensive. In January 2021, the communications team discussed ways for executives to be less conciliatory when responding to crises and decided that there would be less apologizing.[15] Hence, in July of that year, when President Biden said Facebook was "killing people" by spreading COVID-19 misinformation, Guy Rosen, Facebook's vice president for integrity, disputed that characterization in a blog post and pointed out that the White House had missed its own coronavirus vaccination goals. The company also became less transparent by restricting access to company data that allowed academics and journalists to scrutinize how the social network worked. Moreover, Facebook again employed their new offensive strategy in response to a September 2021 investigation by *The Wall Street Journal* based on leaked internal Facebook documents. These documents revealed that Facebook's own researchers were aware that its popular photo-sharing app, Instagram, harmed the self-image and mental health of many teenage girls and that its platform was used in developing countries for human trafficking, drug dealing, and the promotion of ethnic violence.[16] This led Nick Clegg, Facebook's vice president for global affairs and communications, to write a blog post that denounced the premise of the *Journal*'s investigation and claimed that the idea that Facebook executives repeatedly ignored warnings about these problems was "just plain false."[17]

I doubt that many of us would condone Facebook's new tactics. The concerns about Facebook's approach to managing the many tensions between its pursuit of profit and the public's welfare are quite serious, and this broad change in public relations strategy offered little confidence that the company would work harder to address these problems. However, the company's decision to shift from apologies to denials really shouldn't surprise any of us. Like it or not, it was a natural response to how little its former, more conciliatory, approach did to improve its public standing. Despite how shortsighted their new strategy might seem, at the core, the company was simply responding to the feedback it was getting and trying something else.

Of course, there are times when denial really is the preferred choice. As the science reporter Ben Carey discussed in an article for *The New York Times*,[18] many psychologists today would argue that denial can serve as a protective defense against unbearable news, such as a cancer diagnosis, and help us manage grief and trauma. In the short term, denial can protect us from getting too overwhelmed and give our minds the opportunity to unconsciously process distressing information at a pace that won't send us into a psychological tailspin.

Moreover, different forms of denial can sometimes enable more durable benefits as well. Carey, for example, quotes psychologist Michael McCullough, who explains, "We really do want to be moral people, but the fact is that we cut corners to get individual advantage, and we rely on the room that denial gives us to get by, to wiggle out of speeding tickets, and to forgive others for doing the same." This approach to denial may help explain why romantic couples who engaged in a blend of denial and rationalizations to portray their partner's flaws in more positive terms, as we saw in chapter 2, were likelier to stay together and report being more satisfied in their relationship than those who did not.

However, when it comes to what people would prefer from those who have violated their trust, people generally expect, and even demand, apologies. Amy Dickinson, writer of the syndicated column Ask Amy for the *Chicago Tribune,* made this observation when she was interviewed by Neal Conan for NPR. She said, "I'm surprised at how often I get letters from people who want me to give them the words so that they can demand and then get an apology many, many, many years later for an affront that happened a long time ago."[19] Psychotherapist Beverly Engel explained this sentiment by noting that apologies are "an important social ritual, a way of showing respect and empathy for the wronged person or persons . . . [It] shows that we care about the other person's feelings . . . that we are capable of taking responsibility for our actions." She added that this response also allows apology recipients to feel that the apologizer is no longer a threat to them and it, furthermore, validates their feelings and perceptions.[20]

Yet if apologies really are what we want, the findings from my studies raise a very serious concern. By considering those who apologize for integrity-based violations less trustworthy and becoming less willing to make ourselves vulnerable to them in the future, we are telling those who might have otherwise sought to provide this response not to bother. Our reactions make it loud and clear that they would be better off if they simply denied guilt for the incident. And it is in this sense that our reactions to these kinds of trust violations can be self-defeating.

The incentive problems we create for those accused of a violation also don't stop there. Let's revisit the job interview study we discussed earlier, in which a job candidate is accused of filing an incorrect tax return at her prior job and either apologized or denied culpability for that incident. Now, let's also suppose that after the interview, you then obtained incontrovertible proof from a reliable source that this person had been lying. How would this affect your view of that candidate?

My guess is that if the candidate denied culpability for the incident but was then found to be guilty, you would be particularly disinclined to trust that person. Likewise, if that candidate apologized for the incident but was then proven innocent, this would also damage that person's credibility (and perhaps also raise other red flags about that person's grip on reality), which should lower your trust in the candidate as well. Thus, it seems natural to expect that efforts to repair trust with a dishonest response would damage trust even further if that lie is discovered.

My research team tested this premise in a follow-up experiment that asked participants to rate their trust in a job candidate twice—first, immediately after she offered an apology or denial for either of the accounting-related allegations I mentioned previously, and then after receiving the results of an official inquiry, which concluded that the candidate was either innocent or guilty.[21] As we expected, the findings from that study made clear that when the candidate's response was proven false by subsequent evidence, this significantly lowered trust.

However, we found a much more insidious side to this story as well. The results also revealed that although having a response refuted by the facts can significantly damage trust, this didn't lower trust any more than if the respondent had offered an honest but suboptimal response from the beginning. Thus, when the candidate denied guilt for an integrity-based violation and subsequent evidence proved that denial to be a lie, trust in that candidate was certainly lowered. However, trust was not lowered any more from that lie than if the candidate had apologized for the integrity-based violation in the first place. This was because being guilty of an integrity-based violation was so harmful for trust that, even if one was found to have clearly lied about that guilt as well, there was essentially no room for trust to be lowered further.

This is where perceivers again create a terrible incentive for those accused of a violation. If we were to consider how the job candidate should address the allegation, my guess is that few of us are likely to say that we would want that person to lie about it afterward. We also reflect that preference, to some degree, by exhibiting less trust in the candidate if we discover that this person lied. However, if the cost we impose for that lie is no greater than if the candidate had been honest from the beginning, then it shouldn't be a surprise that this person would wonder if lying is worth the risk. What would the candidate have to lose?

This issue reminds me of a scene from the 2001 heist film *Ocean's Eleven,* where Tess Ocean (played by Julia Roberts) criticizes her ex-con former husband, Danny Ocean (played by George Clooney), with the accusation, "You're a thief and a liar." And in response, Danny explains, "I only lied about being a thief." What makes this moment funny is that Danny's response offers an element of truth. If you're already a convicted thief, what does it matter if you lied about being one as well? The latter offense can seem trivial in comparison, and that's what makes Tess's twofold criticism seem amusingly petty.

But is it petty? Don't we care about people lying to us as well? We clearly do. Michelle Mays, the founder of PartnerHope and the Center for Relational Recovery, notes that for most romantic partners who have experienced sexual betrayal, for example, the lying is at least as painful as the sexual behaviors that might have instigated it. She writes, "While the sex is a huge breach in trust, the lying feels like an even deeper betrayal. When your partner lies to you, it creates a sense that you cannot know what reality is. You cannot believe that what he says to you is true, authentic, and real."[22]

It certainly is the case that as with denials, we do not always consider lies bad. Organizational psychologists Emma Levine and Maurice Schweitzer, for example, conducted experiments that randomly assigned two people to the role of either Sender or Receiver and asked them to play a game with financial payoffs that would be determined by the outcome of a computer-simulated coin flip and the choices the participants made. The game would only inform the Sender the results of that coin flip. Hence, Senders had an opportunity to send their Receivers either a dishonest message about the outcome of the coin flip (that would likely benefit the Receiver and prove costly to the Sender) or an honest message about that outcome (that would likely benefit the Sender and prove costly to the Receiver). When Receivers learned whether the Sender had lied after the game was completed, their responses revealed that they viewed Senders who lied to benefit the Receiver to be more trustworthy and moral than those who told the truth.[23]

However, in the absence of such clear prosocial goals, lies are of course generally considered to be harmful. Lies involve a deliberate choice to fabricate the truth. They represent an intentional decision to violate the principle of honesty that most of us consider important. Thus, in the absence of any countervailing principle that we might find equally important (such as helping others), lies represent clear integrity-based violations that typically damage trust.

Yet if we ultimately do care about violators lying to us, the evidence from my own experiment suggests that we are not doing enough to discourage it. If the repercussions are the same regardless of whether someone offers a false denial for an integrity-based violation and is then found to have lied or admits guilt and apologizes for that transgression from the beginning, then there's little objective reason for them *not* to lie. We have created the incentive for them to do so through our reactions, especially if there's a chance that the lie won't be discovered.

The incentive problems we can create for those who have been accused of a transgression, furthermore, don't end there. What if someone is obviously guilty of a violation and thus cannot deny it outright? That person still has the choice of responding in ways that assume full blame for what happened or by making excuses that try to shift at least part of the blame to other things. The offender, for example, could argue that the incident occurred due to pressure from peers, orders from a boss, or a host of other factors.

In these instances, the prevailing wisdom (again consistent with the takeaway from the Tylenol pill-tampering case in chapter 3) is that the best thing to do is to take full ownership for what happened rather than provide an excuse. The logic here makes sense if we consider how the acceptance of full blame can offer a stronger signal that the violator recognizes and intends to rectify the failing. The problem, however, is that this logic again considers only one side of the coin. It does not account for how people also respond to information about guilt.

Another variant of the job interview studies my research team conducted sought to investigate this issue by having the job candidate, who had been accused of a violation, either accept full blame or try to shift some of that blame to external factors.[24] The violation again either concerned matters of competence (filing an incorrect tax return due to inadequate knowledge of the tax codes) or integrity (filing the incorrect tax return intentionally to satisfy an important client). But this time, the candidate always apologized for the incident and promised that it would not happen again. The only difference was whether, in addition to apologizing, the candidate took full or partial responsibility for what happened. In the latter case, she attributed the rest of this responsibility to the influence of higher-level managers at her prior job (i.e., either bad advice regarding the implementation of tax codes or pressure to misreport some of the tax return's numbers, respectively, depending on whether the violation concerned matters of competence or integrity).

Now, let's say you were evaluating these responses. Which one would you prefer? If you are like most of us, you would probably have a strong preference for that guilty candidate to take full responsibility for the incident than to make excuses, regardless of the type of violation that occurred. Yet the findings from this study revealed that although accepting full blame can help repair trust after a competence-based violation, doing so is much less helpful after an integrity-based violation. The findings revealed that being guilty of the integrity-based violation was so harmful for trust that the candidate was evaluated more favorably if she instead offered an excuse for what happened (in this case, by stating she had been pressured by managers to misreport the tax numbers).

The irony here is that, as we discussed in chapter 3, people intuitively believe that those with high integrity would act with integrity regardless of the situation. Thus, we tend to discount claims that integrity-based violations were caused by external factors rather than one's own deficiency. Yet the evidence indicates that being guilty of an integrity-based violation is so harmful for trust that any excuse, even one that perceivers are likely to question, can help. This underscores how, to the extent that most of us would prefer having violators take full ownership for what happened rather than pass the buck, our reactions are again encouraging the exact opposite of that preference.

In this regard, it is worth noting that the U.S. legal system has implemented practices to counteract these kinds of issues. If someone is indicted for a crime, the defendant is given a more lenient sentence if that person admits guilt. Likewise, parole is likelier to be granted for the convicted who take full responsibility for their crimes rather than make excuses. These legal practices certainly have their own problems, some of which I will cover in chapter 6. Most obviously, these practices will do little to help when someone has been falsely accused of a crime, as with the five boys at the start of this chapter who were charged with beating and raping a woman in Central Park. However, these legal practices can at least help counteract some of the downsides of how we tend to deal with these responses on our own.

Our challenge, though, is that most trust-related judgments don't occur through the legal system. Moreover, even when a law tells us one thing, our gut can tell us another. For example, consider the right against self-incrimination. It turns out that despite widespread recognition of this right, as well as the many legitimate reasons why those accused may not offer an immediate response to an allegation, the evidence from other experiments my collaborators and I have conducted reveals that not offering an immediate response tends to be the most harmful response of all.[25] In particular, we found that (for those seeking to repair trust) offering no response was as harmful as apologizing for integrity-based violations, while also being as harmful as denying culpability for competence-based violations. In short, staying silent may be a good way to protect yourself in legal situations, but it will also make you look untrustworthy, regardless of whether you are guilty or not.

This is due to another wrinkle in how people tend to make judgments. Most of us believe that when making a judgment, we would carefully weigh the pros and cons of all the information available before reaching a conclusion. But that's not how the real process happens. Rather than evaluate this information in a systematic manner before reaching a conclusion, the evidence from the studies my collaborators and I have conducted on the effects of silence suggests that we instead act far more impetuously by immediately reaching a conclusion based on the information we first consider and then only later revising that conclusion if we have the opportunity and inclination to consider more.

In other words, we first "believe" and then "disbelieve," with the latter only occurring under certain conditions, such as when we have enough time, information, and motivation to examine why the initial belief might not be true. This approach can work reasonably well when decisions are insignificant or when time is of the essence. If a waiter tells you that the oysters the restaurant is serving are not quite fresh, for example, not much is lost by ordering something else from the menu, and the stakes only grow if you attempt to verify that claim by trying some for yourself. But this approach can create serious problems when the target of evaluation is another human being rather than questionable shellfish, and we are gauging our trust in that person after an alleged transgression.

In such cases, the information we first consider is the fact that this person has been accused of a violation. And our tendency is to start by believing it. Thus, the question becomes how that belief might be addressed by the alleged offender. Apologies can do that by signaling that the problem underlying the offense will be corrected, and this kind of compensating signal can certainly help for matters of competence. Alternatively, denials offer the option of directly challenging both the perception of untrustworthiness and subsequent need to be redeemed, and this can help address integrity-related violations (particularly when we are not guilty).

Offering no response, in contrast, entails the worst of both worlds. It neither promises redemption nor refutes the allegation itself. Thus, since it gives no reason to "disbelieve" the initial premise of untrustworthiness that the allegation triggered, we are simply left believing the allegation is true. This is how we can leave alleged offenders with an awkward choice (at least in the short term when exculpatory evidence is not available) between exercising their legal right to remain silent or addressing people's essentially automatic presumption, based on the accusation, that trust is not deserved.

Yet efforts to be more explicit can create a different type of problem. This can be understood by taking a closer look at a legendary example of how explicit details have been used to distinguish between those who can be trusted from those who cannot. When the rock band Van Halen rose to prominence in the 1970s, they provided the concert promoter with a contract "rider" whenever they were hired to play a show, which outlined specific things the promoter was responsible for addressing. This included standard clauses such as sound and lighting requirements, instructions for setting up the backstage area, security needs, and nutritional requests for the band and crew. These details could range from being as critical as the precise weight of the speakers that would be used, to ensure the girders and stage floor would support the weight, to as trivial as the specific brand of toilet paper that the band wanted in the backstage washroom. The rider, thus, became an unwieldy tome that few would be inclined to read in detail.

That is why, as a little test, the band included in the technical aspect of the rider, in the middle of nowhere, a clause stating, "There will be no brown M&M's in the backstage area, upon pain of forfeiture of the show, with full compensation." This additional clause provided an easy way for the band to gauge whether the promoter had bothered to read the contract. As David Lee Roth, the lead singer for the band, recounted in his book, *Crazy from the Heat,*[26] "So, when I would walk backstage, if I saw a brown M&M in that bowl . . . Guaranteed you'd run into a problem. Sometimes it would threaten to just destroy the whole show. Something like, literally, life-threatening." He proceeded to describe an incident in Pueblo, Colorado, where he found some brown M&M's and responded by trashing the dressing room. "Dumped the buffet, kicked a hole in the door, twelve hundred dollars' worth of fun." He explained that because they didn't bother to look at the weight requirements in the rider, the production's staging sank through their new flooring and did $80,000 worth of damage.

Van Halen's use of the "no brown M&M's" contract clause has been broadly portrayed as a brilliant move.[27] There seems little reason to doubt Roth's claim that, when the discovery of brown M&M's in their backstage bowl would prompt a line-check of the entire production, this was "guaranteed" to reveal a technical error. I also suspect that this seemingly capricious M&M clause, combined with the destructive havoc his band unleashed backstage if that clause was not fulfilled, helped contribute to Van Halen's bad boy reputation and gave the band some measure of free publicity.

However, this account raises some nagging questions for me as well. As Roth tells it, their band's show was the biggest production ever, and in many cases, "the venues were too outdated or inadequately prepared to set up the band's sophisticated stage."[28] Thus, there were "many, many technical errors—whether it was the girders couldn't support the weight, or the flooring would sink in, or the doors weren't big enough to move the gear through." If so, this makes me wonder whether Van Halen's sneaky clause would have necessarily screened out all those technical problems, even in the instances when the brown M&M's had been removed.

Roth never addresses that possibility, only that technical errors were "guaranteed" if he did see brown M&M's in the bowl. But if the complexity of their production made technical errors quite likely with every concert venue, and the band simply didn't embark on the same kind of line-item search for such problems when the brown M&M's had been removed, then it is not clear how useful a test that "no brown M&M's" clause provided. All we have to justify the value of that clause is one vivid anecdote about their production staging sinking through the stage floor in Pueblo, Colorado, to give us the impression this happened far more often when brown M&M's were present. But we don't have the data to know if that was really the case, let alone whether such an incident couldn't have been just as likely to occur even when the "no brown M&M's" clause had been followed, because the band's sampling methods were inherently skewed. Rock and roll doesn't train you to be a social scientist.

To illustrate how Van Halen's conclusion may be faulty, let's put ourselves in the position of a harried concert promoter struggling to overcome the difficulties posed by the outdated concert venue and this highly demanding rock band. Imagine that prior to the event, you received the band's extremely lengthy contract rider, which Roth himself acknowledged was overwhelmingly tedious and difficult to read. If you have only limited time, resources, and mental bandwidth for addressing all these contract terms, which of them are you likelier to prioritize?

For some of us, the choice might be to focus on the things that really matter, such as the kinds of safety-related concerns Roth tried to underscore in his recounting, at the expense of seemingly silly demands like "no brown M&M's" in the backstage bowl. But for others, the choice might be to prioritize the contract terms that are most easily addressed, are most easily noticed, and also happen to be accompanied by the most serious threats, such as the demand for no brown M&M's in the backstage bowl "under pain of forfeiture of the show, with full compensation." Better that than engage in the costly and time-consuming retrofits for flooring and girders whose carrying capacity can only be assessed with special equipment and that you suspect would likely hold up just fine for this concert anyway, just as they have for many other productions.

In either case, the "no brown M&M's" test would lead to the wrong conclusion. It can either lead to a false sense of danger when brown M&M's are found or a false sense of security when they are not. In fact, the only cases in which the results of this test may prove valid are the occasions in which the promoter has somehow managed to address every one of the myriad clauses that were detailed in Van Halen's lengthy contract rider. And though that is theoretically possible, I suspect that was far from the norm. Instead, a likelier consequence of Van Halen embedding that hidden "gotcha" in its contracts may have simply been to promote misunderstandings and mistrust through these encounters.

The second experiment in the contracting study I described in chapter 3, where contractors and subcontractors were tasked with building a house, provides some insight into how such misunderstandings can happen.[29] This follow-up experiment sought to address a question that had been raised about whether violations of documented expectations (letter violations) would still be considered more intentional than violations of undocumented expectations (spirit violations) if the contract was more complex. This question was based on the notion that we should all understand how much easier it can be to miss even explicitly documented expectations as contracts become more complicated and overwhelm the ability of contracting parties to keep track of those details. Thus, we should be less inclined to consider letter violations more intentional than spirit violations as the complexity of the contract grows.

I tested this possibility by creating different versions of a short-term contract people use to rent vacation homes and asking participants to play the role of a property owner who had rented their home to a tenant. Participants would be informed that they had drafted a contract, which the tenant had read and signed, and they were given a copy of the contract, which was either quite lengthy and complex or short and simple, so participants could read it themselves. In the high-complexity condition, the contract was three pages long and contained twenty-four detailed terms. However, in the low-complexity condition, the contract was just one page long and contained only six of the terms that were contained in the more complex version. Moreover, regardless of the contract's complexity, each of the contracts contained the following documented expectation: "The maximum occupancy is 8. No additional persons are permitted to spend

the night. Persons on the property are the sole responsibility of the Tenant." This served as the basis for the contract violations that were enacted in the study.

Specifically, after reading the contract, participants were informed, "During the tenant's stay, however, you discovered that they held a large party during the day with roughly 30 people. This led to two toilets getting clogged, a rosebush being trampled, a broken gate, and a noise complaint, which took time and money to rectify." In the letter violation condition, participants would then be told, "The contract explicitly documents that the maximum occupancy for the property was 8, but the tenant violated the contract term by having more than 30 people at the home." However, in the spirit violation condition, participants would be told, "Even though the term referring to the maximum occupancy of 8 did not explicitly state that it applied to visitors during the day, the tenant violated the intent of that contract term by having more than 30 people at the home." In each case, participants were also informed that they received an email from the tenant a day after that renter left stating, "I'm really sorry. This was my fault. If there is anything I can do, please let me know." Then, after receiving this information, participants would be asked to gauge the intentionality of the incident, as well as their trust in and willingness to punish that tenant through legal action.

How do you think contract complexity would have affected these assessments? If you are like most, your guess would probably be that people would be more understanding of violations that concern explicitly documented expectations when contracts become more complex. This is because most of us understand how easy it can be for people to miss a detail as the complexity of a task grows. However, that was not the case. Contract complexity did not have any discernible effect on how intentional the violation was perceived to be. Hence, people still considered letter violations to be more intentional than spirit violations in general and were, thus, more inclined to punish the apologetic tenant when the violation concerned a documented, rather than undocumented, term.

These findings raise serious red flags for anyone seeking to distinguish those who can be trusted from those who cannot by adding sneaky traps, like Van Halen's "no brown M&M's" clause, to complex contracts. By adding such hidden clauses, and thereby making contracts even more complex, chances are quite high that they will be overlooked. Indeed, the more complicated the contract, the more difficult it will be for even the most earnest individual to address everything. Yet the results from this experiment reveal that we will fail to account for how the contract's complexity may be responsible for these oversights happening and instead just blame the violator when that hidden clause has not been addressed. Thus, one consequence of this hidden clause approach is that it can ultimately lead us to place less trust in others than they might deserve.

If so, the natural question becomes: What would be the alternative? Well, in Van Halen's case, the answer seems simple. Roth's recounting suggests that the band's clear priority was safety (for example, making sure the stage floor and girders could support their equipment's massive weight). If so, why not put that priority front and center at the top of the contract, detail how those major safety issues must be verified "under pain of forfeiture of the show, with full compensation," and *not* distract the concert promoter from addressing those mission-critical items with trivial demands like "no brown M&M's" and a specific brand of toilet paper in the backstage washroom? Wouldn't that do more to ensure their clear priorities had been satisfied?

These questions aren't meant to claim that Van Halen's tactic was necessarily foolish. I certainly don't have experience with the kinds of challenges this band faced on a regular basis, and it's possible that there were other particulars about these concert riders that really did make the band's use of its "no brown M&M's" clause a clever choice. However, I raise these concerns based on several of my own contracting experiences, where I have dutifully waded through pages of contract legalese to make sure I live up to my part of the agreement, only to find that I had taken the contract details more seriously than even the ones who had proposed it.

Each time, I have found explicit terms that have been embedded, often as boilerplate language from long ago, that the counterpart presenting the contract had overlooked and eventually suggested we disregard. The most alarming example of this occurred with the covenants, conditions, and restrictions (CC&Rs) for a home I purchased years ago that, to the community's embarrassment, still included explicit restrictions against Blacks and Asians, like myself, owning property in the neighborhood. Those CC&Rs are still used by that community today, with the only difference (at least in the copy I received) being that someone crossed out that restrictive language with a pen and added a handwritten note claiming that this text had been "deleted on April 4, 195x" (with the x illegible due to bad photocopying).

It is unclear whether the cross-outs and handwritten note were added by someone in an official capacity or not. There is no official seal, signature, or even a set of initials next to them to let me know one way or the other. Moreover, even though I have received official documentation of these CC&Rs being modified in other ways, none of those changes mention anything about those racial restrictions being removed. This leads me to believe that the restrictions still reside in those official documents and that the community has simply turned a blind eye to that discriminatory language, with the takeaway being that even explicitly documented expectations aren't necessarily representative of what any of the contracting parties might really want. I, for one, put far more stock in the welcome I felt from my neighbors and the growing diversity I have seen in that community than some antiquated, and ultimately unenforceable, language in a document almost no one reads.

The bottom line is that it would be a mistake to assume that increasing the amount of documentation will necessarily help you. It can just as often lead to other types of problems, such as confusion, vestiges from past agreements that have little to do with the current situation, unnecessary discussions over clause clarifications and markups, greater difficulty keeping track of all those details, and greater mistrust if those documented expectations are violated. Thus, by insisting on greater documentation in our agreements to protect ourselves, we can sometimes make things even worse.

These considerations, in turn, further underscore the broader message from this chapter—namely, that the repair of trust is not just the alleged violator's responsibility. Perceivers play a major role in the trust-repair process as well. Perceivers can make an enormous difference by affecting not only how violations are addressed but also how the violation is viewed and ultimately the extent to which efforts to repair trust would be successful.

This doesn't mean that perceivers should simply assume that trust is always worth repairing. There may certainly be times when the repair of trust is not warranted, just like there may be times when it is. However, what these observations do suggest is that perceivers should give more careful consideration to how they make those judgments, because they can affect what occurs after trust has been violated in more ways than they might think. At some point, all of us are violators and all of us are perceivers. Thus, the questions each of us needs to answer are: How well do we play each of these roles, and what can we do to get better?

5

THE SEDUCTION OF SIMPLISTIC STORIES

t may be tempting to infer from the prior chapters that the best course of action, when trust has been violated, would be for offenders to just offer the response that would be most effective for the type of violation that occurred. In other words, is the lesson that they should simply be more strategic, by apologizing for competence-based violations, but denying and shirking blame for integrity-based violations? My emphatic answer is no. Beyond the basic fact that most of us would consider such an approach unethical, it can also be quite risky and ineffective at repairing trust when the response can be refuted. Even if getting caught falsely denying one's guilt for an integrity-based violation, for example, makes the offender no worse off than honestly admitting that guilt from the beginning, the end result for each approach remains that trust has not been repaired. In either case, the violator would be considered guilty of an integrity-based violation, and perceivers will consider that guilt to be more diagnostic than any positive signals of repentance that violator might convey. This is not only evident from the research findings but can also be illustrated by many real-life incidents. The case of President Bill Clinton's impeachment in 1998, when the discovery of Monica Lewinsky's stained blue dress proved his denial of their alleged affair to be a lie, is just one example.

Rather, there is a far more meaningful implication from this research. It stems from the fact that, in each of the studies, the underlying transgressions being tested, such as the filing of an incorrect tax return, were really the same. They had been framed as a matter of competence or integrity. Yet this simple difference in how the same offense had been framed was enough to produce dramatically different reactions to the same trust-repair efforts.

The importance of such framing can be seen by comparing Bill Clinton's experience, when he ultimately admitted and apologized for his affair, with that of Arnold Schwarzenegger, when, during his campaign for governor of California in 2003, six women came forward with accusations of groping and humiliation that spanned decades prior.[1] Schwarzenegger also apologized, and he did so for what could be considered far more egregious behavior. Whereas Clinton's scandal involved one willing partner, Schwarzenegger's actions involved multiple unwilling victims. Yet Clinton was impeached for his behavior, whereas Schwarzenegger won his bid for gubernatorial office.

I recall hearing discussions on the radio after Schwarzenegger's victory by political pundits who wondered whether this meant that the public was no longer as concerned about sex scandals as it had been during Clinton's time. This premise seems doubtful given the public's reactions to a litany of sex scandals that have occurred since, including the 2009 censure and two impeachment resolutions for Mark Sanford (then governor of South Carolina) for using state funds to pursue an extramarital affair, the 2017 firings of journalists Charlie Rose and Matt Lauer for sexual harassment, and the 2020 sentencing of film producer Harvey Weinstein to twenty-three years in prison for sexual abuse and rape.

The Schwarzenegger case differs from these other incidents in another way. All the other scandals were considered clear breaches of integrity. And we know that even if these public figures offered an apology (as most did), the apology would be ineffective for addressing integrity-based violations. However, Schwarzenegger also did something else. Before he apologized, he reframed the incident in a critical way.[2] He said, "Yes, I have behaved badly sometimes. Yes, it is true that I was on rowdy movie sets . . . and I have done things I thought were playful that now I recognize that I have offended people." It was only after those statements that he also said, "I am deeply sorry about that and I apologize."

In short, he first reframed the violation as a competence-related issue—namely, a faulty social barometer that led him to misunderstand and misbehave in these situations. We also know that for competence-based violations, an apology can be far more effective. It's not clear whether this was enough to sway any of Schwarzenegger's accusers, and I wouldn't be surprised if it didn't (for reasons that I will detail later in this and other chapters). However, it was enough to convince a sufficient number of voters to avoid the potentially devastating inference that Schwarzenegger lacked integrity, in favor of the view that this was a potentially correctable problem (regarding his limited understanding of certain social cues), for him to win the election.

This doesn't mean that this kind of reframing is always feasible, easy, or warranted. It may just be a coincidence, but since the science journalist Shankar Vedantam, who had been at *The Washington Post* and is now host and creator of the podcast *Hidden Brain,* was the first to report some of my research findings on this matter,[3] I have noticed several ham-fisted attempts by public figures and organizations to do precisely that. For example, when Fox News was caught having used a photo of sex trafficker Jeffrey Epstein and his alleged accomplice Ghislaine Maxwell that cropped President Donald Trump out of the image, Fox News responded on July 5, 2020, by stating that the president's image had been cropped "mistakenly" and added, "we regret the error."[4]

Yet the claim that a major news network like Fox would somehow crop Trump's image out of the photo by mistake seems particularly hard to believe, given Fox's well-established reputation for distorting news for political purposes.[5] When the motive is obvious, it becomes harder to rule out intent, and the incident becomes more clearly a matter of integrity. That is why I would also suspect that, to the extent that other news organizations across the political spectrum develop their own reputations for journalistic bias, they too will find it harder to reframe any misreporting consistent with that bias as "mistakes."

Efforts to reframe a transgression can, furthermore, fail even when it is hard to identify a clear motive for the violation. For example, let's revisit the case of Dolce & Gabbana in 2018, in which the company released a promotional video that many considered racist and disrespectful of Chinese culture, and this was followed by the release of Instagram messages allegedly sent from Gabbana's account disparaging China. It is hard to imagine how the founders of D&G could have wanted to offend the Chinese public. Businesses generally don't profit from insulting their customers.

Nevertheless, when Dolce & Gabbana apologized and twice sought to characterize these incidents as "mistakes," those attempts to reframe what happened from matters of integrity to competence didn't work either. As Shaun Rein, founder and managing director of China Market Research Group, stated to CNN, "If you say something publicly but then allegedly say 'Chinese are s**t' in private, then who's going to believe you?"[6] The Chinese public believed that it had a very clear glimpse into the company's real views about China and its culture through Gabbana's private Instagram messages. Thus, when D&G's apology was released, some internet users observed that "D&G is just apologizing to Chinese people's wallets."[7]

That view illustrates how even if violators do not have a motive to violate trust, they typically have a motive to repair it—to maintain their relationships and all the benefits those relationships might afford. The latter motive can, furthermore, prove just as problematic for violators who seek to reframe their transgressions as the motive to commit the offense in the first place. Perceivers are often suspicious of reframing attempts, particularly when the reframing might serve the violator's interests, and this can lead them to push back against such efforts.

These considerations point to how the matter of whether a transgression should be viewed as a matter of competence or integrity can be just as much a subject of contention as whether the offender offers an apology or denial. Perceivers are not just blank slates. The information they already have about the violation, their past experiences, the assumptions they have made, and a host of other factors we will consider later in this book can all affect whether they will be open to reframing attempts or not. Thus, we ultimately need to understand why efforts to reframe a violation might be more successful in some cases than others. Why did Arnold Schwarzenegger's attempt to reframe his transgressions from matters of integrity to competence succeed, for example, when similar attempts by others who have since been accused in the #MeToo era failed? I suspect there were several reasons.

First, the incidents involving Schwarzenegger (one occurring in the 1970s, two in the 1980s, two in the 1990s, and one in 2000) spanned almost thirty years, starting in the 1970s when "a lot of crazy things happened," before he was married, said Schwarzenegger.[8] Further, the more recent of those incidents occurred in studio offices and on movie sets that tend "to be rowdy and permissive," as some stressed when they were interviewed for an article about these allegations in the *Los Angeles Times*.[9] Thus, the implicit message those sentiments conveyed was that we shouldn't consider his actions breaches of integrity or violations of principles we believe should be upheld, because the standards people lived by at those times and in those settings were different. Many simply expected that kind of behavior to occur without social or professional repercussions. Of course, we don't know what percentage of the public might have been persuaded by such claims, but that percentage probably wasn't zero. Moreover, regardless of what that percentage might have been, it is certainly true that the public is far less tolerant of sexual harassment today, even in the film industry, as Harvey Weinstein eventually discovered.

Second, Maria Shriver—his wife, a journalist, and member of the Kennedy family—became his most vocal defender. As someone who presumably knew Schwarzenegger better than anyone, she vouched for his integrity. For example, she said in a speech to a Republican women's group in Orange County, "You can listen to all the negativity, and you can listen to people who have never met Arnold, or who met him for five seconds thirty years ago. Or you can listen to me."[10] Evidence from a study by researchers Ying Yu, Yan Yang, and Fengjie Jing supports the notion that these kinds of persuasive efforts by third parties can help repair trust with an alleged violator.[11]

Third, Schwarzenegger was an extremely popular public figure. He had built an enormous following from his bodybuilding and film careers, and he was virtually certain to win the recall election, despite the enormous number of other candidates on the ballot, before the allegations were raised. Most voters wanted him to be the next California governor. They were motivated to see that happen. Moreover, as we observed in chapter 2, that kind of pro-relationship motivation can affect how we interpret others' transgressions, to see them as less serious, less damning of the relationships we wish to preserve. This, too, could have made many in the public more receptive to the idea that his actions were mistakes rather than evidence of low integrity.

Finally, it probably also helped that Schwarzenegger had never held political office. Of course, he certainly had ample exposure to that world. He had married into the Kennedy family, after all, and he had previously been appointed by President George H. W. Bush as chairman of the President's Council on Physical Fitness and Sports, in addition to serving later as chairman of the California Governor's Council on Physical Fitness and Sports under Governor Pete Wilson. But at the time the allegations were raised, he was still a political outsider running in a California recall election on a ballot containing a total of 135 candidates, including child actor Gary Coleman and pornographer Larry Flynt.[12]

This outsider status is important because it has implications for power. A large body of research has made clear that our perception of power depends on a host of considerations that can differ quite substantially depending on the context.[13] Although Schwarzenegger had plenty of power in the film industry, in the context of politics, he was not an established player. He had less power than those who had already made politics their career. As a result, the public may have viewed his transgressions differently, by being less inclined to believe his transgressions were intentional, than if he had been an established politician whose power was high (as chapter 7 will detail). If he had been an established politician, it would have been easier to infer that he would have known his actions were inappropriate for someone seeking that kind of position and decided to use his power to act on his impulses anyway.

Of course, this is all just speculation. As with any case study, we can only try to make sense of what happened based on our inferences and attempts to associate the details of that incident with insights that have been obtained through other, hopefully more systematic, means. Thus, I wouldn't claim that this list is exhaustive or that any of those factors alone would have been sufficient to alter how Schwarzenegger's transgressions were viewed. It is, furthermore, quite possible that those factors may not all need to be in one's favor for this kind of reframing effort to work.

For example, when CNN's chief political correspondent Dana Bash interviewed Carla Hall, who had been one of the reporters of the Schwarzenegger harassment allegations for the *Los Angeles Times,* Hall pointed to Donald Trump's own harassment scandal during his presidential campaign. She observed that Trump was caught on the microphone during an interview for *Access Hollywood* "saying things about women and grabbing them and that kind of thing . . . he had to go on camera and make an apology of sorts and he survived that."[14] Trump didn't have the benefit of claims that the incident occurred decades ago. However, Trump was a political outsider, his wife defended him by stating, "This does not represent the man that I know. He has the heart and mind of a leader. I hope people will accept his apology, as I have,"[15] and he clearly had a fervent following willing to overlook virtually anything.

That seems to have been sufficient to convince enough voters that his statements were just "locker room banter" (rather than a reflection of his character) for him to survive that scandal.[16] This illustrates how, depending on the circumstances, reframing efforts can sometimes still work today. As Hall observed for CNN, "It often boils down to 'I was being playful. I was being rowdy. I had no idea I was offending somebody. I'm really sorry if I offended somebody.' And then they manage to go on."

The bottom line is that researchers do not yet have a thorough understanding of what might affect the success of efforts to alter how a transgression might be viewed. We know it is possible but also far from easy. The evidence thus far suggests that it is likely to depend on a range of considerations, some of which may not be under the violator's control. We also know that perceivers can either facilitate or impede those reframing efforts depending on what they want their future relationship with that violator to be. But this is just a starting point, with many studies still needing to be done.

Nevertheless, these considerations suggest that we should at least give more thought to our tendency to make largely automatic and simplistic attributions for these kinds of incidents and think more carefully about how our responses would have differed if other attributions had been used. For example, consider the kinds of violations I tested in some of my job interview studies, such as the case where an accountant filed a client's tax return incorrectly due to inadequate knowledge of the relevant tax codes. This can seem like a clear-cut competence-based violation. However, couldn't this lack of knowledge stem from this accountant not bothering to learn those tax codes properly in the first place, a matter of intentional negligence? Or consider how we portrayed the integrity-based violation by stating that this incorrect tax return was filed intentionally to satisfy an important client. Satisfying an important client is not an inherently bad thing. Moreover, accountants make plenty of decisions that are not black and white. There can also be shades of gray. And this can often require judgment calls by people who may do their best to strike the right balance but fail (a matter of competence).

An example of how this can happen can be found in the experience of John Vandemoer, who coached sailing at Stanford for eleven years. When federal agents uncovered a vast college admissions scheme in 2019, called Operation Varsity Blues, Vandemoer became the first person convicted for his involvement when he took a plea deal. This scheme involved dozens of wealthy and powerful parents who paid a private admissions counselor, William Singer, a total of $25 million nationwide to guarantee their children admission to top-tier schools, such as Stanford University, Yale University, and Georgetown University, as well as my own institution, the University of Southern California.

The scam worked by having parents donate a large sum of money, typically between $250,000 and $400,000, to Singer's foundation, which they could deduct from their taxes. The ostensible purpose of that donation was to "unlock the door to academic, social, personal, and career success" for underprivileged youth, according to Singer's now-defunct website. However, Singer would instead funnel the money to college coaches and athletic administrators as bribes to designate these students as recruited athletes and thus dramatically increase their chances of gaining admission, despite none of these applicants being skilled at the sports for which they were being "recruited."

Yet unlike the many coaches and administrators who personally benefited from those bribes, Vandemoer had simply handed the checks that he received from Singer, totaling $770,000, to Stanford development officers, who planned to use the money for new sailing team boats. These administrators raised few questions about the source of the gifts and made clear to Vandemoer that Singer was both well known by the senior administration and had everyone's blessing. Moreover, even though Vandemoer did wind up designating two of Singer's applicants as athletic recruits without evaluating them, no students ever entered Stanford because of Vandemoer.

This doesn't absolve Vandemoer of blame, even from his own perspective. Before sentencing, he told himself he deserved to go to jail, and he chides himself for letting Singer persuade him to classify two students as sailing recruits without vetting them first. He said, "I used shame as a warm blanket," and he believes that he should have asked more questions and shown greater skepticism about the donations.[17]

Nevertheless, in contrast to those who pocketed Singer's bribes to fund their personal lifestyles, a case can be made that Vandemoer's transgression arose from an error in judgment, a matter of competence rather than integrity, based on his impression that Stanford had already vetted Singer. Further, even though Vandemoer's plea deal allowed him to avoid a lengthy prison sentence, I find it hard to reconcile the notion that he would be fired and will have to live the rest of his life with the stigma of a felony conviction when senior Stanford officials, who were aware of the arrangement with Singer all along, avoided blame entirely. Should those officials really be absolved by their strategic ignorance, which allowed them to obtain the money they wanted while conveniently distancing themselves from the source? In their case, their purported lack of knowledge may just as easily be considered an intentional tactic meant to skirt the rules without getting their own hands dirty, a matter of integrity rather than competence.

It's possible that some may view this level of scrutiny as needless hairsplitting. After all, Vandemoer did admit to classifying two students as sailing recruits without vetting them first, and he ultimately did plead guilty for the role he played in this scandal. Moreover, for those of us who believe college admissions should be fair and meritocratic, the notion that the wealthy would pay bribes for their already privileged children to gain entry to elite schools through side and back doors is hard to see as anything but unethical.

Yet for those accused of such violations and perceivers who want real (rather than just the illusion of) justice, this kind of hairsplitting can make an enormous difference. At the very least, this finer-grained scrutiny can help us view Vandemoer's role in the college admissions scandal with greater empathy and compassion than he has tended to receive through more superficial accounts of his involvement. As he observed in an article for *The New York Times,* "Right now, I'm on Google being painted with the same brush as coaches who bought houses, took vacations and paid tuition with the money. I turned the money over to my employer, who is somehow a victim in this. It's been devastating."[18] In my view, and despite all the well-justified outrage this scandal has caused, I do think we should appreciate that difference.

Moving beyond the kinds of simplistic black-and-white characterizations that are so easy to make about those accused of a violation is critical, not only because each of us can be vulnerable to these kinds of allegations but also because it can be essential for healing afterward. This is often evident, for example, in cases of marital infidelity. Marriage counselors often advise couples seeking to mend their relationship after an affair of the need to move beyond finger-pointing to develop deeper insight into why that betrayal happened. And this can frequently involve having both members in the couple take some responsibility for what occurred.[19]

As researcher and bestselling author Brené Brown observed in her book *Daring Greatly,* long before infidelity occurs, there has usually been another form of betrayal.[20] She writes, "When the people we love or with whom we have a deep connection stop caring, stop paying attention, stop investing and fighting for the relationship, trust begins to slip away and hurt starts seeping in. Disengagement triggers shame and our greatest fears—the fears of being abandoned, unworthy, and unlovable." This form of betrayal is also much more insidious. There is no dramatic event, so it can be harder to point to this source of pain. Yet until we do, until we really try to move beyond more simplistic accounts to take stock of the part one's own disengagement might have played in the subsequent affair, we will not understand why that affair happened or regain the sense of control we might need to make ourselves vulnerable to that partner again.

It is also worth taking a closer look at whether the inferences we might have made about the violator based on what happened are even valid. As we've previously observed, people intuitively believe that those with high integrity would refrain from unethical behavior in any situation, whereas those with low integrity may behave either ethically or unethically depending on their incentives and opportunities. That is why we tend to weigh negative information about integrity much more heavily than positive information about integrity when judging others.

However, numerous studies have also made clear that this basic intuition that guides so much of how we perceive our social worlds is simply untrue. Some of this research is probably familiar to anyone who has taken a course in introductory psychology at some point in their lives. These studies include the famous Milgram experiments, which revealed how readily otherwise regular people who varied in age, occupation, and education would obey an authority figure who instructed them to administer what they believed to be painful electric shocks to another person, with voltages that gradually increased to levels that would have been fatal had they been real. The mere presence of an authority figure, dressed in a lab coat, and prodding the participant with statements such as "Please continue" and "The experiment requires that you continue" were enough to get 65 percent of the participants to administer the experiment's final massive 450-volt shock.[21]

But the Milgram experiments are far from the only example of how inadequate our integrity can be in preventing us from making ethically questionable decisions. An even more revealing illustration can be found in a classic study involving Princeton theology students.[22] Psychologists John Darley and Daniel Batson were interested in what might affect this expressly pious group's willingness to help others. So, they designed a study in which they asked these students to give a short talk at another building on campus. Along the way, the students encountered a shabbily dressed person slumped by the side of the road, clearly in need of help. And the researchers altered certain features of the situation to explore what might affect whether that help was offered.

Their study revealed that the kinds of things most of us might think would encourage these seminarians to help this person in need did not. Darley and Batson did not find relationships between the participants' level of religiosity and whether they helped that victim. Moreover, participants who were asked to give a talk about helping others, specifically the parable of the Good Samaritan (i.e., the biblical story about someone seeing a stranger by the side of the road in need of help and indeed helping), were not likelier to help either. In fact, there were several occasions in which the seminary students "literally stepped over the victim" on their way to speaking about that parable. In the end, the only thing that made a difference in whether these participants helped was the amount of time pressure they felt. Sixty-three percent stopped to help in the study's low hurry condition (where participants had ample time to help and then give the talk), whereas 45 percent stopped to help in the medium hurry condition, and only 10 percent stopped to help in the high hurry condition.

Putting aside the rather troubling observation that, despite those participants all having decided to dedicate their lives to God, only 63 percent chose to help the stranger in need when given ample time to do so, this study further underscores how specific features of the situation (such as the amount of time available) can ultimately make a much bigger difference in whether we choose to do the right thing than differences in our character. The notion that individuals with high integrity will refrain from doing ethically questionable things regardless of the situation is simply wrong. Whether it concerns the application of electric shocks, choosing not to help someone in need, our willingness to denigrate others, or our decisions to cheat or steal, countless empirical studies have made clear by now that it is quite easy to get good people to behave in ways most of us would consider unethical. It just depends on the situation.

Psychologists have long recognized that when considering the extent to which an individual's behavior was caused by the person, as opposed to the situation, we try to subtract out the effect of the situation and attribute what remains to the individual. This approach is based on the notion that individual and situational influences operate in a hydraulic manner, so that as situational forces grow stronger, the role of the individual would become weaker. We probably wouldn't blame someone for stealing, for example, if that was caused by that person having a gun pointed to their head, whereas we would hold that person far more responsible if that theft had not been coerced. However, this approach to making inferences about how much responsibility a person should hold for their behavior can also create problems because we generally aren't good at understanding the situational constraints and pressures others face.[23] These problems can, furthermore, create different implications for how we view that person depending on whether a violation concerns matters of integrity or competence.

The good news is that our difficulties understanding the situational constraints and pressures others face are likely to pose less of a concern after a competence-related transgression. For example, if a coworker makes a serious error in your team's report that you need to work overtime to fix because that person was struggling with personal issues at home, you may not be aware of those personal struggles. However, you will also be less inclined to make strong inferences about that coworker's abilities based on that one error if you believe it's a matter of competence, because we tend to weigh negative information about competence much less heavily than positive information about competence. Thus, even if we are quite often unaware of situational influences that might underlie a competence-related transgression, we are nonetheless inclined to discount that failure anyway because we tend to believe many things can keep even competent people from performing well. In effect, these two tendencies can offset each other after a competence-based violation to mitigate the errors we might make when trying to draw inferences about that person. Thus, even if you don't know what's going on with that teammate, you may recognize that they usually do a good job and believe this person will ultimately rectify the problem.

But for integrity-related violations, our tendencies to overlook situational influences and weigh positive and negative information differently can become an explosive mix. Most of us would distinguish between stealing to get what you want and stealing because you are poor and starving. Most would not equate lies that seek to exploit a victim with lies that are in response to being threatened. And most of us also think it matters whether an assault is directed toward an innocent bystander or at someone who has inflicted grievous harm on one's family.

However, instigating forces like hunger, fear, and injustice are quite likely to escape our awareness, even if they played a key role in the violation, because they tend to be far less salient to those perceiving the transgression than to the offenders themselves. This discrepancy, furthermore, becomes particularly problematic for matters of integrity because (as we noted earlier) people tend to consider negative information about integrity far more diagnostic than positive information about integrity. Thus, even a single integrity-related transgression can be enough for others to consider the person committing the act irredeemably unethical, despite the situational pressures that person might have faced. We simply tend to overlook such influences and act as if those situational influences shouldn't have mattered anyway.

Of course, these observations aren't meant to imply that *any* situational influence would constitute a legitimate excuse. The experience of social pressure certainly differs depending on whether it comes from one's employer or one's peers, and neither is equivalent to having a gun pointed at our heads. Likewise, the extent to which we would discount the violator's culpability based on those factors is likely to be greater for relatively mild offenses than offenses that are quite serious.

Instead, the point is simply to underscore the need to delve into these particulars, to recognize that we are unlikely to have all the information required to make good judgments (particularly after an integrity-based violation), and to consider how additional efforts to account for these details might either clarify or alter how the violator might be viewed. Far too often, we simply don't engage in this kind of scrutiny as thoroughly as we might think. And the failure to do that, not only from the standpoint of those who have had their trust violated but also from the standpoint of those who might have committed those infractions, can make a major difference in determining the extent to which subsequent efforts to repair trust ultimately work.

Consider, for example, Facebook's attempts to address the scandal that engulfed the company after whistleblower Frances Haugen leaked thousands of internal documents in the fall of 2021. Those documents revealed that:

1) Facebook's own research found that its subsidiary Instagram harmed the mental health of many girls; 2) the company knew its Facebook platform was used in developing countries for human trafficking, drug dealing, and ethnic violence; and 3) Facebook was aware that its algorithms promoted divisive and sensationalist content. The message was clear—Facebook consistently prioritized its profits over the safety and well-being of its users. This led Mark Zuckerberg, Facebook's founder and CEO, to release a statement that contended that "the argument that we deliberately push content that makes people angry for profit is deeply illogical . . . I don't know any tech company that sets out to build products that make people angry or depressed."[24] Zuckerberg also sought to dispute Haugen's claims by pointing to Facebook's efforts to improve safety, transparency, and research into its platform's effects on people. His strategy was to deny the claim that the company put profits ahead of the safety and well-being of its users and to argue that even if some Facebook users had been harmed by its platform, this had certainly not been its intent. This represents a very specific type of denial, a denial not of the damage the company might have caused but rather of Haugen's explanation for why that harm happened. It was an attempt to reframe the violation as a matter of competence rather than integrity.

However, that reframing effort completely failed to assuage the public. What made Facebook's response a source of immediate and widespread criticism was that it did not address the core concerns the incident raised. The leaked documents did not suggest that Facebook deliberately sought to push harmful content for profit or build products that would elicit negative emotions. Instead, the violation concerned Facebook's intentional choice not to course-correct when those harms were discovered, due to concerns that this would depress user engagement and growth. As Aaron Mak observed in an article for *Slate,* "It's a sin not of action, but rather inaction."[25] This was made loud and clear by Facebook's own leaked documents, which detailed how Zuckerberg himself was well aware of these problems but didn't do anything meaningful about them.[26]

Thus, it shouldn't be a surprise that these and similar efforts by other

Facebook executives to reframe the company's transgressions have been widely criticized. Rather than address the core concern regarding its deliberate neglect of harm to Facebook users to advance its own profits, Facebook largely tried to sidestep this problem based on the hope that the public wouldn't notice their sleight of hand. But when the details about the transgression are clear, due largely to the leak of Facebook's own internal documents, it doesn't help the company to defend itself by glossing over the core problem and attacking a straw man. Instead, the primary effect of Facebook's crisis management response was to leave the core concern unaddressed. And as my own past research on the effects of silence has found, this would at least implicitly confirm that the company is guilty of the core integrity-based transgression, provide no assurance that this problem would be meaningfully addressed, and ultimately fail to repair trust with the public.[27]

We can likewise delve further into Dolce & Gabbana's 2018 scandal in mainland China to gain clearer insight into why their apology failed to resolve that incident. That scandal arose not only from a series of promotional videos it released, which were widely criticized as racist and disrespectful of Chinese culture, but also from private messages allegedly sent from cofounder Stefano Gabbana's Instagram account that contained a series of derogatory remarks about China and Chinese people. However, when Dolce and Gabbana released their apology video, they did not distinguish between these two offenses. They simply treated them as the same underlying transgression when they apologized and sought forgiveness for what they called "mistakes" in interpreting Chinese culture and in the way they expressed themselves.

The problem, however, is that these two offenses were quite different. If the scandal involved the disrespectful promotional videos on their own, D&G's apology would have probably been much more effective. This can be illustrated by a more recent scandal, in which the South Korean broadcaster MBC used stereotypical and offensive images to represent different countries during the opening ceremony of the 2021 summer Olympics.[28] Those images included pizza for Italy, Dracula for

Romania, an image of protests for Haiti (at a time when the country was grappling with the recent assassination of its president), and an image of Chernobyl for Ukraine to remind viewers of the 1986 nuclear disaster.

This incident went viral, and the broadcasting company quickly responded by apologizing on the front page of its website, as well as through a news conference that was held by its chief executive, Park Sung-jae.[29] Even though this was not the first time MBC had made this misstep during the Olympics, with the broadcaster having been penalized by the Korea Communications Commission for disparaging countries in the 2008 Beijing Olympics with its captions,[30] the company's 2021 apology managed to quell public outrage. The incident was largely seen as just another example of cross-cultural bumbling many of us have experienced around the world. Thus, it was easier to see this offense as a competence-related violation, for which an apology would be effective. In fact, the only repercussion this broadcaster ultimately faced for its offensive images during the 2021 Olympics was nonbinding administrative guidance from the Korea Communications Standards Commission that amounted to a slap on the wrist.[31]

Stefano Gabbana's derogatory Instagram messages were not viewed in the same way as D&G's promotional videos. Evidence from another set of studies I have conducted (which I will detail in chapter 7) reveals that people tend to believe the sentiments others express in private are more authentic than those they express in public.[32] This suggests that when the alleged leaks of Gabbana's private messages described China as "the country of . . ." followed by a string of excrement emojis and used the phrase "China Ignorant Dirty Smelling Mafia,"[33] the subsequent claim he made with Domenico Dolce that they made "mistakes" in the way they had expressed themselves was almost certain to fall on deaf ears.

The private messages already made clear to the public that Gabbana held negative sentiments about China and its people, and his holding of those sentiments is what the public considered an integrity-based violation. The matter of whether he might have made "mistakes" in how he expressed those sentiments, in contrast, was considered largely irrelevant, because his genuine beliefs are what really mattered. Thus, the failure of D&G's apology video stemmed from the fact that, like Facebook, D&G did not address the public's core concern. It neglected to address the fact that the alleged leaks of Gabbana's private Instagram messages made a very compelling case that he really held those harmful sentiments, a matter of integrity for which an apology was unlikely to work. This problem was also compounded by the fact that the private nature of those leaked messages made them appear much more diagnostic of Gabbana's underlying views than any public statements he might, and did, subsequently make regarding his respect for China and its people. Hence, it should not be a surprise that some, like Shaun Rein of the China Market Research Group, considered D&G's efforts to repair trust in China a lost cause. He told CNN, "It's probably the only brand that I've seen the Chinese stay angry at for so long."

But we should also recognize that the need to move beyond the seduction of simplistic stories goes both ways. Perceivers need to dig more deeply into what happened to make sure they understand the nature of the violation as well.

There is a moment in Bruce Springsteen's memoir *Born to Run* that describes what this can mean on a very personal level as he recounts the arc of his journey from childhood through his induction into the Rock & Roll Hall of Fame.[34] He spends the early part of his book detailing the difficulties of his homelife, with particular attention to his fraught relationship with his psychologically abusive father. Springsteen wrote that his home was filled with his father's epic silences, distant disapproval of a sensitive son who did not fit his tough mold, and booze-fueled rages, all of which left emotional scars that still haven't fully healed.

Things started to change, however, after his parents left for California and left him in New Jersey at the age of nineteen to fend for himself. Springsteen recalled signs of his father's mental illness, later diagnosed as paranoid schizophrenia, a condition that ran in his family. He experienced his own struggles with mental illness, serious bouts of depression, and two emotional breakdowns, which would require decades of ongoing therapy and medications to treat. He eventually also saw how his own inner demons contributed to his first marriage falling apart.

This personal journey culminated in a visit in the days before Bruce Springsteen himself was about to become a father with his second wife. He had kept in touch with his parents and visited them on occasion, and their roles gradually shifted as he became an increasingly important source of support for them over the years. So, on that day, his dad drove hundreds of miles down from his home in San Mateo to Los Angeles because he "just wanted to say hi." Then, as the two of them sat at a table in a small dining area of Springsteen's LA home trying to make small talk, his father suddenly said, "Bruce, you've been very good to us . . . And I wasn't very good to you."

There was a small silence at that moment. Then Springsteen said, "You did the best you could." He later wrote, "That was it. It was all I needed." After all those painful years, his father had come to tell him, on the eve of his own transition to fatherhood, that he loved him and to warn him to be careful, to do better, to not make the same painful mistakes he'd made.

This is the same sentiment I have heard from other adults I have known who have shared stories about their own parents. Many have even expressed that sentiment with the same kind of phrase. "He did the best he could." "She did the best she could." "They didn't know any better." It is a sentiment based on recognizing how many things can cause those who meant to do well to fall short. It is based on seeing how easily we too can let people down, despite our efforts. It is an awareness of our shared humanity and all the imperfections that can entail.

That recognition may not be enough to fully heal every wound, and some of these relationships may simply be beyond salvaging. As Springsteen himself observed, "There are sins which aren't redeemable and there are lives that can't be reframed." But as his own testimony reveals, there are also times when this kind of awareness can make a real difference.

Digging beneath the simplistic story, to understand all the things that might have shaped what happened, can help at least some of us move beyond attributions of harmful intent that can be so devastating to relationships. This may allow us to reach a state of grace from which we might mend some of those bonds. It is also through that process that we may ultimately start healing ourselves. For those of us who manage to do that before it's too late—if we can somehow find that semblance of peace before that parent passes, despite the scars we still bear—maybe it's at least in this small way that we can finally consider ourselves fortunate.

6

YOUR BALANCE SHEET IS BROKEN

When Gregory Boyle became pastor of Dolores Mission Church, it was the poorest Catholic parish in Los Angeles. The parish included the largest public housing projects west of the Mississippi, Aliso Village and Pico Gardens, as well as the highest concentration of gang activity in Los Angeles, a city then known as the gang capital of the world. At the time, in 1986, the prevailing efforts to address the gang violence focused on law enforcement and mass incarceration. Yet they clearly weren't working. Gang violence remained a serious problem, and those who had been convicted of crimes and completed prison sentences were quite likely to commit crimes again.

That is why Father Greg founded Homeboy Industries, which has grown to become the largest gang intervention, rehabilitation, and reentry program in the world. In 2014, it launched a global network with four hundred other organizations that are striving for social justice, advocating for marginalized populations, working to break the recidivism cycle, and seeking to address the collateral consequences of serving time in prison. And in 2018 alone, it served almost seven thousand members of the immediate Los Angeles community and offered its flagship eighteen-month employment and reentry program to over four hundred men and women.[1]

Homeboy Industries is a story of remarkable success. It is also a story of society's abject failure. This is because one of the biggest reasons why Homeboy Industries has thrived is that our stance toward reintegrating offenders into society is so deeply conflicted. That has meant that most of those who have been helped by this organization would have had no other recourse if it hadn't existed. We would have simply cast them aside.

Public debate on how to treat criminal offenders remains heated to this day, with questions of trust in those who committed the crimes, as well as the justice systems we have in place, lying at the center of these arguments. Should we punish for the sake of retribution or deterrence? Or should the goal be rehabilitation of the offender or some form of reparation to the victim? Society has shifted from one view to another and back over time because, in practical terms, none of them are entirely adequate, and these goals often come into conflict with one another. A harsh sentence designed for retribution, for example, may do little to rehabilitate the offender and even increase the likelihood of recidivism, whereas a sentence designed to rehabilitate may fail to express society's repudiation of the behavior or provide an effective deterrent to others. And the unfortunate truth is that as we struggle with these dilemmas, the U.S. has become the world's leader in incarceration (with 2.2 million people in the nation's prisons, a 500 percent increase over the last forty years, overcrowded prisons, and significant state fiscal burdens) due primarily to changes in law and policy rather than changes in crime rates.[2]

Part of the problem stems from the fact that our notions of justice itself can be so conflicted. Justice, at the broadest level, is simply about people getting what they deserve. Yet the pursuit of this seemingly straightforward principle represents one of the most fundamental and thorny societal challenges we deal with every day. This is because even if we can agree that justice is about people getting what they deserve, we quite often disagree about what that really means.

Justice can be distinguished into two broad types. *Distributive justice* concerns the allocation of rewards, whereas *retributive justice* is concerned with how people are punished. Moreover, both types of justice can affect trust and its repair after its violation. For example, some of my own research has found that justifying a transgression as an attempt to achieve distributive justice can help repair trust if they point to distributive justice principles people consider important.[3] As with the legend of Robin Hood, it can sometimes seem reasonable to steal, for example, if that is meant to help others. However, because the principles that determine how people are punished are quite different from those used to distribute rewards, and matters of punishment tend to be particularly salient after a violation, I will focus on matters of retributive justice for this chapter.

The traditional view of retributive justice, or the punishments people deserve for their wrongdoing, can be found in the principle expressed in Exodus 21:24 as an "eye for an eye." The German philosopher Immanuel Kant articulates this stance best by arguing that perpetrators should be punished in proportion to the moral offensiveness of their actions and that the imperative to punish derives not from the future consequences of the punishment but rather from a universal goal of giving people what they deserve.[4] From this perspective, punishment needs no justification beyond the deservingness of the perpetrator based on the harm they committed, and any future consequences of the punishment are irrelevant. Thus, if some consequence *is* achieved from punishing the offender, we might view it more as a matter of restoring some abstract sense of cosmic fairness and balance rather than a specific societal end.

Utilitarians like the English philosopher Jeremy Bentham, however, contend that justice should ultimately be about maximizing the overall welfare of society.[5] They claim that the primary way this can be achieved is by using credible threats of punishment that are sufficiently severe to lead potential wrongdoers to make different choices (i.e., deterrence) and for past wrongdoers to stop doing bad things (i.e., rehabilitation). Moreover, unlike the traditional retributive perspective, which asserts that only the guilty should be punished and that this should be in proportion to the harm that was committed, proponents of this utilitarian view suggest that it can sometimes make sense to punish the innocent or inflict disproportionately severe punishments on the guilty if this produces a better societal result. For example, this perspective suggests that it would make sense to execute a few people who have exceeded traffic speed limits on national television if this saves enough other lives through the deterrence of speeding to save more lives overall.[6]

Yet despite these often-lengthy debates about what our approach to justice *should* be, it remained unclear which of these views is more consistent with how people intuitively make these judgments. Psychologist Kevin Carlsmith, thus, sought to address this question with several experiments. The experimenter would inform participants a crime had been committed, tell them they were responsible for recommending a sentence, and then give them the option of learning about different categories of information about the crime, each of which was uniquely relevant to deterrence, incapacitation, or retribution.[7] For example, the deterrence-related information could concern the extent to which the punishment would be made public, whereas the information pertinent to incapacitation could concern the offender's likelihood of violence, and the retribution-related information could concern the amount of harm the crime had caused.

Carlsmith's studies revealed that participants overwhelmingly prioritized information pertinent to retribution, with 97 percent of participants requesting that kind of information first, and that they only sought deterrence-related information pertinent to the utilitarian view, such as the extent to which the punishment would be made public, after the other types of information had already been exhausted. The evidence also revealed that retribution-related information increased participants' confidence in the punishments they assigned more than any other information type. Thus, both Carlsmith and psychologist John Darley (who conducted the classic study about the helping behavior of Princeton theology students described in chapter 5) have concluded based on these and related findings that people's intuitions are more closely aligned with the traditional, rather than utilitarian, view of retributive justice.[8] Rather than punish to maximize the overall welfare of society, they do so primarily for the sake of an eye for an eye.

This doesn't mean that people will necessarily reject the utilitarian perspective. People can engage in a more deliberate, rather than intuitive, form of reasoning as well, and that kind of deliberate reasoning may lead them to conclude that utilitarian principles like deterrence are sufficiently important to override their intuitive inclinations. However, as the Nobel Prize–winning psychologist Daniel Kahneman aptly detailed in his bestselling book *Thinking, Fast and Slow*,[9] a wealth of evidence has made clear that our intuitions are much more immediate and automatic, and that deliberate reasoning can only override those intuitions in certain cases, such as when we have the time, mental resources, motivation, and opportunity to engage in that more effortful type of thinking.

This reasoning suggests that the moral outrage we feel when someone commits an offense represents our immediate intuitive response to instances of wrongdoing. We can then engage in more deliberate reasoning about the broader consequences of that punishment to countermand those initial impulses in some cases. However, because that kind of deliberate reasoning takes more time and effort and thus tends to be used more sparingly, our intuitive inclination to rely on the more traditional ("eye for an eye") form of retributive justice quite often prevails.

This dual-process approach to reasoning is evident even in brain-imaging studies. In these experiments, neuroscientist Joshua Greene and his collaborators told participants a story that ended with an action the protagonist could take and asked them to decide whether the action was appropriate or inappropriate.[10,11] In some cases, you would be told a runaway trolley was about to kill five people standing on the tracks and that you needed to decide whether to flip a switch to divert it onto another track where it would instead kill one person. Or in other cases, you would be asked to imagine a scenario in which enemy soldiers had taken over your village with orders to kill all remaining civilians and where you and some of the townspeople were hiding in the cellar of a large house. Then as the soldiers come to that house to search for valuables, your baby would begin to cry loudly, and you must decide whether to smother your child to save yourself and the other townspeople or not.

The neural imaging studies found that these scenarios could activate very different regions of the brain, depending on the type of reasoning people used. One region, which was activated quite rapidly and generated quick assessments about the appropriateness of a given harm, involved areas of the brain that have been associated with both emotion and social cognition activities. The other region, which was activated when participants responded in a more utilitarian manner (based on whether their decision would serve the greater good), involved abstract reasoning centers in the brain and areas associated with the engagement of cognitive control. That second, abstract-reasoning brain region developed later in our evolution and has been found to produce responses that conflict with the intuitions produced by the first brain region. However, its chances of limiting or overriding those intuitions ultimately depend on the extent to which each of those brain regions is activated.

These considerations suggest that at least one reason why our approach to criminal justice is so often conflicted can be found in ourselves. On the whole, we don't necessarily subscribe to one theory of retributive justice or another, whether this be the more traditional view of "an eye for an eye" or a utilitarian approach that seeks to maximize the greater good. Instead, our preferences can switch back and forth between these views depending on the situation (e.g., due to the time, motivation, mental resources, and opportunity we have available), as if we suffer from a type of dissociative identity disorder.

Moreover, because our default intuitions about punishment tend to be more consistent with the traditional ("an eye for an eye") perspective on retributive justice, they often conflict with the laws of the U.S. justice system, which psychologists Carlsmith and Darley observe has become increasingly utilitarian in nature.[12] That discrepancy, they argue, is what leads people to lose respect for the law. They lose trust in the legal system; hence, they don't rely on the law's guidance in ambiguous situations where the appropriate response is unclear. When the legal system tells us one thing, but our intuition tells us another, we are often more inclined to trust our gut. And though communication efforts may help mitigate this conflict in some cases by helping people appreciate the utilitarian bases for those laws and override their intuitions, they may not always do so completely. Thus, there are likely to remain many cases in which some level of conflict between our intuitions and our legal institutions in the pursuit of retributive justice continues.

Our dissatisfaction with society's approach to retributive justice seems to stem from another problem as well. If justice is ultimately about how we deal with matters of guilt and redemption, the dominant approaches to retributive justice we have considered don't seem to have given the latter concern much attention at all.* Thus, it should not be a surprise that there

---

* This is certainly the case with the traditional "an eye for an eye" perspective on retributive justice, which is only concerned with punishing perpetrators in proportion to the harm they have caused (and without regard to the punishment's consequences). However, this is also true for the utilitarian perspective, despite its concern with advancing the overall welfare of society, since it treats the prospect of wrongdoer rehabilitation simply as a subtype of deterrence, in which the punishment is severe enough to dissuade the wrongdoer from committing the offense again.

has been a growing recognition by the public of the need to rectify this problem. The April 2016 National Survey of Victims' Views,[13] which polled the opinions of eight hundred victims of violent or property crimes pooled from a nationally representative sample of over three thousand respondents, found that even crime victims want to see shorter prison sentences, less spending on prisons, and a greater focus on the rehabilitation of criminals. Fifty-two percent of victims said that prison makes people likelier to commit crimes again, whereas only 19 percent said that prison helps rehabilitate people into better citizens. Thus, by well over a two-to-one margin, the people surveyed believed the criminal justice system should focus on rehabilitating people who commit crimes rather than on punishing them. They also preferred shorter prison sentences over keeping criminals incarcerated "as long as possible" by similar margins. Moreover, they preferred holding people accountable through options beyond prison (such as rehabilitation, mental health treatment, drug treatment, community supervision, or community service) by a margin of three to one.

Another notable feature of the findings is that these opinions cut across demographic and political groups, with most Democrats, Republicans, and Independents supporting these reforms regardless of how the questions were asked. This pattern is consistent with the results of a 2012 survey by the Pew Charitable Trusts, in which 84 percent of the public, including strong majorities of Democrats, Republicans, and Independents, agreed that money should be shifted from locking up nonviolent inmates to alternative programs like probation and parole.[14] But the results of the 2016 National Survey of Victims' Views, which included actual crime victims, including victims of violent crimes, provided the strongest call for change yet. As Judy Martin, an Ohio woman whose twenty-four-year-old son was shot and killed in a parking lot was quoted stating in that survey, "The way our criminal justice system is set up currently doesn't allow for redemption . . . We must treat each other, even those among us who have made serious mistakes, with more humanity. It's the only way forward."

That view is consistent with a growing interest in "restorative justice" approaches that have focused on repairing the harm caused by the criminal behavior.[15] Psychologist Albert Eglash pioneered this approach in the 1950s through his extensive work with prisoners, by viewing crime not only as a violation of the law but also as a violation of human relationships that injures victims, communities, and even offenders themselves. This approach asks, "Who has been hurt? And how can we bring together offenders and victims to acknowledge and repair the damage?"[16] Thus, it holds the offender accountable to victims, their families, and the community by getting the wrongdoer to make amends rather than by simply having the wrongdoer suffer.

Yet though studies of restorative justice programs suggest that they can improve victim satisfaction, increase offender accountability, and decrease recidivism compared to more traditional criminal justice responses, the data remains far from conclusive. For example, it remains unclear how much of this effect is due to a self-selection bias, in which the results may have arisen from inherent differences between those who agree to participate in such programs and those who do not.[17] Moreover, even if we take these benefits at face value, efforts to pursue restorative justice must ultimately confront the fact that our intuitions can still lead us to prefer more traditional "retributive" approaches to justice in many cases.

Consider, for example, the case of Brock Turner, a Stanford University undergraduate and member of the school's swimming team who was convicted in March 2016 on three felony counts for sexually assaulting an unconscious woman on campus (sexual assault of an unconscious person, sexual assault of an intoxicated person, and sexual assault with intent to commit rape).[18] He attacked Chanel Miller, the then-unidentified twenty-three-year-old victim who has since revealed her identity, behind a dumpster and was lying on top of her unconscious, partly clothed body when witnesses intervened and held Turner for the police. Prosecutors in the case had sought a sentence of six years in prison. However, Superior Court judge Aaron Persky sentenced Turner to just six months in county jail and three years of probation, due to Turner's lack of criminal history, the harm he had already suffered from the intense media coverage, and his belief that "a prison sentence would have a severe impact on him. I think he will not be a danger to others."

That reasoning seems consistent with the opinions respondents expressed in the 2012 survey by the Pew Charitable Trusts and the 2016 National Survey of Victims' Views. It favors both leniency and the likelihood of rehabilitation over punishment. Moreover, consistent with the focus by advocates of restorative justice on making amends, Brock Turner's father released a statement in which he said his son planned to use the time on probation to educate college students "about the dangers of alcohol consumption and sexual promiscuity" so that he could "give back to society in a net positive way."

Yet that sentence sparked widespread outrage in the public. The Santa Clara, California, district attorney, Jeff Rosen, released a statement that said the sentence "did not fit the crime" and called Turner a "predatory offender" who refused to take responsibility or show remorse. *The San Jose Mercury News* published an editorial that called the sentence "a slap on the wrist" and a "setback for the movement to take campus rape seriously." The sentence also sparked a campaign to recall the lenient judge, which succeeded in June 2018 when Persky became the first California judge to be recalled in over eighty years.[19]

Advocates of restorative justice might reasonably argue that the outrage does not represent a problem with restorative justice principles per se. Restorative justice programs typically encourage victims to take an active role in the restorative process by engaging in a dialogue with their offenders and encourage offenders to take responsibility for their actions, neither of which occurred here. Turner, for example, admitted drinking but had not acknowledged any fault in the attack, insisting the episode had been consensual. Moreover, whereas restorative justice involves the offender rectifying the harm to the victim in some way, the sentence itself was widely believed to favor the needs of the offender over those of the victim.

But the backlash to Turner's light sentence also underscores the major role our retributive intuitions can continue to play in our quest for justice. Even though we may espouse the values of leniency and rehabilitation, our desire to punish, to seek "an eye for an eye," remains our immediate and default response to these kinds of incidents. Thus, the question becomes how we might seek to address these potential conflicts between our espoused and underlying preferences for those who have committed a transgression.

One way to make sense of how we typically navigate these concerns is by thinking about how people evaluate moral character more generally. Developmental psychologist Mordecai Nisan observed that people tend to treat the implications of their good and bad acts over time much like a bank account, in which their good acts add to the account (as credits) and their bad acts subtract from that account (as debits).[20] This metaphor suggests that if someone does something bad, that person would incur a debit that would need to be rectified in some way. And it is only when we expect this person to pay this debt and avoid similar debits in the future that we would consider the offender redeemed and consider trusting that person again.

The problem, however, is that we are quite bad at gauging whether that redemption would occur. Without a true window into an offender's soul, we make our best guess based on the assumption that harsher punishments would foster this redemption by increasing the offender's repentance for the transgression and the hope that such repentance would, in turn, lead the offender to make sufficient amends. This may explain why people sometimes dismiss apologies as "cheap talk" and demand more substantive remedies from those who have committed a transgression.

Yet this perception of repentance, as a means toward redemption, can be noisy and skewed. There are times when verbal responses can make a significant difference, such as after adverse medical events, where doctors who apologize have been found to experience fewer legal claims and lower defense, settlement, and total liability costs than those who adopt traditional "deny and defend" approaches.[21,22] But there are also times when more substantive responses that include decisions to resign from office do little to repair trust, such as in June 2011, when New York congressman Anthony Weiner announced that painful decision after a sexting scandal in which he was caught sending sexually explicit photos and messages to several women before and during his marriage, only for a heckler to cry out, "Yeah! Bye-bye, pervert!"[23]

This is because we are ultimately concerned not with the substantive costs such responses might inflict on the offender but with the extent to which those responses elicit repentance. We can see this from several experiments I conducted with my collaborators to investigate the effects of trust-repair efforts that are more substantive in nature.[24] One of these experiments, for example, was based on an incident involving Donald J. Carty, who was the CEO of American Airlines in 2003. The airline had sought wage and benefit concessions from its unions to avoid a bankruptcy filing. But after the unionized workers finished voting to accept the concessions, they learned that the company had decided to give seven executives, including Carty, cash bonuses equal to twice their base salaries if they stayed until January 2005, as well as $41 million in pension funding guarantees for an even larger number of executives. This discovery destroyed the union's fragile support for the concession contracts and forced the two sides back to the bargaining table, despite Carty's subsequent apologies and the company's decision to cancel the executive bonuses (but not the pension guarantees). Carty himself was forced to resign.[25]

My collaborators and I wanted to disentangle this complex set of events by comparing what might have happened if the trust-repair effort had involved the apology on its own versus just paying a financial penalty or deciding instead to implement some other form of substantive response (such as regulations that would prevent similar transgressions in the future). I took advantage of my university's Los Angeles location by reaching out to USC's dedicated television studio to hold a casting call for Hollywood actors and creating a series of video newscasts that would report on these events. These videos were created to allow each of the participants to view just one of these different types of attempts to address the scandal. Participants saw either reports of the CEO offering: 1) only an acknowledgment that the allegations were true; 2) just an apology; or a substantive response that involved either 3) some form of financial penance or 4) concrete steps to prevent such incidents from happening again. And the question was how participants would view the CEO who took those actions.

The findings from this research revealed that, despite their surface-level

differences, each of these trust-repair efforts worked in the same way. Their effects all hinged on the extent to which they elicited perceptions of repentance. This repentance was also easier to convey when the violation concerned matters of competence rather than integrity, consistent with this book's previous discussions of how much harder it can be to address integrity-based violations. However, these findings can also explain why a sincere apology can be as effective as more substantive responses, particularly if the substantive response seems insincere or strategic.

The results suggest that, for those who are guilty of a transgression, the question is not what price the offender pays but rather that person's level of repentance, because that latter sentiment will play a more direct role in determining whether the problem would be rectified in the future. If it seemed like the CEO was truly sorry for the trust violation, regardless of how that was expressed, participants were likelier to accept their gestures as a sign that they could be trusted again. Yet because the perception of repentance is ultimately in the mind of the beholder, it can be shaped by factors that can have little to do with the offender's actual repentance or likelihood of redemption. This is the reason why it can be easier to resort to harsher punishments and demand our pound of flesh than to consider what might truly enable trust repair.

The irony, however, is that this focus on punishments can make things even worse because we are also quite terrible at gauging how much punishment would be appropriate. This can be understood by considering an additional nuance in the bank account metaphor we considered earlier. In particular, that metaphor not only suggests that we would incur debits for behaving badly but also that we would have leeway to engage in occasional bad acts if we have done good things in the past, so long as the balance in our moral bank accounts does not fall below zero (to make us "morally bankrupt").

Our reliance on this kind of logic has been supported by at least two streams of empirical research. Psychologists Benoît Monin and Dale Miller, for example, reported three studies, which revealed that when people were first given opportunities to act in ways that would establish credentials as nonprejudiced persons, they would subsequently become more willing to

express attitudes that could be viewed as prejudiced.[26] In one of their studies, for example, participants were given photos, names, grade point averages, and majors for five job applicants for a starting position at a large consulting firm and asked to indicate which one they would hire. Of these, the fourth applicant was designed to be the most attractive, with a degree from a prestigious institution, a major in economics, and the highest GPA. The study also altered the gender and ethnicity of that fourth applicant with the photo and name so that person was either a white woman, a Black man, or a white man (with all four of the other applicants being white men). Then after selecting an applicant, participants were presented with a dilemma that was designed to elicit the expression of prejudice, by having them gauge the extent to which it would make sense to select someone who was female (in the gender condition) or Black (in the ethnicity condition) for a job in another setting that seemed less inclined to accept members of that stereotyped group. The results revealed that participants were likelier to favor a white man in that second task if they had established a credential as a nonprejudiced person (by selecting a white woman or Black man in the prior task) than if they had not.

This approach to moral accounting is also suggested by a series of experiments by behavioral economists Nina Mažar, On Amir, and Dan Ariely, which gave participants a financial incentive to misreport their task performance.[27] One of these experiments, for example, gave participants twenty matrices, with each containing twelve three-digit numbers. The participants were given four minutes to find two numbers within each matrix that added up to ten. They were also told that two randomly selected participants from the experiment would earn ten dollars for each correctly solved matrix. Then when that time was up, the study either had the experimenter verify participants' answers on the matrix task and write down the number of correctly solved matrices on a separate answer sheet for them (in the control condition) or asked participants to indicate the total number of correctly solved matrices on the separate answer sheet themselves and to submit only the answer sheet (in the experimental condition), so participants could keep the solved and unsolved matrices in their possession and thus have an opportunity to cheat. The results revealed that participants did cheat when they were given the opportunity to do so, by reporting significantly more matrices solved in the experimental than control condition. However, participants also cheated far less than they could have to avoid having that cheating threaten their positive views of themselves as honest individuals.

The problem, however, is that, as some of my latest findings with researchers Alyssa Han, Alexandra Mislin, and Ece Tuncel suggest, those witnessing such acts may account for those behaviors in a very different way.[28] We asked participants to consider something good or bad a person might have done or a sequence in which one of those deeds was followed by the other. In one of these experiments, for example, my collaborators and I presented participants with an adaptation of an incident that the author Walter Isaacson reported in his biography *Steve Jobs* to have occurred between Jobs and Steve Wozniak, the cofounders of Apple.[29]

Before founding that company, Wozniak was working for Hewlett-Packard and Jobs was working for Atari, and the two had already been friends for some time. Thus, when Jobs was tasked with developing a sequel to Atari's classic game *Pong,* a single-player game called *Breakout* that would be released in 1975, he recruited Wozniak (who was known on the market as the better engineer) for help. Wozniak was grateful to Jobs for the opportunity, but it turned out that Jobs had lied to him about the work.

Jobs told Wozniak they had only four days to complete the assignment and that they needed to use as few chips as possible. However, he never told Wozniak there was a bonus for using fewer chips and that the four-day deadline was self-imposed by Jobs so he could get back to his commune farm to help bring in the apple harvest. Moreover, despite the fact that these deceptions forced Wozniak to work around the clock to balance both his day job and this extra work for Jobs, with Jobs doing relatively little, Jobs gave Wozniak only half the pay, kept the other half, and also kept the entire bonus for himself.[30]

Wozniak only found out the truth ten years later. Yet even well after the two achieved extraordinary success and prosperity with Apple, Wozniak admitted that this incident still caused him pain. Wozniak said that it was not about the money. "If he had told me he needed the money, he should have known I would have just given it to him," he said. Jobs was his friend, and he had given Wozniak the opportunity to work on an exciting project (one he would have worked on for free), but Jobs also took advantage of his friend in a serious way. Thus, the questions for my team in our experiments were how people would perceive those who might engage in these kinds of good and bad acts (such as Jobs offering Wozniak an exciting work opportunity and then lying to him about it, respectively) and whether this might differ from how those engaging in those acts would perceive themselves.*

The findings from this research ultimately revealed a very serious problem. The studies revealed that whereas those engaging in these acts tended to believe that their prior good deeds would persist as moral credits to offset the implications of their subsequent transgression, those observing such actions instead reacted to the transgression by revisiting the prior good deeds and questioning whether those deeds were good after all. This led observers to see the initial good deeds not as moral credits but rather as nefarious attempts to set them up for the bad deed the offender had planned all along. And those effects ultimately led observers to consider their offenders to be much less moral and trustworthy than the offenders expected.

For example, in the case of Jobs and Wozniak, the results suggest that it would have been natural for Wozniak to have much greater difficulty seeing Jobs as a moral and trustworthy person than Jobs saw himself. Jobs would likely have had little difficulty rationalizing his deceptive actions as just a small blip in their extraordinarily successful relationship—a blip that was easily outweighed by all the opportunities Jobs brought Wozniak and the enormous fortune those opportunities allowed Wozniak to earn. But for Wozniak, that deception represented a very serious betrayal that raised fundamental concerns about Jobs and their relationship, at least in part because this would have made Wozniak question whether there were ulterior motives underlying the other good things Jobs might have done as well.

Yet even if Wozniak believed his trust had been violated and tried to express that sentiment, this would have likely been difficult for Jobs to fully understand. If Jobs believed his prior good deeds offset his harmful action,

---

* Other versions of these experiments involved different types of good deeds, such as helping a coworker complete a report despite the competitive nature of the workplace, as well as different types of bad deeds, such as stealing an item from a coffee shop or engaging in a cover-up that gets an innocent third party fired.

this would have encouraged him to view Wozniak's sense of betrayal as at least somewhat overblown. This would have also increased the likelihood, if Wozniak had expressed his views, that any attempts Jobs might have made to repair the relationship would have been inadequate and even prompted him to lose patience with Wozniak for demanding too much before things could return to normal.

That kind of frustration is a common problem in cases of spousal infidelity, for example. Counselors report that the cheating spouse can become exasperated in their attempts to repair the marriage and wind up telling their partner to just get over it or say they don't want to talk about it anymore.[31] They may take responsibility for what they have done but consider that affair at least partially offset by their many good deeds over the course of their relationship. Thus, even as they seek to repair the relationship and try to make amends, they can eventually reach a point where they believe they have paid enough of a price for their cheating and lose patience with their partner's failure to move on. But that problem may be due to the cheater not seeing the world through the eyes of their partner, and their failure to see how that betrayal may have raised serious questions about whether there were other secrets, betrayals, and underlying nefarious motives that might explain their good deeds in the past as well.

This failure to consider how others might reinterpret one's past actions can also create another problem. Because the observers in my studies had less trust in the offenders after the subsequent transgression (less than the offenders themselves thought was deserved), the observers also behaved in ways that reflected that sentiment. For example, they were less likely to recommend the offender for an important position, allocate resources to that person, or put that offender in charge of handling relations with important clients than the offenders expected. And this, ironically enough, has the potential to lead offenders to believe those observers have punished them unfairly and ultimately to regard those punishers to be untrustworthy in turn.

All these considerations ultimately help explain why we gravitate so readily toward retribution. Even if most of us would like to believe we are fair and consistent, the evidence suggests that we are ultimately quite inconsistent in how we make judgments of others as compared to ourselves. We believe that others would have less moral standing than we would hold after the same set of actions. Moreover, we are far likelier to discount the signals of repentance others might convey than the repentance we might personally experience. This puts others at more of a deficit in their moral bank accounts, from which they might seek to repair trust, and creates more of an uphill battle in which punishment may be considered the only means through which we can feel like they have experienced sufficient remorse.

It is no wonder then that Father Greg's efforts, from the start of this chapter, to reintegrate former gang members into society are so important or why the criminal defense lawyer Bryan Stevenson takes such pains to stress in his bestselling book *Just Mercy* that "each of us is more than the worst thing we've ever done."[32] My findings suggest that in the eyes of others, we are often *not* more than that worst thing. The results highlight how readily observers can take that worst thing as the truest sign of one's character, use that moment to reconsider anything else about the offender that might have been good, and punish that person far more harshly as a result. This is a fundamental problem with how we make moral judgments. And until we address it, we will continue to preclude a realistic path toward redemption for those who might deserve a second chance.

7

THE POTENTATE'S CURSE

O f all those responsible for the opioid crisis, an ongoing public health emergency in the U.S., none are more culpable than the Sackler family. As journalist Patrick Radden Keefe detailed in an article for *The New Yorker,*[1] the Sacklers' company, Purdue Pharma, was the first in the 1990s to persuade the American medical establishment that strong opioids should be much more widely prescribed and to dismiss physicians' fears about the addictive nature of such drugs. When Purdue launched OxyContin in 1995, the company unleashed an unprecedented marketing campaign that pushed the use of this powerful opioid for an enormous range of ailments while claiming that this drug led to addiction in "fewer than 1 percent" of patients.

Yet that assertion proved disastrously false. OxyContin, and the competing products that drug spurred other pharmaceutical companies to introduce, has lured millions of Americans into a cycle of opioid use and an accelerating increase in overdose deaths. The opioid crisis has killed at least 450,000 people since 1999 and cost the American economy at least $2.15 trillion as states struggle to address this problem.[2] Yet by 2020, OxyContin had also earned Purdue approximately $30 billion in revenue and made the Sacklers one of the richest families in the United States. The Sacklers have, furthermore, been able to keep the vast bulk of that fortune through financial and legal maneuvers, despite the devastating wreckage to American lives their drug has caused. To protect themselves from their day of reckoning, they had siphoned most of the money from Purdue to offshore accounts that were beyond the reach of U.S. authorities. That left only the carcass of a company when Purdue eventually filed for bankruptcy protection and reached a revised settlement in 2022 that many states, as well as the U.S.

Department of Justice, have criticized for letting both the company and the Sackler family off too lightly.[3]

This is an example of a story we know all too well. Most of us are well aware of incidents where the powerful get off too easy. With deep pockets and connections, the powerful can hire expensive lawyers, public relations experts, and crisis management consultants who can identify legal loopholes, run self-serving media campaigns, and either wear down or pay off those who might get in their way. Thus, it is not a surprise that so many of us look upon the powerful with suspicion and are so eager to hold those who commit offenses to account.

But we also need to consider another side of this coin. Despite all the harm the Sackler family caused, we need to recognize that decent people can wind up in positions of power too. And sometimes even those we might highly admire can do the wrong thing.

How does one reconcile the fact that Franklin D. Roosevelt, for example, led the United States through two of the greatest crises of the twentieth century (the Great Depression and World War II) but also forced the relocation and internment of about 120,000 innocent Japanese Americans (more than two-thirds of whom were native-born U.S. citizens) in concentration camps for years without due process during the Second World War? How should we view Maria Theresa, the only woman to rule Austria and the broader Habsburg dominions, who inherited control of a penniless and poorly governed country, turned around the economy, revitalized the military, and instituted mandatory public education for both boys and girls, but also sought to expel the Jews on multiple occasions and wrote, "I know of no greater plague than this race . . . the Jews are to be kept away and avoided"?[4] And how do we make sense of Martin Luther King Jr.'s historic fight for civil rights in light of vetted summaries of FBI audiotapes, sealed until 2027, that reveal King's affairs with more than forty women?[5]

Reasonable people may disagree about how to make sense of these legacies, and the specifics in each case make them quite different. Yet as we struggle to weigh all the good against the bad, vile, and inexcusable in these otherwise great leaders through the rearview mirror of history, we also need to consider the ways power can affect how we make those judgments.

The advantages of power can be obvious. Social scientists have typically defined power as the ability to exert one's will despite resistance.[6] It is about being able to achieve what you want even though other forces might stand in the way. Moreover, given that most people tend to want things that benefit themselves, it should be no surprise that the powerful generally wind up better off. My own research with organizational psychologist Alison Fragale, for example, has found that negotiators who have greater power relative to their counterparts are able to obtain a significantly larger share of benefits from their agreements.[7]

This kind of advantage can help explain why the Sackler family was able to reach such favorable terms in their opioid case settlement. They had already siphoned most of the money from Purdue to offshore accounts that were beyond the reach of U.S. authorities. Thus, they controlled access to funds U.S. states desperately needed to manage the opioid crisis, and this would have naturally created significant pressure for many of those states to make the distasteful decision to accept the inadequate financial settlement rather than oppose the agreement without a clear prospect of getting more.

Further, just like we can be motivated to preserve our close interpersonal relationships, we can be similarly motivated to preserve our relationships with those who have power. Of course, that isn't always the case, since people can possess power for a variety of reasons, including their ability to inflict punishments, that do not necessarily make them attractive relationship partners. However, to the extent that this power is based on the ability to bring things to the table that we cannot obtain elsewhere, it is natural that we would want to maintain our relationship with that party and the benefits that relationship would afford, even if that means rationalizing, discounting, or even denying offenses that party might have committed. This is true regardless of whether that powerful party is an individual, group, institution, or business.

Take Facebook, for example. Despite its numerous transgressions and the loss of trust its behavior has created, this social media platform has remained viable. Even before the latest wave of scandals that was mentioned in this book's earlier chapters, a survey in October and November 2019 by the Pew Research Center found that 59 percent of adults said they distrusted the platform as a source for political and election news, while only 15 percent said they trusted it.[8] Yet other Pew data reveals that there has been no statistically significant change in the share of adults who used the platform (69 percent) from 2016 through early 2021.[9] This can make sense, however, when we consider the fact that Facebook has dominated the social media landscape with a much larger share of social media users than any platform other than YouTube, and how this can create a motivation to remain in that network due to the benefits that might accrue from that network's scale.

We can likewise see this motivation to maintain relationships with the powerful in how some have responded to Martin Luther King Jr.'s infidelities.[10] Michael Honey, who teaches civil rights history at the University of Washington Tacoma, acknowledged that it was widely known King had many affairs. But when Honey's students became disillusioned by King's affairs, he would point out that King was on the road three hundred days a year, only seeing his wife periodically, and having marital fights and stress. He would then tell his students, "Well, just think about it for a minute, you know? What do normal people do? They have sex."

I'm not sure if everyone would agree with Honey's attempts to normalize King's affairs in this way. It shouldn't be so hard to accept the notion that marital infidelity is wrong. However, it may be easier to understand that attempt to diminish the significance of King's infidelities as a form of denial, based on the motivation to keep his affairs from diminishing his legacy and contributions to civil rights.

More broadly, these observations illustrate how power affords at least two distinct advantages for those who have committed a transgression. It can not only enable them to get their way due to their greater influence on how disputes might be resolved but also motivate those who depend on the powerful to maintain those relationships even after a transgression has occurred (even if that means discounting the significance of the wrongdoing or denying it altogether). But the effects of power are not just one-sided. These benefits must ultimately be balanced against the ways in which power can also make the repair of trust more difficult.

One of the ways in which power can exacerbate the challenges of addressing trust violations stems from the fact that we typically assume that the powerful have more control over what happens than they really do. We tend to assume this about other people as well, as we will consider more thoroughly in chapter 9. However, as organizational researchers James Meindl, Sanford Ehrlich, and Janet Dukerich have found, through a combination of archival and experimental studies, this tendency is accentuated with leaders.[11] Their work suggests that society has developed and nurtured a romanticized view of leadership that treats it as a larger-than-life characteristic worthy of glorification. Thus, we tend to exhibit an unrealistic faith in what leaders can do, what they can accomplish, and how they can affect our lives that leads us to focus on leaders as the reason why things might have succeeded or failed, regardless of what the true impact of those leaders might have been.

This view of leaders as having the power to control whatever happens can, furthermore, lead us to attribute more intent to their actions. We can see this in studies by organizational psychologists Jennifer Overbeck, Larissa Tiedens, and Sebastien Brion, who asked participants to read about and explain the actions of people with more or less power. For example, when presented with a scenario in which an employee went to work on a Saturday, respondents attributed this action to personal motivation when told that the employee was a manager, but attributed it to outside influences when the employee was an assistant.[12] They also found that this effect stemmed, at least in part, from a biased perception in which perceivers systematically underestimated the situational constraints on the powerful and overestimated the constraints on the powerless.

These findings suggest that although power can afford important advantages, it can also become a serious liability when trust has been violated. We tend to consider the powerful more responsible (than those with less power) for such offenses and assume their transgressions were more intentional. Moreover, as we've previously considered, this tendency to attribute greater intent for the offenses of the powerful suggests that if they are guilty, their efforts to repair trust with an apology or more substantive responses are far less likely to work.

An example of this occurred quite close to home for me on August 20, 2020, and briefly made national news. As journalist Conor Friedersdorf reported in *The Atlantic,*[13] Greg Patton, another professor at my university, was teaching an online class on communication, which covered the importance of avoiding filler words such as *um* or *er*. Thus, to be more inclusive of international students, he gave another example of a filler word. He said, "Like in China it might be nèi-ge—nèi-ge, nèi-ge, nèi-ge. So there's different words that you'll hear in different countries."

However, some of the students thought this Mandarin word sounded too much like the N-word. They sent a letter of complaint to administrators and underscored their grievance in a meeting. This complaint led Patton to offer a prompt apology for what happened, but this did not quell the furor. Instead, the complaint resulted in a formal investigation and Patton's removal as instructor for the course.

These events can be understood by taking a closer look at the letter of complaint the students submitted. The letter not only claimed that Patton mispronounced the Chinese word in a way that would be more harmful to the students but also alleged that in each class session, he would "conveniently stop the Zoom recording right before saying the word, then resume the Zoom recording afterwards," and asserted that this made clear "that his actions were calculated." Thus, the students had immediately framed the offense as an intentional act. And we have already underscored how apologies tend to be far less effective at repairing trust after integrity-based violations.

The allegation that Patton stopped the Zoom recordings right before saying the offending word was subsequently proven false, since recordings of Patton using that word in one of those classes surfaced quickly online. Yet this evidence did not deter the claim that Patton inflicted intentional harm. And part of the reason why may be found in the fact that Patton had taught this same course for years, as a *communications* professor, and was (in the eyes of students) someone with greater experience, expertise, and ultimately power. All these considerations can make it easy to infer that Patton knew what he was doing and that he was quite aware of the harm that Chinese word would cause.

Other professors (as well as much of the broader public and eventually even those who conducted the formal investigation of this incident at the university), however, interpreted this situation quite differently. One of the things professors have well learned from the need to move courses online since 2020, due to the onset of the COVID crisis, has been how much more challenging it can be to assess the body language and mood of a virtual class. Moreover, even the very best instructors tend to treat their courses as ongoing works in progress that involve regular tweaking, experimentation, and improvement. That's how we make our courses better. Thus, there are often moments when we are not sure a lesson will work and where we make mental notes of things to fix afterward, and these efforts can be made even more difficult as we strive to teach larger and more diverse sets of audiences with different tastes, sensibilities, and attention spans.

In the face of such challenges, it can be difficult for even the most experienced and successful teachers to anticipate all the ways in which our statements might be received. We are human too. And if we somehow offend even just a few of our students, all we can really do is try to rectify that through our subsequent words and actions. Thus, when I read Patton's letter to the business school's Graduate Student Association, which stated that when he learned that some students were upset, "my heart dropped, and I have felt terrible ever since," I believed he felt sincere remorse.

However, several studies I have led with an international team of researchers from the United States, the Netherlands, and Israel suggest that the students he offended would have been less likely to share that view. My own appraisal of Patton's remorse involved the evaluation of a peer, someone with whom I could empathize based on my own experiences navigating the many thrills, challenges, and pitfalls that can arise in a classroom. But when Patton's students considered his expression of remorse, Patton's power relative to theirs may have led them to interpret that response quite differently.

I examined this possibility with my collaborators by asking study participants to observe either high-power or low-power individuals who had been accused of a violation express one of several emotions (sadness, anger, fear, happiness, or an entirely neutral expression) and then both evaluate that expression and indicate their trust in that person afterward.[14] Some of the experiments involved still photos of these individuals expressing the target emotion, whereas others involved video recordings we had made or edited. The transgressions also ranged from hypothetical financial and legal offenses to real-life cases. One of those real-life cases, for example, involved the CEO of Toyota America testifying before Congress in 2010 regarding the deaths and injuries caused by the sudden acceleration of their cars. The other involved the CEO of Lululemon expressing sadness in 2013 after a scandal in which he tried to shift blame for complaints about their yoga pants being too sheer with the argument that some women's bodies weren't suited to wearing athletic clothing. In each case, we presented participants with the exact same photo or video and simply told them that the person was either a CEO or a lower-level subordinate.

Yet even though the expression participants viewed for each emotion we studied was identical, the results revealed that participants perceived the display to be much less authentic when they believed that person's power was high rather than low. We also found that this occurred because people tend to believe that those who attain positions of power have greater control over their emotions and that this emotional control makes them likelier to express those emotions strategically. This leads them to discount the authenticity of the emotions the powerful might express in response to a transgression and ultimately remain less willing to trust them afterward.

Related markers of success have been found to harm the perception of authenticity and how people respond to transgressions in other arenas as well. For example, in the context of stand-up comedy, one of the dangers comics routinely face is the potential for joke theft. Sociologist Patrick Reilly, who conducted qualitative research as a participant-observer in the Los Angeles stand-up comic community, has found, however, that whether someone is accused of joke theft has little to do with the similarity of the joke; it depends far more on whether other comics view the potential joke thief as authentic to the community.[15] Specifically, those who are most vulnerable to such allegations are the ones who have enjoyed commercial success despite low peer esteem. Few people respected them as peers and were, therefore, less willing to grant them leeway. Thus, as with my own research, the findings from this subsequent study highlight how external forms of success can become a double-edged sword. Such success can bring power and other benefits. But as Patton experienced with his attempt to apologize for using an offending word, that success can also make one's transgressions seem more intentional and harder to overcome, at least in part because the remorse one might subsequently express will seem less authentic.

The only exceptions I've found in my research for this tendency to discount the emotional authenticity of the powerful are when the emotion is expressed in settings that aren't strategically beneficial or when the powerful have a history of being bad at managing their emotions. In one of these studies, for example, we showed participants a photo of someone expressing sadness and again told them this person was either a CEO (high power) or a lower-level employee (low power). However, we also told participants that they either witnessed this expression in a company meeting (in public) or when they glanced into this person's office where he was sitting alone (in private). The study revealed that the type of background information participants received made a marked difference in how this expression was viewed. When the expression was made in public, where the expressor might have had a strategic motivation to manage impressions, people viewed the emotion to be far less authentic when the expressor's power was high than when it was low. However, this effect of power vanished when the expression occurred in private and there was little reason to be strategic.

Similarly, in another study, we altered this background information to manipulate the expressor's perceived level of emotional control. To do so, we either described this person as having "a reputation for skillfully managing his nonverbal expressions" (high emotional control) or having "a reputation for wearing his heart on his sleeve" (low emotional control). The results revealed that when the expressor was described as having high emotional control, the exact same expression was considered less authentic when the expressor's power was high than when it was low. However, when the expressor was described as having low emotional control, the expressor's power had no effect on how authentic the emotion was perceived to be.

The bottom line is that, because our tendency to consider the powerful less emotionally authentic stems from the belief that a) they are more emotionally skilled and thus b) likelier to express emotions strategically, breaking either link in this causal chain can circumvent this problem. And there is perhaps no better illustration of this phenomenon than how former president Donald J. Trump has been viewed by his base. As someone who has been described as lacking the temperament to be president[16] and who has routinely engaged in strategically nonsensical acts like admitting that Russia helped him win the presidency only to deny it twenty minutes later,[17] it is hard to infer that Trump's outbursts are anything but a real window into his psyche. In the eyes of his supporters, Trump might sometimes shoot himself in the foot, but there is no question in their minds that he is being authentic. This, in turn, can make them far more inclined to trust him than the more polished (and hence less authentic) political establishment.

It is important to note, however, that other studies have revealed that, on the whole, those with power not only are more emotionally skilled[18] but also tend to be more authentic.[19] That greater authenticity, furthermore, seems to arise precisely because those with power have greater freedom to do what they want. The issue is simply that most of us are also aware that the powerful possess these emotional capabilities and are thus inclined to discount their expressions so dramatically. Hence, as with so many other aspects of trust, it may ultimately be the balance between perception and reality that makes the difference in whether these beliefs about emotional authenticity are warranted or not.

More broadly, the findings underscore the highly conflicted minefield of forces that can affect how we view those with power. Some of those forces can create important advantages, such as the motivation to maintain relationships with those individuals (due to the benefits those relationships might provide), whereas other forces can create serious liabilities, such as our belief that they have more control over what happens than they really do. Thus, it would be natural for efforts to evaluate leaders who might have troubling details in their past to produce very different opinions, and it is ultimately up to each of us to make our own judgments about how those sentiments should be tallied.

Nevertheless, some insight into what that approach might entail can be found in historian Barbara Ransby's reference to a warning by Ella Baker, who worked alongside Martin Luther King Jr. for many years, about the dangers of putting individual leaders on pedestals.[20] Ransby wrote, "They are human beings like the rest of us. We can criticize their failings and still find value in their contributions, so long as we are learning lessons and not looking for someone to worship."

That warning hints at the ethical accounting problem we considered in the last chapter. What we do when we believe someone is guilty of an intentional offense is to start questioning all the good things that person might have also done. Those good deeds stop being taken at face value; they become infected by the breach of integrity as we start wondering what sorts of nefarious motives might explain those good deeds as well. Although this kind of questioning can also occur when we evaluate others more generally (even if we don't do that for ourselves), it is likely to be more problematic for leaders, because we tend to believe they have the power to do what they want and that their transgressions are thus more intentional. This can lead us to consider even one bad act by a leader sufficient to erase an entire legacy of good things that person might have done, to find them contradicting our unrealistically romanticized view of what a leader should be, and thereby conclude they were unfit to have led us at all.

Thus, faced with that prospect, those who want to maintain faith in their heroes often choose the alternative path of denying that those transgressions occurred. Their defenders may attempt to discount the significance of the violation or do their best to deny the possibility that it even happened. Those reactions are understandable if we accept the notion that being guilty of such transgressions should wipe out all the good things that person might have done. However, they ultimately belie the wisdom in the point that Ransby and others have at least implicitly made when they assert that we can both criticize leaders' failings and find value in their contributions, so long as we recognize they are human beings rather than start looking for someone to worship.

What that claim suggests is that we should *not* treat their transgressions as sufficient to wipe out all the good things a person might have also done. Because if we don't, then we would not have to work so hard to deny those transgressions in the first place. Denial only becomes necessary if we insist on maintaining an unrealistically romantic view of leaders as heroes who can do no wrong. But if we accept that those leaders, as well as each one of us, can do both good and bad things, then we can be more honest with ourselves about what each of their implications would have been.

This seems particularly important as we struggle with the many sordid revelations of so many historical figures today. One thing we have learned, for example, is that George Washington owned and bought slaves. As historian Mary V. Thompson details in her book *The Only Unavoidable Subject of Regret,* there is even a record of him ordering an enslaved man to be whipped for walking on the lawn, he aggressively pursued runaways, and he also took steps to prevent his slaves from being freed while visiting free states.[21] We should be able to acknowledge that part of his legacy, while also being able to acknowledge his extraordinary leadership during the Revolutionary War and as the first U.S. president. Both things can be true at the same time.

Likewise, with Franklin D. Roosevelt, I will forever admire him as a beacon of hope for the poor, disenfranchised, and vulnerable through some of the darkest times of the twentieth century. But I will also remember that by issuing Executive Order 9066, to compel the relocation of innocent Japanese Americans to concentration camps, he ultimately accepted the premise that Americans of Asian heritage were less than equal and less deserving of civil rights. His actions reveal how he still saw us as the "other," no matter how long we have made this country our home.

And as for Martin Luther King Jr., it is clear based on accounts of King's life that, as a *Time* magazine profile observed,[22] "King developed from his earliest years a raw-nerved sensitivity that bordered on self-destruction," that he made two suicide attempts before the age of thirteen, and that he cheated on his wife on numerous occasions.[23] That shouldn't diminish the fact that he also rose to the call of history when he was needed, that his eloquence and vision helped inspire a nation, and that generations since remain indebted to that service.

Recognizing both the good and bad doesn't require that we become indifferent. We can still weigh these facts as we see fit and use them to reach some overarching judgment, and there are certainly plenty of cases where the harm clearly outweighs anything else, as in the case of the Sackler family. But if we don't try to account for each side of the ledger first, if we deny the basic premise that "in all good is the possibility of evil, and in all evil the possibility of good,"[24] then the judgments we make will be based on distorted caricatures rather than human beings with real limitations and flaws.

That reliance on caricatures seems to lie at the core of why our trust in the powerful can go to such extremes. Those tendencies may also help explain why so many leaders experience such a dramatic rise and fall. We tend to exhibit an unrealistic faith in leaders until something we can't dismiss shatters that illusion. Then, once that occurs, trust becomes almost impossible for them to repair, because we are likely to believe the offense had been intentional and that their remorse was insincere. Thus, our main recourse is to conclude that they were unfit to have led us after all and, when possible, simply to cast them aside for someone else who might better fit this heroic mold. It is in this sense that we may be at least partly to blame when our trust in leaders dramatically changes. It ultimately stems from our efforts to nurture highly romanticized views of what leaders should be that virtually no one can fulfill.

8

BEWARE THE HIVE MIND

On the evening of Friday, August 11, 2017, a column of mostly young white men began to stretch across a field behind the Memorial Gymnasium at the University of Virginia in Charlottesville. They lit kerosene-filled torches and marched at a brisk pace to converge on a statue of the school's founder, Thomas Jefferson, while yelling slogans like "Blood and soil!" "You will not replace us!" "Jews will not replace us!" There, they met a group of about thirty UVA students, both white and nonwhite, who locked their arms around the base of the statue to face down the hundreds of torchbearers. The marchers circled these students, with some making monkey noises at the Black counterprotesters, and then began chanting, "White lives matter!" Within moments, chaos ensued with shoves, punches, and both sides spraying pepper spray and similar chemical irritants.

These clashes escalated early on the next day, with self-identified members of the alt-right, neo-Confederates, neo-fascists, white nationalists, neo-Nazis, Ku Klux Klan, and various right-wing militias arriving in contingents with nationalist banners. Many of them also wielded shields, clubs, and guns. When the counterprotesters were joined by local residents, members of church groups, civil rights leaders, and onlookers early that same morning, some of them had sticks and shields as well. And by the time the Unite the Right rally ended, less than twenty-four hours after the start of the torchlight march, three people had died and at least thirty-three others were injured, with one of the deaths and nineteen of the injuries caused by a single driver who deliberately rammed them with his vehicle.[1]

These kinds of clashes have become all too familiar. Plenty of others have occurred before and since, not just between protest groups but also between protesters and police. You don't need me to add to the numerous commentaries that have already been made about these specific incidents.

However, it is worth examining the deeper causes of intergroup conflict that helped fuel this rally to reveal the challenges they can pose for trust and its repair.

Our understanding of intergroup conflict is based on decades of research in the social sciences that has offered crucial insights about how events like the one in Charlottesville can happen. We know that arbitrary differences, such as eye color or even preference for abstract art, can quickly become the basis for people to sort themselves into different groups, to distinguish "us" from "them." We also know that through such distinctions, people wind up favoring members of their own group at the expense of those outside it.[2] This affects not only how we allocate resources and other benefits but also how we perceive the world, with people viewing the exact same confrontation, for example, firmly believing the other side was to blame.[3]

These tendencies can make it far easier to build trust within groups than to build trust between groups, and likewise produce similar effects when trust has been violated and efforts are made to repair it. A few years ago, for example, I was presenting some of my research at a business school conference when the school's dean, who had been in the audience, responded to my findings by recounting her own experience with a group of CEOs and other top executives from around the country. She mentioned that their overwhelming sentiment was that the best way to address a crisis was to apologize and assume full responsibility for what happened. We already know from the prior chapters how this kind of "one size fits all" approach to addressing trust violations can go disastrously wrong, and I was able to draw on that research evidence to convince both the dean and the rest of the audience to rethink their assumptions. However, there is a reason why the executives themselves might have been more resistant to such findings, an implication that stems from the nature of groups.

At issue is the fact that these top executive discussions of how best to address their transgressions took place among participants who were highly similar. They were a group of like-minded individuals leading major companies and with a common interest in continuing education to hone their skills. Thus, their natural inclination would be to look upon their fellow group members favorably by inferring that if any one of them were to commit a transgression, it would have to be by mistake. We have already considered how apologies can be effective for addressing competence-based violations.

The problem, however, is that most of those evaluating their transgressions would not be part of their select group. They would be employees, customers, the media, and the public, who would likely consider these executives to be quite unlike themselves. The evidence also makes clear that we tend to be much less favorable toward people who are different. This broader set of people may, thus, be far more willing to infer that the transgression had been deliberate than the executives would have assumed. And if so, efforts to apologize and accept full ownership for the incident would not help, and could even make things worse, because others would simply see this as confirmation that those who committed the transgression lacked integrity.

These tendencies can thus compound the effects of power the previous chapter detailed. They suggest that we are not only likelier to believe a violation was intentional if the offender has greater power but also likelier to do so if the offender represents a different group. Hence, to the extent that an offender meets both criteria, as we can imagine would be the case for these executives, there may be particularly little hope for them to change that view.

This tendency to favor one's in-group over the out-group, which psychologists have referred to as *intergroup bias,* also creates another complication. That bias can be magnified when the out-group is perceived as a threat. These kinds of dynamics can take many forms, some of which can be relatively benign. Each fall, for example, my university campus bears witness to its own form of symbolic war, when it fights its crosstown neighbor UCLA in a football game. This is an entertaining event that stirs up school spirit at each campus, and it can certainly feel good to root for one's team and share in the camaraderie that relatively harmless rivalry can instill.

But history tells us that previously unimportant distinctions can just as easily grow in significance and lead members to commit extraordinary atrocities against one another. Consider, for example, what happened in August 1947, when the British finally ended their colonial rule over India. Mahatma

Gandhi considered British rule one of the great evils afflicting India and led a multi-decade-long nonviolent movement to oppose it. Yet as their Independence Day on August 15, 1947, approached, and their common enemy of British rule was no longer a threat, Hindus and Muslims in that country quickly turned against one another. They engaged in a terrifying outbreak of looting, rape, and murder, which led millions to flee their homes and cross the borders into what would become a Hindu-majority India and the new Muslim nation of Pakistan.

As Nisid Hajari writes in his book *Midnight's Furies,* "Gangs of killers set whole villages aflame, hacking to death men and children and the aged while carrying off young women to be raped . . . pregnant women had their breasts cut off and babies hacked out of their bellies; infants were found literally roasted on spits."[4] He also notes that some British soldiers and journalists who had witnessed the Nazi death camps claimed that the brutalities they witnessed during that time in India were worse. This is a conclusion that William Dalrymple supports in his article in *The New Yorker* about this period of Indian Partition.[5] He observes, "The comparison with the death camps is not so far-fetched as it may seem. Partition is as central to modern identity in the Indian subcontinent as the Holocaust is to identity among Jews, branded painfully onto the regional consciousness by memories of almost unimaginable violence."

Dalrymple also illuminates how the hostility between Hindus and Muslims only took hold during the previous two decades. Before then, the practice of the two faiths in India "came close to blending into one." He notes that in the nineteenth century, "India was still a place where traditions, languages, and cultures cut across religious groupings, and where people did not define themselves primarily through their religious faith."

But the British gradually eroded this integration in their efforts to maintain control over India by making proposals that aggravated Indian religious (and caste) divisions. They started to define communities based on religious identity and set up local governments with separate electorates where each religion would vote for its own politicians.[6] Historians don't necessarily view those steps as deliberate attempts to stoke infighting between these religious groups to keep them from uniting against British concerns.[7] However, the actions were ultimately consistent with the British empire's broader policy of "divide and rule," which involved breaking larger concentrations of power into pieces that were easier to control,[8] and they eventually caused what had previously been a relatively unimportant religious distinction to take on outsize significance as these religious groups started to vie for political power.

Thus, it should not be a surprise that, as the British lost their grip on India and oppression from British rule stopped serving the role of common enemy against which Hindus and Muslims could unite, these religious groups would turn on one another as the new salient threat. There is no better way to galvanize and find solidarity with one's group than by depicting outsiders as monsters. Whether we see them as trying to harm something we value (such as one's religious beliefs, rights, or ideals) or competing to take things we value away from us (such as property, privilege, or political power), those who face the same predicament have reason to fight together against that threat and to find pride, fellowship, and purpose through that shared cause. But this comes at the cost of clarifying why others don't belong, diminishing what we might have in common with those outsiders, and quite often denigrating them to convince ourselves we are more deserving.

These intergroup influences raise the need to consider another wrinkle as well. The same underlying mechanisms that can facilitate the repair of trust within a group can also exacerbate mistrust between groups. This is not only because we can interpret the offenses of in-group members more favorably than those of out-group members but also because we can expect those in-group members to behave more favorably to us in turn. As people identify more with a group and feel a greater sense of interdependence with the other members, the group can develop norms of looking out for one another and doing things that serve the group's interests. And this, in turn, can create a breeding ground for corruption.

Organizational psychologists Priyanka Joshi, Nathaniel Fast, and I have investigated how this can occur with several studies. In one, we analyzed archival data on National Collegiate Athletic Association (NCAA) violations and found that universities with a stronger culture of interdependence engaged in less monitoring of their athletic programs and ultimately more frequent and severe violations of NCAA rules. We also found through additional studies that these effects could be explained by group members' feelings of interdependence leading them to protect one another based on their belief that the offenses were intended to benefit their group. The problem with that reasoning, however, is that those outside that group are much less likely to consider that kind of protection warranted. Instead, they are likely to consider it to be far less justified and believe that it reflects the corruption of all its members.[9]

One particularly troubling way in which these group-level influences have been underscored is through the different reactions of the public and the police unions to the 2020 killings of Breonna Taylor and George Floyd. Each of these cases involved the egregious deaths of African Americans at the hands of police officers. The public responded to those incidents with outrage, demands to convict those responsible, and calls to change and even defund the police. These were just the latest of many examples of police violence against the African American community, after all, and many believed that if something major wasn't done even in response to these particularly outrageous acts, this meant the police system was fundamentally broken.

Police unions, on the other hand, viewed these incidents quite differently. When Ryan Nichols, the president of the Fraternal Order of Police chapter that represents the Louisville Metro Police Department, spoke to Gayle King of *CBS This Morning* about Breonna Taylor's death, he said, "The officers were definitely justified in returning fire." When King asked how the police could be justified in firing thirty-two shots into the apartment, Nichols responded by stating that in these kinds of high-stress situations, "typically you may not be aware of how many rounds someone else is firing, how many other officers are firing. And perhaps you may not have an accurate count of the rounds you fired." Moreover, when asked to address how the incident report could have claimed there was no forced entry in the apartment when that was clearly untrue and how this indicates a cover-up, Nichols replied, "Can I definitely say affirmatively that no mistakes on anything were made? Obviously not. But I don't believe that there was any type of cover-up."[10]

Both the public and the police unions considered Breonna Taylor's death a tragedy, but their interpretations of this event completely differed. Whereas much of the public saw this death as a flagrant and unjustified abuse of power that officers deliberately sought to conceal, representatives of the police union attributed what happened to officers' natural limitations in the face of such high-stress situations and mistakes—matters of competence rather than integrity. The police union representative furthermore stressed that "nothing illegal occurred," that his fellow officers "don't want citizens to live in fear of violence of any kind," and that when it comes to change, his union is always interested in fair and balanced reforms that enhance policing. In his view, police officers were fundamentally good people doing their best in the face of very difficult circumstances. That is why he believed morale in his police department was low and found the public's outrage "very frustrating."

My goal is not to judge the merits of these views but rather to underscore how such tendencies to interpret offenses as intentional acts committed by bad people, as opposed to honest mistakes made by those who mean well, can be a natural result of how we tend to see those within versus outside our group. There is, furthermore, another way in which our group memberships can distort how we perceive these kinds of incidents. This can be revealed by comparing people's reactions to Breonna Taylor's killing with the video-recorded murder of George Floyd.

Unlike how the police union responded to the Louisville officers' role in Breonna Taylor's killing, the Minneapolis Police Officers Federation chose not to defend the actions of Derek Chauvin once the video of George Floyd's death was made public. The video had clearly shown that police officer kneeling on Floyd's neck for approximately nine minutes even after he cried out for his mother, his body went limp, and bystanders repeatedly called for the officers to stop.[11] This made it quite difficult for anyone to claim this killing had not been deliberate. Thus, the federation ultimately decided it wouldn't try to have Chauvin reinstated, even if he requested it and was acquitted of the murder and manslaughter charges he was facing.[12]

However, the federation did do something else. The union leaders next to the federation president, two women and a Black officer, said that although the video of Chauvin was horrific, it was not representative of the entire force. Moreover, they did not consider it a racial issue. In fact, Anna Hedberg, a sergeant and director of the federation, said, "As far as race goes, you have a white cop, you have a Black cop, you have an Asian cop, you have another white cop." Thus, she didn't see race as a factor in what happened, despite Floyd's death representing such a vivid example of police brutality against Black men.

In the eyes of the federation, Chauvin was a bad apple rather than a reflection of the entire police department. (The other three officers involved in the incident still had the union's backing.) Thus, they considered the loud demands from the public to reform, and even defund and abolish the police, unjustified. They were furthermore outraged when rioters set fire to the city's Third Precinct police headquarters, forcing fifty-four officers (who had not been involved in Floyd's killing) to scramble to get their belongings out before it fell, and when those officers were subsequently "chased down the street because the failed politicians allowed [the rioters] to be there."[13]

What's notable about these union complaints is that they sought not to affect how the public interpreted Chauvin's actions but rather to engage in a strategy of differentiation. The federation did not defend Floyd's killing but instead made clear that the police force was not a homogeneous group. In their view, the police force was comprised of officers with different racial backgrounds and most had nothing to do with Floyd's murder at all. Thus, they considered it quite unfair for the entire police force to be punished for the actions of one of its members, in contrast to many in the public, who were inclined to see this incident as a reflection of the broader police force.

This difference illustrates another well-established phenomenon with groups. That research has long ago made clear that whereas people tend to recognize and appreciate differences within their own group, they tend to see members of other groups as homogeneous. One study by psychologists Bernadette Park and Myron Rothbart, for example, which asked ninety members of three campus sororities to judge the degree of intragroup similarity for their own and the other two sorority groups, found that participants judged members of their own group to be significantly more dissimilar to one another than members of other groups perceived them to be.[14] We can likewise observe that just as the federation lamented the public's efforts to villainize the police force as a whole, based on the actions of one bad apple, it also levied its own complaint against the actions of "politicians" as an undifferentiated group for not doing more to defend police officers. As this example illustrates, the underlying tendency to differentiate within one's own group but treat other groups as homogeneous is so insidious and pervasive that we can find ourselves doing both at the same time without even realizing it.

This tendency to view other groups as more homogeneous than one's own can, in turn, affect the kinds of remedies we consider appropriate. It suggests that if a breach of trust occurs, people will consider it reasonable to implement more targeted remedies within their own group and find it particularly unfair when efforts are made to impose larger-scale interventions that harm the group as a whole (e.g., since many fellow group members may not have been involved in the incident and may perhaps have as much in common with the victims as the offenders). However, they are also likely to prefer broader remedies for other groups, since they will tend to believe the offense reflects upon all of them and are less likely to think that any of the group's members are truly innocent. Thus, even if both sides agree that an offense has been committed and interpret it in the same way, they can still disagree about what to do about it. Moreover, when this occurs, this can become yet another source of conflict.

A case in point can be found in how my own university, the University of Southern California, has struggled in the wake of numerous high-profile scandals. As journalist Jason McGahan reported in *Los Angeles Magazine*,[15] USC had the dubious distinction of being more involved than any other school in the Varsity Blues college admissions scandal we discussed earlier, by letting in twice as many falsified athletic recruits as all the other schools combined. Moreover, in July 2017, reporter Paul Pringle and his team of investigators detailed how the dean of the Keck School of Medicine, Carmen A. Puliafito, had "kept company with a circle of criminals and drug users who said he used methamphetamine and other drugs with them."[16] This eventually led to an incident in a hotel room on March 4, 2016, when Puliafito called 911 after the twenty-one-year-old sex worker with whom he was taking drugs had overdosed. Later in 2017, an FBI probe also uncovered a massive college basketball scandal, in which the men's basketball assistant coach, Tony Bland, was caught pocketing thousands of dollars in bribes from a sports agent.[17] This was then followed by the most shocking scandal of all, when Harriet Ryan and her fellow reporters published an article on May 16, 2018, in the *Los Angeles Times,* which investigated how campus gynecologist George Tyndall had sexually abused hundreds of young patients over three decades, despite complaints about him that began in the 1990s (before many of the doctor's later victims were even born).[18]

As crazy as this may seem, this is only a sampling of incidents that eventually led USC president Max Nikias to step down in the fall of 2018. Indeed, McGahan described the breadth and frequency of these incidents over that two-year period as "unprecedented in the annals of American higher education."[19] When McGahan interviewed Michael Useem, a professor of management at the University of Pennsylvania's Wharton School who specializes in catastrophic risk management and corporate governance, for his *Los Angeles Magazine* article about these scandals, Useem said, "I can't think of anything close . . . There are very few examples where you've had so many different parts of a university affected at almost the same time."

What's more, despite the installment of a new administration (with Carol Folt as president and Charles "Chip" Zukoski as provost), the scandals have unfortunately continued. For example, on October 13, 2021, the former dean of USC's School of Social Work and Los Angeles politician Mark Ridley-Thomas were charged with a bribery scheme in which Ridley-Thomas promised to steer millions of dollars in contracts to the school if his son got a scholarship and a teaching job at the university.[20] Then on October 21, a USC Department of Public Safety log was published, which revealed six separate reports of female students being drugged (of whom one also reported a sexual assault), while attending parties at the Sigma Nu frater-

answer—all ties with McKinsey should be severed. One professor, further-more, justified that stance in an email exchange by stating, "I believe that when an apple is rotten it is rotten, does not matter which part is rotten. A company's values and culture are reflected in everything it does and to claim that in a decentralized organization one wing's egregious choices should not be held against the others is both naive and dangerous."

These sentiments struck me as both heartfelt and guided by a sincere desire to make the university a better place. Yet if we were to apply that logic to McKinsey, it is hard to see why it shouldn't be applied to USC as well. Our scandals have revealed not just one rotten part of the apple; parts were rotten from its campus doctors up to the dean of the medical school, across a range of its athletic programs, and in at least one other of its professional schools. Yet the faculty voicing their frustrations about these incidents did not suggest that everyone boycott their own institution or that all those associated with the institution, including themselves, should be punished. They believed the blame should be more focused—on the individuals who committed the crimes, the former president, and now the new administration. And this would seem eminently reasonable if it weren't for the fact that they would take such a contradictory stance when viewing institutions other than their own.

The point is that although it would be logically consistent to claim that the scandals at USC and McKinsey & Company should be used to broadly con-demn both organizations or that more targeted remedies would be warranted for each (based on the view that the scandals do not represent the organiza-tions as a whole), it makes less sense to consider targeted remedies appropriate for one's own organization but broader condemnation more appropriate for others. Yet that kind of hypocrisy may be more common than we think and even occur with those who believe they are being entirely consistent. Some of my own theoretical work with Scott Wiltermuth and David Newman, a fellow faculty member and a former doctoral student from my department, respectively, suggests that this is because hypocrisy can stem not only from self-serving motivations but also from the fact that we generally have more information about ourselves than we do about others.[27]

We can see this in the aforementioned op-ed in the *Los Angeles Times*, in

nity between September 27 and October 20 of that year, with the
announcing the fraternity's temporary suspension only the night
DPS log was released.

That last set of incidents prompted the chair of a group called C
Faculty of USC, which originally organized to pressure former i
president Nikias to step down after the previous set of scandals, to
op-ed for the *Los Angeles Times*.[21] This letter blasted the new admii
for maintaining a toxic culture based on its "pattern of secrecy ai
in handling fallout" from these kinds of cases. That lack of transpa
been a matter of debate, with the new president, Folt, promptly re:
to the allegation by sharing links to several online websites that ha
to address those transparency concerns over the previous two years
it is ultimately not my goal to weigh in on this specific issue.

However, what I do wish to explore is this op-ed's attempt to un
its claim that "this administration continues to cover up rather th
clean" by sarcastically pointing to the administration's reliance on "tl
ethical experts McKinsey & Co." for two years to advise the new p
on improving USC's culture, despite this consultancy's "role in i
oid crisis and immigrant detention facilities, and for its involveme
Enron." McKinsey had advised pharmaceutical companies, such as
Pharma, to push the addictive OxyContin painkiller onto the marl
eventually agreed to pay a $574 million settlement to U.S. author
its role).[24] McKinsey had worked with U.S. Immigration and Custo
forcement (ICE) to cut costs at its detention facilities through m
the agency's own staff sometimes viewed as too harsh on immigran
as by spending less on food and medical care for detainees.[25] The co
had also previously lauded the off–balance sheet accounting practic
were central to the energy trader Enron's massive accounting fraud an
collapse.[26]

The message here was simple. How can you hope to address t
ministration's toxic culture by relying on consultants who are themse
ethically compromised? In short, how can USC ever rebuild trust i
way? This is a natural question for which many at USC had an imm

which the head of the group of concerned faculty observed, "My students, faculty and staff colleagues are some of the best, most hard-working and most ethical people I have ever known. Indeed, one of the silver linings for me of my involvement in protesting the university administration's actions over the last few years as the chair of Concerned Faculty of USC has been getting to know them better." It can, therefore, seem reasonable for the writer to differentiate those ethical people from those at McKinsey and in the USC administration, whom the letter portrayed as "rotten from the top" when assigning blame. Yet this person is unlikely to have had comparable exposure to the internal discussions at McKinsey & Company, in which ethical members of that organization might have expressed similar concerns. The same limitation also applies to having access to the internal discussions of the new USC administration. Thus, it would be natural for that writer to see no reason to differentiate the good from the bad in those other groups and seek to blame them in their entirety.

We firmly believe these inconsistent responses to scandals by our own versus other groups are justified based on the information we have available. All it takes to sustain that belief is to overlook or dismiss the fact that this information is quite likely to be skewed. That simple step is what allows us to act like hypocrites without even realizing it, to believe that we have been fair and consistent in applying our principles while failing to account for fundamental informational distortions in the arenas where those principles are "consistently" applied. And this can ultimately lead us to consider the exact same effort to address wrongdoing and repair trust to be less adequate when it is meant to address the transgressions of other groups than one's own.

This negative reaction to seeing others respond to transgressions in ways we consider inadequate can, furthermore, be strengthened when we discuss those opinions within our own group. Another well-documented finding in the social sciences is that people's opinions can become more extreme when they talk to others who hold similar views.[28] Their opinions polarize as they exchange those sentiments with one another, and this can strengthen and magnify the beliefs they might have initially held.

This is a major reason why social media sites like Facebook and YouTube can be so dangerous. By using algorithms that continually expose people to viewpoints they already hold, they often exacerbate those sentiments by allowing users to endorse one another's views, even when those views are unfounded or extreme. All it takes is a handful of like-minded others in the billions of Facebook or YouTube users around the globe to feel like our opinions, no matter how far-fetched, are legitimate, that they are no longer on the fringe but part of a growing movement. We support, exchange, and embellish our supportive arguments and thus find them more convincing. We either ignore or denigrate opposing viewpoints, which none in this curated circle of like-minded users have any desire to defend. And we feel pressured to support even more extreme versions of these sentiments than we might have initially believed, because not doing so would be considered disloyal.

This is an ideal breeding ground for radicalization, regardless of what those initial beliefs might have been. When we venture into these kinds of interpretive bubbles, either intentionally or through the guidance of social media algorithms, they can become the primary means through which we make sense of our worlds. They become self-reinforcing systems that both promote and depend on the polarization of their members. And as we considered earlier in this chapter, there is no better way to galvanize and find solidarity with one's group than by depicting those outside the group as monsters. We can see this again and again in our political discourse with the rise of hate-filled language, as well as in the rise of conspiracy theories like Pizzagate, which absurdly claimed that emails published by WikiLeaks in November 2016 contained coded messages of high-ranking Democratic Party officials engaging in a human trafficking and child sex ring in a Washington, D.C., pizza restaurant.[29]

I was, therefore, curious to see how this group polarization phenomenon might affect people's reactions to different kinds of trust-repair efforts. This led me to design an experiment with my collaborators to investigate whether and how such reactions might differ when those repair efforts were being judged by individuals versus groups.[30] This research drew on the job interview paradigm I mentioned in the earlier chapters, where the job candidate is accused of committing a competence- or integrity-based transgression and responds with an apology or a denial. However, when we asked participants to evaluate the candidate afterward, we had them do that both individually and as part of a group. They either first evaluated the candidate individually and then again as a group of three to six participants (who were asked to discuss their opinions with one another to reach a collective judgment), or they first evaluated the candidate as a group and then again individually. The instructions also made clear that they could revise their initial opinions when evaluating the candidate for the second time if they wished.

This study found that, on the whole, people were generally harsher in their assessments of the job candidate's trustworthiness when they evaluated the candidate as a group than as individuals, because people are generally disinclined to trust those who have been accused of a violation, and (consistent with past findings) that sentiment was generally strengthened when they discussed those sentiments as a group. However, closer scrutiny of the results revealed that this only occurred in specific cases. It turns out that groups were not any harsher than individuals in their judgments when the violator addressed the transgression in ways group members considered adequate. It was only when the candidate responded in ways that were considered inadequate, specifically by apologizing when the violation concerned matters of integrity or by denying culpability when the violation concerned matters of competence (as we have previously considered) that groups became relatively harsh. This effect arose because the group context allowed participants to convince one another, when the trust-repair response was considered poor, that a harsher judgment was deserved. Thus, the sequencing of these evaluations mattered, such that participants' initial individual evaluations could become harsher when they subsequently evaluated the candidate as a group, but the harshness of initial group evaluations was not tempered even when participants subsequently evaluated the candidate as individuals.

The sense of inadequacy can hinge on more than the verbal response one might provide. It can also stem from a broader array of sentiments in society about what is appropriate or not. As the reporters Evan McMorris-Santoro and Yon Pomrenze detailed for CNN, this is a problem Kelsey and Chris Waits confronted in Hastings, Minnesota, when their youngest child, who had been assigned male at birth, began to identify as a girl.[31] Kelsey had been active in local Republican politics as a young woman, she had served on the Hastings school board since 2017, and she had been elected school board chair in January 2020, just two years into her first term.

Then COVID hit, and residents quickly divided into camps that were either in favor of or against children wearing masks in schools. The anti-mask residents formed a closed Facebook group called Conservative Parents of Hastings, subsequently renamed Concerned Parents of Hastings a few weeks later, which sought to undermine Kelsey as board chair. Kelsey said she was fine with that. "That's politics," she said. "People can say they're frustrated with me, I understand that. Completely fine."

Yet we know by now that the group wouldn't just stop there. It would polarize as its members fed on and became increasingly emboldened by their shared opinions. After one parent posted a long complaint about a host of things involving Kelsey, another parent took the next step by writing, "She should be locked up for child abuse . . . Her younger 'daughter' is actually a boy." Then other parents joined in by attacking both Waitses as "woke parents" who had pushed their views onto their child.

When Kelsey learned this was being written, she dropped to the floor and cried. "This was my most precious secret," she said. "The thing I protected most and the thing I was most afraid of ever being used in a political way because for me, this isn't political. This is my family, this is my child." She tried to appeal to decency in a letter to the editor of the local paper,[32] in which she wrote, "Local politicians are a part of the community . . . If we want to see political division end, it begins with us. It begins by treating each other as humans. It begins in recognizing that there are boundaries that should not be crossed." But some of the "Concerned Parents" reacted to this letter with glee for the free press it gave to that group's efforts. The hate just continued to magnify.

Thus, for Kelsey Waits, "every interaction we have with new people is me trying to figure out if my child is safe." She worries about how having a child outed before they're ready can increase their risk of suicide. She said, "This is not about my parenting practices. This is about the lives of kids." Moreover, even though Kelsey eventually lost her bid for reelection, this did not end the abuse in this community. Her husband, Chris, says he was told by another parent the day after the election that a middle schooler was approached by another student and told, "My mom says that we won so now we can deal with sickos like you." The Waitses have, thus, chosen to move from their neighborhood to find more privacy, and hopefully safety, in a new address that has not been publicized.

Yet despite the harm they have caused, these "Concerned Parents" probably consider their actions entirely justified. They probably believe they are on the side of right fighting against "indecency" and "perversion." They probably see themselves as upstanding citizens who care about their community, their families, and doing the right thing. Most probably hold steady jobs, pay their bills on time, and even identify with a religious faith. Even so, these same people found it reasonable to expose the most private aspect of an eight-year-old child's identity, to put a spotlight on the most vulnerable among us with a rallying cry of hate, and then celebrate those deeds as hallmarks of their decency. It is the modern version of binding the limbs of a woman and letting her drown to prove she wasn't a witch.[33]

All it takes is a scenario that raises one's ire and the ability to share that opinion with like-minded others for a group to turn into a mob. To turn into a self-righteous collective monster that magnifies the ugliest parts of ourselves. To believe that the opinions and welfare of other human beings who happen to be outsiders are simply less important than our own. This can also occur regardless of where one stands on the political spectrum—it happens on both the Left and Right.* No matter the form the intolerance might take, these amplifying effects of polarization are like pouring gasoline on a fire.

But in this group-polarization effect, we can also find the seed to a solution. The key is to break out of these interpretive bubbles and engage in real dialogues with those whose opinions are different. This, of course, is easier said than done, with so much of our world already polarized to black-and-white extremes and people refusing to think beyond the scope of their own ideological dogmas. Nevertheless, there is reason to believe that this kind

---

* The case from chapter 7 of students from the University of Southern California getting an award-winning professor removed from a course for using a word in Mandarin that, to them, sounded too much like the N-word is just one of many examples of how this can happen with Left-leaning sensibilities as well.

of dialogue with those who hold different views can make a difference, at least for those who are willing to engage and listen.

One study I conducted with organizational psychologists Deborah Gruenfeld and Melissa Thomas-Hunt, for example, examined how exposure to different perspectives in one's group can affect how we think about controversial topics like school busing.[34] To do that, we polled participants on their initial views about this topic and then created groups based on these opinions that were either unanimous (in favor of or against busing) or comprised of members who were in favor of and opposed to this issue. We then asked participants to discuss this topic in their groups, report the group's final decision, and then write a post-decision rationale for their own stance on this busing issue that they expected either to remain private or be made public.

This study revealed, consistent with past findings, that unanimous groups (as well as members of minority factions within nonunanimous groups) tended to think about this issue in more simplistic, unidimensional terms as we might expect from groups that are polarized. However, members of majority factions who were exposed to dissenting minority opinions exhibited much more sophisticated ways of thinking about the problem that recognized others' views and even found ways to integrate those competing opinions into a cohesive whole. Those nonunanimous majorities exhibited what psychologists call greater *integrative complexity*, regardless of which side was pro- or anti-busing. What's more, that greater complexity in those majority factions was not just for show; this effect was found when members believed their post-discussion rationales would be kept private as well. This suggests that having the opportunity to engage with people who hold different views can fundamentally change one's thinking for the better.

These findings suggest that the problem is not with groups themselves but rather with how they tend to be managed. Rather than construct them to reflect and account for the diversity of opinions people might hold, we strain out that richness to find those who share our own views. We short-circuit everything that has the potential to make groups great, such as the wealth of information and perspectives a broader diversity of members might hold, to simplify our deliberations, validate ourselves, and find shared purpose.[35] These are natural tendencies, and they can certainly bolster trust inside our groups. But the high price we pay for that privilege is greater mistrust and more difficulty repairing trust with everyone else.

9

PLAYING THE WRONG
RULES OF THE GAME

At the edge of Tokyo's Hibiya Park, a lush and tranquil place with gurgling fountains and formal gardens, you will find a small, four-story brick library frequented by middle-aged men. They are normally elusive and hard to find, rising early every day to don white shirts and knot their ties before disappearing from their neighborhoods between the morning and evening rush hours. One of them, wearing a blue suit and shiny black shoes, visits the library on Tuesdays. It is not clear where he goes the rest of the week. He can visit other places but can't go too far. He has the money to travel, he says, "but if I start going away a lot, the neighbors will grow suspicious." So he has settled into a fixed routine, much like a prisoner. That may be fitting since he is guilty of an offense from which he will likely never recover.[1]

His offense, like those of the other middle-aged men, was to become a casualty of modern work life. They have either lost their jobs or had their businesses go bankrupt. And in a society that treats such events as an unspeakable failure, nearly all of them have given up hope of redemption. They are middle-aged in a country that primarily hires younger workers and, at least historically, hires them for life. Some, like this man in the blue suit, find it difficult even to seek work at the government unemployment agency, because if an acquaintance saw him there, it would be too difficult to explain. For many, the most honorable solution is suicide,[2] while others are destined to spend the rest of their lives in a prison—one made not of concrete and steel, or even limited to the confines of this library, but of the need to maintain the illusion of being employed to retain some shred of dignity. A prison built from shame.

Most people living in the U.S. would probably find it hard to relate to this predicament. We face job loss and bankruptcy as well, in fact at much higher rates than in Japan. Yet we are also likelier to rebound from such incidents and even put a spotlight on them in our public narratives of eventual success. Steve Jobs was forced out as Apple's founder in 1985 before returning as its CEO in 1997 and leading the company to greatness. Oprah Winfrey was fired early on in her career as an evening news reporter for being "unfit for television news" before starting her famous talk show and building her media conglomerate. Walt Disney was once fired from a studio for not being creative enough before introducing some of the most beloved cartoon characters, stories, and theme parks in the world.[3] Moreover, he and some of the most famous industry tycoons, including Henry Ford and Milton Hershey, are known to have bankrupted their businesses on the way to prosperity,[4] with Hershey doing so twice before starting his chocolate empire.[5]

As these examples reveal, even if we were to view job loss and bankruptcy as personal failures, as so many do in Japan, we are nevertheless far less inclined to treat them as permanent stigmatizing marks. This opportunity for individuals and their businesses to start fresh in the U.S. has been considered an asset to our capitalist system. The ability to find new work after being let go allows us to maintain productive roles in the economy, and a forgiving bankruptcy system encourages the risk-taking necessary for entrepreneurial activity and economic growth. Both serve the larger goal of keeping economic actors alive, active, and productive. This is also something other countries around the world (including Japan) have tried to emulate to spur their own market economies.[6]

Yet as the middle-aged man at the start of this chapter illustrates, efforts to adopt formal systems and laws from the U.S. may do little good if cultural attitudes about job loss and bankruptcy do not support them. Government unemployment agencies and U.S.-style bankruptcy laws won't help if people are unwilling to avail themselves of those options, or if being found to have done so marks those who do with an unforgivable blight.[7] Thus, we should be sobered by the fact that as hard as it can be to address our failures to fulfill promises and expectations in the U.S., it is far worse in Japan, at least for these kinds of work-related incidents. And there is reason to believe that culture can affect how people address matters of guilt and redemption for a broader range of "offenses" as well.

One reason why the experience of job loss or bankruptcy can be harder to overcome in Japan can be found in the fact that Japan represents a collectivist culture. A large body of evidence has revealed that members of collectivist cultures like Japan's tend to see themselves as connected to others and focus on the needs and goals of the group over the needs and desires of individuals. This contrasts with individualist cultures like that of the United States, whose members tend to see themselves as more separate from others, define themselves based on personal traits, and stress the rights and goals of individuals.

Yet in contrast to what cultural psychologists initially assumed, perhaps due to most of them coming from North America and Europe, greater collectivism does not necessarily engender high trust.[8] Collectivists may see one another as more of a family, with more of a shared identity than those in the U.S., and this can encourage them to be more cooperative. But that orientation also leads its members to emphasize the duties and responsibilities they have to one another, become more vigilant to ensure those norms aren't broken, and sanction those who do break those norms more severely.[9] In that vein, those in Japan who lose their jobs or bankrupt their businesses are being punished not for their lack of individual success but rather because they let those around them down—by failing to remain economically productive members of society, by not paying back what their businesses owed, and by failing to provide for and ultimately bringing shame on their families.

Indeed, evidence suggests that a transgression in collectivist cultures can cast a stain not just on the offender but also on that person's entire group. For example, research by Tanya Menon and her colleagues comparing how newspapers in the U.S. and Japan discussed the same high-profile corporate scandals has found that whereas U.S. news stories focused on how the individual offenders managed to commit the offense, the same coverage in Japan focused instead on how the broader organization allowed this kind of incident to happen.[10] This finding suggests that whereas Americans were likelier to blame the individual offender, the Japanese were likelier to blame the entire collective. This is because those in the U.S. are more inclined to believe that individuals control their own actions, whereas the Japanese tend to be more attuned to how factors outside their control (including norms and pressures to address their group's needs and goals) can affect their behavior.

Curiously, these cultural differences can also lead the Japanese to apologize for transgressions they did not even commit. I recall chatting with a young woman from Japan in 2011 about the Fukushima nuclear disaster that occurred there earlier that year. She had not worked at that plant, had not done anything related to the nuclear industry, and didn't even live near Fukushima. So I was surprised when at the end of that conversation, she concluded by apologizing for what happened.

Now, it's possible that I just have a secret gift for making people feel bad about themselves. However, it seems likelier that she was apologizing for a different reason. In particular, my sense is that she apologized not for her personal actions but rather on behalf of her collective and her sense that there was some responsibility they all shared for what happened.

This may strike many of us as both strange and unnecessary. Why wouldn't it make more sense to focus blame on those who are actually responsible? Wouldn't that do more to address and prevent these kinds of incidents? The problem with these seemingly reasonable questions, however, is that they rest on a premise that is fundamentally flawed—the notion that a person's actions depend primarily on the individual rather than the social and environmental forces the individual faces.

We have already touched on this phenomenon earlier, when we considered how people assume that leaders have more control over what happens than they really do. Although this tendency is particularly pronounced with leaders, Westerners tend to make this assumption about others as well. It turns out that people in the West, such as in the United States, tend to oversubscribe to the notion that individuals determine their actions. In fact, this is such a well-known tendency that social psychologists have spent well over half a century demonstrating all the ways in which this belief can be wrong. Members of many East Asian cultures, however, have been found to be less susceptible to this error, because they tend to be more conscious of the situational influences that can drive what people do.[11]

Thus, when Japanese newspapers ask how the organization could have allowed one of its employees to commit a transgression rather than focus on how that individual personally managed to commit it, the data is on their side. For example, if we read about the Wells Fargo Bank account fraud scandal that was first widely reported in late 2016, in which employees created millions of fraudulent savings and checking accounts on behalf of its clients without their consent, we can now find reports of how the company itself promoted such actions. The reporter Emily Flitter of *The New York Times,* for example, described how the scandal was caused by "a pressure-cooker environment at the bank, where low-level employees were squeezed tighter and tighter each year by sales goals that senior executives methodically raised, while ignoring signs that they were unrealistic."[12]

Yet it is also the case that when this scandal was first reported, blame was placed squarely on those low-level branch workers rather than the unreasonable demands they faced. The American public erred, as we typically do, by placing blame on those who committed the actions rather than on all the pressures, incentives, and failures by those who should have known better but still promoted these actions, even if they did not engage in the activities themselves. Thus, thinking more broadly about what might have caused a violation, as the Japanese tend to do, can be a good thing if we really want to understand how such incidents arose and might have been prevented.

These kinds of differences have also been found to affect attitudes toward trust within these cultures. We have already considered in chapter 1 the difference between whether people a) choose to make themselves vulnerable despite the risk it would entail, or b) exhibit that same behavior because its associated risk and vulnerability have been removed. Whereas the former can be considered a display of trust, the latter allows people simply to act as if they trust one another even when they do not trust one another at all. In this regard, evidence from a cross-national survey (including 1,136 Japanese and 501 U.S. respondents) by cross-cultural trust researchers Toshio Yamagishi and Midori Yamagishi suggests that the Japanese are likelier to gravitate toward the latter approach (i.e., by reducing their risk and vulnerability) than those in the U.S.[13] For this reason, they ultimately found the Japanese to be less inclined to trust and less inclined to leave their social networks (which would deter potential violations) than their U.S. counterparts.

These cultural differences may, furthermore, help explain why apologies can be both more common and less meaningful in Japan than in the U.S.[14] Because collectivists tend to see themselves in terms of their relationships with other group members, their greater vigilance against norm violations can lead them to apologize more frequently in their daily interactions. This contrition can be beneficial by serving as a "social lubricant" that highlights their sensitivity to potential offenses that might disrupt group harmony. However, because collectivists are also more conscious of how social and environmental influences can drive one's actions, they are also less inclined to treat apologies as explicit acknowledgments of personal culpability than as general expressions of remorse.

Some of my own cross-cultural research with organizational psychologists William Maddux, Tetsu Okumura, and Jeanne Brett provides evidence to support this reasoning.[15] This research began with a survey of participants in Japan and the U.S., which provided empirical support for the notion that the Japanese apologize more often and are likelier to do so for actions in which they were not personally involved, whereas Americans apologize less often and are likelier to equate apologizing with personal blame. We then conducted an experiment to investigate how such differences might affect people's trust in those who offer an apology after an offense that involved matters of competence or integrity, using the job candidate interview paradigm from some of my earlier studies.

The results revealed that, because the Japanese are less likely to interpret apologies as a confirmation of guilt, apologizing for integrity-based violations (in this case, filing an incorrect tax return to please an important client) repaired trust more effectively in Japan than in the U.S. However, since the Japanese also believe that individuals have less control over their own actions than do Americans, apologizing for competence-based violations (in this case, filing an incorrect tax return due to inadequate knowledge of the relevant tax codes) was less effective in Japan than the U.S., presumably because the Japanese had less faith that the apologizer could personally correct that problem. These findings, thus, underscore how our cultural perspective can make a major difference not only in how we interpret the causes and consequences of a transgression but also in how we respond to the subsequent trust-repair effort.

Moreover, though I started this chapter by describing how cultural perspectives can differ between nations, it is important to recognize that cultures can differ within different subgroups in the same country as well. Different geographical regions, different companies and organizations, and even different political groups in that country can vary in the extent to which they emphasize individualistic versus collective values, as well as a host of other values, beliefs, and norms. Such differences also don't just influence how frequently we apologize or where we place blame; they can ultimately affect what people even consider to be integrity-based transgression.

The matter of integrity concerns whether you believe others adhere to principles you find acceptable. Yet what is acceptable to one group may not be acceptable to another. Psychologists Jesse Graham, Jonathan Haidt, and their colleagues, for example, have observed that these judgments are based on five underlying moral intuitions.[16] These are:

1. **Care,** which concerns the ability to feel and dislike the pain of others and encompasses the virtues of kindness, gentleness, and nurturance.
2. **Fairness,** which concerns the value we place on cooperation, as captured by the concept of doing unto others as we would have done to us and encompasses the virtues of justice and trustworthiness.
3. **Loyalty,** which relates to our history as tribal creatures and encompasses the virtues of patriotism and self-sacrifice.
4. **Authority,** which is based on our primate history of hierarchical social interactions and encompasses the virtues of obedience and deference.
5. **Sanctity,** which concerns matters of disgust and contamination, as captured by the idea that we should live in elevated, less carnal, and nobler ways, and encompasses the virtues of chastity, piety, and cleanliness.

This research has also found that different cultural groups (both between and within countries) can prioritize these five moral intuitions quite differently. For example, people in Eastern cultures have been found to be likelier to value the principles of loyalty and sanctity than people in Western cultures. Likewise, women have been found to be more concerned about care, fairness, and sanctity than men. Moreover, comparisons of liberals and conservatives in the U.S. revealed that whereas liberals tend to prioritize the principles of care and fairness, conservatives (especially religious conservatives) tend to prioritize the principles of loyalty, authority, and sanctity.[17]

These differences are important because they can dramatically alter how people's actions are viewed. For example, I wouldn't consider myself politically liberal or conservative, preferring instead a more cautious approach to public policy based on what we can glean from the data, which probably puts me closer to the center. However, as someone who immigrated to the U.S. as a child, it is particularly hard for me not to react to the Trump administration's child separation policy at the U.S.-Mexico border with outrage and horror. When I think of the trauma this policy has caused for those families and the serious (and likely permanent) harm it has inflicted on their children, my immediate reaction is to consider it a deliberate breach of basic human decency and to see those who champion that policy as immoral.

But if I were to put on my social scientist hat, I would also have to recognize that this reaction is based on the premise that the principle of not doing harm (and caring for those in need) is of paramount importance and that others may not necessarily share that view. Those more inclined to support that family separation policy could argue, for example, that although the harm it has inflicted is regrettable, this must be balanced against the goals of protecting the interests of U.S. citizens (loyalty), getting other countries to help solve these problems (fairness), making sure the U.S. isn't overrun by "criminals" and other "undesirable" elements (sanctity), and respecting the will of the administration, because "elections have consequences" (authority). And though I could respond to such claims by explaining that those goals could have been achieved in other ways, through methods that would not have required such serious harm to this policy's victims, it is not clear that such arguments would work. That would require venturing into the realm of policy wonks who analyze and debate these issues for a living, and probably losing the attention of everyone else.

More broadly, these considerations point to how the principles we hold can become a double-edged sword. Principles consist of rules or standards that enable us to distinguish right from wrong. Thus, we generally view principles in a positive light, as the means through which we can make judgments of integrity, trustworthiness, and the appropriateness of different actions. But as people's highly polarized reactions to the child separation policy at the U.S.-Mexico border illustrate, our principles can also lead us to talk past and point fingers at one another, with each side firmly believing it is right. That possibility is perhaps most famously captured by the sentiment "The first thing a principle does is to kill somebody," in Dorothy Sayers's novel *Gaudy Night*.[18] And it raises the need to understand the ways in which these different implications of principles might arise if we wish to address these kinds of social and political divides and the mistrust they so often engender.

Consider Pat Buchanan's 1992 speech at the Republican National Convention,[19] in which he declared that the United States was engaged in a "cultural war" that was "as critical to the kind of nation we shall be as the Cold War itself." Adding fire to a thesis first laid out by James Davison Hunter in his book *Culture Wars*,[20] Buchanan contrasted two moral visions of America. On one side, there were those who championed the virtues of American exceptionalism, traditional families and institutions, and Judeo-Christian sexual propriety. And on the other side were those Buchanan dismissively characterized as determined to undermine those institutions and values through the support of "unrestricted abortion on demand"; gay rights; the right to discriminate against religious schools, sue one's parents, and put women in combat; and attempts to "put birds and rats and insects ahead of families, workers, and jobs."

This cultural divide between conservative and liberal moral sensibilities (between those who adhere to what Hunter called "orthodox" or "progressive" worldviews) has only become deeper and more entrenched in American politics in the decades since Buchanan's speech. That demarcation has clarified for each side how the other does not adhere to principles it considers acceptable and, thus, lacks integrity. This has stoked mistrust and escalated conflicts, as each side has advocated policies it considered eminently reasonable but the other considered misguided and inappropriate. Moreover, efforts to resolve these disputes through reason and debate have increasingly fallen on deaf ears, as each side makes ever more impassioned arguments to support its point of view that the other side seems unable or unwilling to understand.

This is because, in the face of competing principles, we are no longer choosing between right and wrong but rather between right and right, between alternative moral standards that may each have some merit. And though we might hope to reconcile these differences by persuading others of the superiority of our own stance, that approach seems to misunderstand the process through which our principled views tend to be formed. We generally believe that the moral principles we hold are based on rationality and logic. But as we have already considered in chapter 6 with respect to people's views about retributive justice, evidence suggests that our moral principles are likewise not as grounded on deliberate forms of reasoning as we would like to think.

Psychologist Jonathan Haidt illustrated this point by asking readers to consider the following scenario.[21]

> Julie and Mark are brother and sister. They are traveling together in France on summer vacation from college. One night they are staying alone in a cabin near the beach. They decide that it would be interesting and fun if they tried making love. At the very least it would be a new experience for each of them. Julie was already taking birth control pills, but Mark uses a condom too, just to be safe. They both enjoy making love, but they decide not to do it again. They keep that night as a special secret, which makes them feel even closer to each other. What do you think about that? Was it OK for them to make love?

Haidt reports that most people who are asked to read and express their opinions about this scenario state immediately that it was wrong for the siblings to have sex, but then struggle to search for reasons. They might point out the dangers of inbreeding, for example, until they remember the siblings used two forms of birth control. They might argue that the siblings will be hurt, even though the story makes clear the experience only strengthened their relationship. Or they might speculate that others will be hurt if they learn of this incident, despite the siblings deciding to keep it a secret. Eventually, many reach a point where they say something like, "I don't know, I can't explain it, I just know it's wrong."

These findings suggest that deliberate moral reasoning does not provide the basis for moral judgment (i.e., for the principles we choose to uphold). Instead, that reasoning tends to be something that happens *after* moral judgment, based on our intuitions, has been reached. People in Haidt's study made their moral judgments immediately—and you may have too— but then they struggled to find a viable reason for their intuitions afterward. This means that efforts to use rational arguments to challenge the moral principles they might hold are unlikely to work, because they would only target the consequences of those moral judgments rather than their cause.

The bottom line is that it generally doesn't help to argue that others' moral sensibilities are wrong. Those sensibilities tend to be based on largely automatic and visceral reactions that have been imprinted by our evolutionary history and shaped by the specifics of our cultural upbringing. This can lead different cultural groups to uphold very different sets of values, to find their own set of principles eminently reasonable, and to diminish the moral sensibilities others might hold. This can also create major problems when people deal with controversial issues in real life, since it can lead some to believe that a serious offense has been intentionally committed (based on their own moral intuitions), while those committing such acts believe they are being unfairly maligned for behavior they think is completely justified. That can make it particularly difficult to repair trust, since it can mean those involved may not even agree on whether a transgression has been committed.

This problem is also compounded by the group polarization effects we considered in chapter 8. As individuals reinforce their views with other members of their group, the principles they hold can become more extreme and represent increasingly important markers of their identity. Thus, they become ever more intransigent, by treating their values as absolute, and by responding to the prospect of those principles being infringed with moral outrage. They can start to see those values as not just important but sacred and become unwilling to resolve their differences, even in practical terms, through negotiation or compromise.

Yet in this problem, there is also the seed to a solution. What so often drives these rifts is the assumption that because our values are right, the other side's values must be wrong. We assume that since those who share our principles have high integrity, the integrity of those who do not share those principles must be low. But as we have noted, the challenge we often face when confronting competing principles stems from the need to choose not between right and wrong but between right and right, between alternative moral standards that may each have some merit.

We can see this in the five moral foundations we considered earlier, the principles of care, fairness, loyalty, authority, and sanctity. Even if some of us consider one or more of those principles more important than others, few are likely to claim that any of those intuitions are irrelevant. We have simply prioritized those principles differently based on our personal and cultural experiences. This suggests that there may be opportunities to reconcile these differences by illustrating how the choice among these principles is often less clear-cut—by having us confront situations where upholding even sacred values can require unacceptable compromises to other values we also hold.

Psychologist Philip Tetlock reports that this approach can alter people's stance on issues they might have otherwise considered sacred, such as the prospect of buying and selling body organs for medical transplants.[22] He found that although most people, including both liberal Democrats and conservative Republicans, are initially appalled by the idea, 40 percent tempered their opposition when they were convinced that this was the only way to save lives that would have otherwise been lost. Thus, even if they might have initially rejected organ sales based on the concern that this would impede access to organs for the poor or force them to sell their organs in deals of desperation (based on the principle of fairness), a sizable proportion would become less ardently opposed to this practice when it required a trade-off against another value they also considered important, such as the principle of care, through the saving of lives that would have otherwise been lost.

We can also find examples of how people can moderate their views even with the kinds of issues Pat Buchanan identified as central to the U.S. "culture war" in his 1992 Republican National Convention speech. Consider the traditional conservative stance against gay marriage. When former president George W. Bush called for a constitutional amendment to ban same-sex marriage in August 2004, his vice president, Dick Cheney, took the unusual step of distancing himself from that effort.[23] Cheney explained his support for gay relationships at a campaign rally in Mississippi by noting that his wife "Lynn and I have a gay daughter, so it's an issue our family is very familiar with." Then in 2013, when his other daughter, Liz Cheney, expressed opposition to gay marriage while campaigning as a Republican for the U.S. Senate, causing a public spat with her lesbian sister, Mary, their father released a statement stating, "Liz has always believed in the traditional definition of marriage" and she "has also always treated her sister and her sister's family with love and respect, exactly as she should have done."[24] Finally, in a 2021 interview for *60 Minutes,* Liz Cheney herself expressed regret for her earlier opposition to same-sex marriage.[25] She said, "I was wrong. I was wrong. I love my sister very much. I love her family very much . . . And my sister and I have had that conversation."

What we can see in this example is how the Cheneys were forced to confront a trade-off between the conservative stance in support of traditional family values and the love and compassion for a member of their own family. It was enough to prompt the second-most-powerful Republican in the country to take the extraordinary step of standing against the orthodoxy of both his political party and the president he served. In time, that trade-off was also enough to convince his ideologically conservative daughter to change her own stance on gay marriage, despite holding a seat as a Republican in the U.S. House of Representatives.

Of course, these illustrations should not be taken to mean that this kind of change in one's moral sensibilities is either common or easy. This is because, in the absence of pressure to confront these trade-offs, people are generally inclined to look away. Hence, they can become easily distracted by rhetorical smoke screens that can allow them to maintain more dogmatic positions. It is thus notable that the Cheney support for gay marriage occurred in the face of a member of their nuclear family who happened to be gay, as this made it difficult to ignore the negative consequences of upholding their political party's traditional antigay marriage stance. It is also notable that, even with a gay family member, it still took Liz Cheney eight years to change her public position on that issue.

A similar set of conditions may also be needed to resolve the conflicts that can arise when competing principles are being espoused by different groups. International relations scholar I. William Zartman observed that people resolve their conflicts only when they are ready to do so, "when alternative, usually unilateral means of achieving a satisfactory result are blocked" and when that deadlock puts them in an uncomfortable and costly predicament.[26] This can create what he called a "ripe moment," where each side to the conflict becomes more receptive to proposals that may have already been in the air but only now appear to offer an attractive way out of that painful stalemate. That doesn't mean the pain each side experiences needs to be equal or that the settlement reached will be perfectly balanced. However, it can make clear how the escalation of conflict will only make things worse, underscore the need to accommodate the other side's view, and motivate the search for a better solution.

Moreover, to the extent that the competing principles are based on the same basic set of moral intuitions we have reviewed, the unacceptable costs people face in this deadlock are likely to involve principles they also hold, even if to a lesser degree. This common ground can lead each side to broaden its conception of integrity by underscoring how a concern with competing moral principles does not necessarily mean that one's integrity is low. It can simply mean that people have prioritized the same set of moral intuitions differently. And if we all share those same ends, this can allow us to shift our focus to the question of means—to how we might pursue each of those principles in ways that would avoid unacceptable compromises to the others.

Zartman also notes, however, that this kind of shift is likely to depend on the balance of power. When either side believes it can impose its moral sensibilities on the other through rational persuasion or force, that is likely to be their preferred choice. It is only when both sides believe they are in a painful deadlock they cannot resolve through escalation that they will reconsider a more accommodative approach. This suggests that there are likely to be long periods of conflict as each side becomes increasingly frustrated in its efforts to use rhetorical claims to convince others that its own judgments of what constitutes integrity are correct and then attempt to impose its views through coercion. Moreover, even when a moment that's ripe for more meaningful reconciliation is reached, it can often be fragile, as each side remains tempted to return to its preferred draconian stance. Those kinds of challenges will become all too evident in the next chapter as we compare efforts to address some of the most devastating gross human rights abuses that have occurred around the world.

—(10)—

BEYOND THE RAVAGES OF HISTORY

Her family's home was burned down in the first weeks of the genocide. So they fled, like thousands of other Tutsis, to seek refuge at
Gatwaro Stadium, where they had been promised the police would
protect them. The reality at that stadium, however, could not have been
more different. "We heard gunshots from far away and saw the Interahamwe
[an extremist Hutu militia] brandishing machetes outside the stadium and
shouting, 'Tomorrow it will be your turn,'" said Mukakamanzi. "We quickly
realized then that death was waiting for us."[1]

On the afternoon of April 18, 1994, the Interahamwe began killing
people in the stadium with guns, machetes, knives, and grenades. Mukakamanzi's elder brother was soon dead, and her father and younger sister
were seriously wounded by grenade shrapnel. Her other brother and two
nephews had disappeared and, she thought, were most likely dead as well.
So Mukakamanzi cried and pleaded with her mother. "They are going to
die . . . we are lucky to be alive, we must leave." But her deeply devout
mother said she had sworn before God "never to leave Daddy, either in
good times or bad."

She relates slowly, with great emotion, how she left her mother kneeling in prayer beside her wounded father and younger sister. "I told her:
'Goodbye, Mama. We'll meet in heaven.'" The Interahamwe stormed the
stadium again that night to finish their work. By the next morning, ten
thousand people who had sought refuge at the stadium were dead. These
are just a few of the eight hundred thousand people who were slaughtered
during a heinous killing spree that occurred during the one hundred days
of the Rwandan genocide.[2] Mukakamanzi was the only one from her family
to survive.

For many of those who experienced such atrocities, reminders of what happened will forever mark their own bodies, in the scars of their assailants' knives, explosives, or bullets. Others will have been severely disfigured by burns or hacked limbs. And even more will likely suffer from some form of psychological trauma and continue to relive the terrors of these events in their nightmares. They have watched their neighbors turn into monsters seeking to harm anyone like them. They have witnessed people they knew and loved brutally attacked and killed. They have also observed how their institutions (including the police, military, and government) failed to protect them and seen how some of the members even facilitated and participated in the crimes.

It is no wonder then that when the massacres finally end, those aware of what happened are left wondering how that society could ever recover. How can its people even come close to addressing such rampant injustice? How can they possibly repair the trust that has been broken—the trust that might allow them to return to living side by side and reforge some semblance of a community again? These are the kinds of questions the world has been forced to confront over and over in the wake of the most horrific crimes against humanity in modern history. In this chapter, we will consider three types of attempts to address these challenges—by comparing the efforts that were made to address gross human rights abuses after Nazi Germany, South Africa's apartheid, and the Rwandan genocide—with the goal of learning what we can from those experiences.

It wasn't until the world's collective revulsion at the horrors of World War II and the atrocities committed in the Holocaust that we began to make serious efforts to apply international standards to address crimes against humanity. Whether through the 1945 Nuremberg Charter, which set the rules and procedures for the Allies to put Nazi leaders on trial between November 20, 1945, and August 31, 1946;[3] the 1993 Statute of the International Criminal Tribunal for the former Yugoslavia; the 1994 Statute of the International Tribunal for Rwanda; and the 1998 Rome Statute of the International Criminal Court, those efforts have sought to define, investigate, and (when warranted) try individuals for those crimes. The template for such efforts has, thus, been courtroom justice. Despite the enormous range of offenses those courtrooms considered, the basic questions to be decided weren't much different from most other crimes, such as theft or fraud. At the core, the process involved using the evidence to determine who committed what crimes and how they should be punished.

But the limitations of this focus on courtroom justice soon became evident. On a practical level, the sheer numbers of offenses associated with these kinds of incidents made it impossible for international courts to investigate and prosecute all those crimes. Thus, they typically focused on only the highest-profile cases. The Nuremberg trials, for example, indicted only twenty-four high-ranking military, political, and industrial leaders. Moreover, even though additional trials of more than fifteen hundred Nazi war criminals were eventually conducted in Europe,[4] and hundreds of those perpetrators were convicted, these tribunals did not force average Germans to confront their own complicity in their country's war crimes or the Holocaust.[5]

A second problem with the pursuit of courtroom justice stems from concerns about the legitimacy of the courts themselves. In the face of mass atrocities, a society's preexisting judicial system is generally poorly suited to prosecuting those crimes because, in many cases, the law and law enforcers may have been major sources of the atrocities that took place, such as in Germany during the Holocaust and in South Africa during apartheid.[6] Moreover, when other court systems are used to fill this judicial role, such as the Nuremberg trials after the Second World War, those trials have often been criticized as a form of "victor's justice," in which the punishments for defeated parties are excessive and unjustified and the victors are given light punishment or clemency for their offenses.

Although the Allies went to great lengths to avoid this criticism of the Nuremberg trials, such as by providing defendants with their choice of counsel and ultimately acquitting three of the twenty-four who were prosecuted,[7] some Germans still accused the Allies of conducting an unfair trial with a predetermined outcome. The charges of victor's justice, furthermore, were not entirely unfounded. The Allies had also committed significant crimes during the war, and the failure to prosecute them with equal vigor introduced notable distortions into the proceedings. This included attempts by Soviet prosecutors to accuse Nazis of the Katyn Forest massacre, in which Soviet soldiers executed nearly twenty-two thousand Polish officers and intelligentsia in 1940 by shooting them in the back of the head.[8] Thus, even though the Nuremberg trials represented an important advance in the effort to pursue accountability (especially when compared to the initial calls by British prime minister Winston Churchill for the summary execution of top Nazi war criminals, as well as Soviet leader Joseph Stalin's proposal for even larger-scale executions), those kinds of distortions still diminished the legitimacy of those efforts.

Finally, as we have already considered in chapter 6, the focus by courtroom justice on accountability and punishment largely ignores the challenge of reconciliation, the need for society to move beyond its ugly past, reintegrate offenders, and find some way for those offenders and their victims to live among one another again. The German historian Norbert Frei, for example, described how in the wake of the Second World War, the Allies not only tried the top Nazi political and military leaders for war crimes but also conducted denazification tribunals through which former Nazis and Nazi sympathizers could be dismissed from their posts, fined, or imprisoned.[9] However, that program faced resistance almost from the beginning. When Chancellor Konrad Adenauer founded West Germany's new federal republic government in 1949, it quickly adopted amnesty laws that absolved many of those guilty of even serious Nazi-era crimes, and it passed a restitution law that mandated reintegrating hundreds of thousands of former Nazi sympathizers the Allies had dismissed (including members of the Gestapo and Waffen-SS) into their former positions.

Frei observes this occurred because excluding hundreds of thousands of former Nazis and Nazi sympathizers would have deprived the new state of needed skills and created potentially dangerous levels of discontent. It soon became apparent, for example, that there would not be enough qualified doctors, lawyers, judges, teachers, or civil servants if former Nazi Party members were excluded from those professions. Such exclusions also prompted public resistance to Adenauer's efforts to integrate West Germany into the Western alliance. Offering the convicted a chance to wipe out the past and start anew provided a way to gain their allegiance to the new government, as well as their support for its international treaties. Frei adds that most West Germans were also strongly in favor of forgetting everything having to do with Nazism, with both politicians and church leaders going out of their way to intercede for those who had been convicted of committing war crimes, and the government paying for their legal defense. Thus, by 1958, all but a handful of the original Nuremberg defendants who had been convicted of war crimes had been pardoned and freed.

These limitations with courtroom justice have prompted a shift by the international community in favor of a more restorative approach, one that would focus on bringing offenders and victims together to acknowledge and repair the damage. In 1990, Chile was the first to launch a national inquest that would call itself a commission for "truth and reconciliation." The country's newly elected president, Patricio Aylwin, was limited in what he could do to address the country's human rights abuses, because his predecessor, Augusto Pinochet, retained his post as supreme commander of the Chilean army after stepping down as president and threatened reprisals if any attempt was made to put his soldiers on trial.[10] Thus, Aylwin sought a more practicable course through which the Chilean commission refrained from even mentioning the names of those who committed the crimes, but named the victims, described the ways that they were killed, made clear that the killers were members of the armed forces, and made it possible for victims to be paid compensatory benefits.[11]

Then in 1995, with the end of apartheid, South Africa took this approach to the next level by forming a commission that fully embraced the idea that one might achieve reconciliation through truth and, in so doing, became a model for the rest of the world.[12] As with other truth commissions, the South African Truth and Reconciliation Commission was empowered to investigate human rights violations, gather testimony, and build a record of the past. However, it also had the power to grant amnesty to anyone who fully disclosed their crimes. It offered amnesty for truth. Proponents of restorative justice, like the late archbishop Desmond Tutu and other Christian South Africans, insisted that this compromise with retribution and the formal court system was worth making for the sake of reconciliation.[13] They believed that the confessions of wrongdoing combined with the leniency of amnesty would facilitate reconciliation not only for victims who at a minimum wanted their tormentors' names and crimes placed into the public record but also for perpetrators who, by being forgiven rather than imprisoned, could have at least some of their own dignity and worth restored.

This path to amnesty, furthermore, was not cost-free. The confessing of one's crimes exposed most perpetrators to harsh public criticism. Moreover, because grants of amnesty were never automatic, subsequent legal prosecution was always a possibility for perpetrators who were found to be telling less than the truth. Thus, whether one believes this system appropriately balanced societal interests in retribution and redemption will depend on how one views the implications of informal sanctions like disapproval and ostracism—on whether the community would or should forgive the offender completely, even if that person avoids prison.

It is also natural, given the retributive nature of people's intuitions that we considered in chapter 6, that at least some societies would prefer a more punitive approach. In 2001, for example, when the Rwandan government initiated its own efforts to address crimes against humanity that were committed during the 1994 genocide there, it was certainly aware of the path South Africa had taken through its Truth and Reconciliation Commission. However, the Rwandan government chose to pursue a different path, one that was more of a hybrid between traditional courtroom justice and South Africa's offer of amnesty for truth.

Rwanda's formal court system was overwhelmed by the number of cases, and its prisons were bursting at the seams with genocide suspects who would likely wait years or even decades for their day in court. Human Rights Watch reports that by 1998, approximately 130,000 prisoners were crammed into space meant for 12,000 to await their trials, resulting in inhumane conditions that claimed thousands of lives.[14] Likewise, although the United Nations Security Council created the International Criminal Tribunal for Rwanda in 1994 to try high-ranking government and army officials in that country who were accused of genocide-related crimes, that tribunal only managed to indict ninety-three individuals and sentence sixty-two of them over the course of seventeen years.[15]

The Rwandan government, therefore, established a novel system of community justice, known as the Gacaca courts, to accelerate those trials. The twelve thousand Gacaca courts, which derive their name from the Kinyarwanda word meaning "grass" (referring to the public space where communities gather to resolve disputes), tried approximately 1.2 million cases between 2005 and 2012 by giving ordinary Rwandans the authority to dispense justice and foster reconciliation. The most serious category of crimes (involving mass murderers, rapists, and leaders who had incited the killings) was still handled by the conventional courts.[16] However, the Gacaca system allowed communities to elect their own local judges to hear trials for other genocide-related crimes and created a forum to bring those accused face-to-face with victims. Punishments from those trials ranged from community service to lengthy prison times. However, these trials also sought to give victims and bystanders the opportunity to speak publicly about what they experienced; to give perpetrators the incentive to confess their crimes, show remorse, and ask for forgiveness in front of their community in exchange for lower sentences; and to provide a means for victims to learn the truth about the deaths of their family members and relatives.

The Nuremberg (and other Allied) trials, South Africa's Truth and Reconciliation Commission, and Rwanda's Gacaca courts thus illustrate three types of attempts to implement what is known as *transitional justice,* a way for countries to address large-scale or systematic human rights violations for which traditional justice systems cannot provide an adequate response.[17] Whereas the Nuremberg trials and other international tribunals remained focused on courtroom justice and punishment, the South African TRC instead focused on reconciliation, and Rwanda's experiment with restorative justice through its Gacaca courts sought a mixture of both. However, they are similar in the sense that each sought to establish the truth of what happened and make it part of the public's awareness and historical record.

The need for truth in each of these cases is underscored by the fact that perpetrators of such atrocities typically have a self-interest in keeping their acts invisible, buried, and publicly forgotten. The Nazis, for example, dismantled and dynamited their death camps at Auschwitz, so nothing remained of those facilities by the time they were abandoned except broken bricks, slabs of concrete, pieces of twisted metal, and the shoes, suitcases, flatware, and hair of those who had been exterminated.[18] In South Africa, thousands did not know the fate of their loved ones who had been abducted during apartheid or where their remains were buried.[19] And in Rwanda, those who did not know the fate of missing family members after its 1994 genocide numbered in the hundreds of thousands, with mass graves containing their remains hidden throughout the country.[20]

In each of these circumstances, the pursuit of transitional justice played an important role in illuminating those crimes. The trials of Nazi war criminals at Nuremberg and elsewhere provided unambiguous judicial acknowledgment of the offenses that officials in the Hitler regime committed. In Rwanda, the testimonials of perpetrators, victims, and bystanders during the Gacaca trials served to increase the amount of evidence and information that was available. Moreover, in South Africa, the stories of both victims and perpetrators served to widen the net of culpability to include perpetrators of varying degrees of responsibility for unjust acts and helped offer a more nuanced account of who was most guilty, who was partly guilty, and who was innocent despite belonging to groups and systems that carried out the atrocity.

South Africa's TRC, and the other truth and reconciliation commissions that it has inspired, also sought to provide more than factual or forensic truth. Its final report distinguished three additional dimensions of truth, which it called *personal* ("narrative"), *social* ("dialogical"), and *healing* ("restorative"), that the TRC deemed essential as well.[21] Personal truth involved granting both victims and perpetrators a chance to share their own truth as they saw it and thereby give meaning to the multilayered experiences of the South African story. Thus, rather than being constrained by the narrow rules of an adversarial court system for what evidence can and cannot be considered, the TRC gave apartheid victims a wide berth to share their stories in their own words. As the South African writer Antjie Krog eloquently recounts in her book *Country of My Skull,* "For me, the Truth Commission microphone with its little red light was the ultimate symbol of the whole process: here the marginalized voice speaks to the public ear;

the unspeakable is spoken and translated; the personal story brought from the innermost depths of the individual binds us anew to the collective."[22]

Social truth, in contrast, represents the truth of experience that is established through interaction, discussion, and debate. It's what emerges when people reconcile different personal truths to form a collective understanding of what happened. In this regard, the ethicist Donald Shriver observed that one of the great services of the South African TRC to the formation of a new national political culture was "its back-and-forth dialogue between victims and perpetrators, who together accumulated the evidence of evil in the apartheid system."[23] He noted that even when perpetrators defended themselves by claiming, "We were obeying legal orders," this served to underscore the evils in the law itself and the institutions that enforced them. Thus, even though many citizens refused to accept any responsibility, including high government officials of the National Party, the combined total of those TRC hearings put the ills of the entire apartheid system on public display. As many white South Africans have testified, "Prior to the TRC we could say, 'We didn't know.' But now there is no excuse for not knowing."

Finally, the TRC described "healing truth" as the kind of truth that places facts and what they mean within the context of human relationships—both among citizens and between the state and its citizens—a kind of truth that would contribute to the reparation of the damage inflicted in the past and to the prevention of similar serious abuses reoccurring in the future. This led the commission to emphasize the role of *acknowledgment,* to placing what is or becomes known on public, national record, and affirming that a person's pain is real and worthy of attention. The TRC considered that central to restoring the dignity of victims.

These four aspects of truth (forensic, personal, social, and healing) can help mitigate some of the challenges identified in this book's earlier chapters that can stand in the way of our efforts to overcome trust violations. The insight gained through the accumulation of facts, personal narratives, and alternative points of view can help counteract our tendency to make automatic and simplistic attributions for what happened, as we considered in chapter 5, by providing a more nuanced account of blame and intentionality. Such efforts to move beyond the simplistic story have revealed, for example, that

Nazi Germany and the Holocaust stemmed from German anger and resentment over being forced to accept the draconian terms set by the 1919 Treaty of Versailles, which ended World War I by blaming Germany for starting that war and burdening the country with massive reparations it could never repay.[24] It was a response to victor's justice. That kind of recognition doesn't require us to absolve Nazis of their crimes. However, it can be essential for both victims and perpetrators to develop a better understanding of how those violations arose and how one might ultimately address them.

More truth can also help mitigate our tendency to view our own groups more favorably than other groups and to treat members of those other groups as homogeneous, which we considered in chapter 8. It can reveal how members of the out-group might have differed in culpability, with some clearly guilty, others partly guilty, and some even putting themselves at risk to protect would-be victims. It can also reveal horrific crimes that were committed by one's own group, as was the case in each of the three examples of gross human rights violations we have considered. Some Allied forces committed crimes against the Nazis, some of the Tutsi minority who were targeted for genocide in Rwanda retaliated violently, and some members of the African National Congress (ANC) sought vengeance against white South Africans during apartheid.

That truth can, furthermore, prompt us to take more careful stock of the moral intuitions from chapter 9 that we might have otherwise taken for granted. We might uphold the moral intuition of authority without question, for example, until we confront the hollow ring of Nazi military executioners or apartheid police torturers trying to justify their crimes by claiming they were just following orders.[25,26] Or we might champion the moral intuition of loyalty until we bear witness to previously unimaginable atrocities that this principle enabled against innocent victims who happened to be different. We might consider the moral intuition of fairness unassailable until we learn how readily many of the perpetrators used self-serving conceptions of fairness to justify their egregious actions. Or we might consider the moral intuition of care to be of paramount importance until we consider how the harm committed through military victory by the Allies against the Nazis or by the Rwandan Patriotic Front (RPF) against the Hutus played a central role in ending those atrocities. And we may even start to reconsider our stance toward the moral intuition of sanctity as the truth reveals the entire society's entanglement in the atrocities that were committed, as was the case in the aftermath of both Nazi Germany and South Africa's apartheid.

As Donald Shriver observed, "Ethical principles are multiple and related, first to each other and second to situations that may shift behavioral priorities from one principle to another."[27] That is, each principle's importance ultimately depends on the costs it would impose on our other principles, if it were pursued, as well as the particulars of each situation. Thus, he reasoned that "more justice almost always results from decisions that respect the complexity of justice," by trying to account for these different trade-offs and contingencies. That approach can help mitigate our tendency to assume that our own moral intuitions are beyond question. It can prevent us from maintaining overly narrow views of how the world should work, by overlooking or forgetting the tragic consequences of taking such dogmatic stands, as it opens our eyes to the difficult trade-offs our intuitions can confront in practice. This, in turn, can spur more substantive dialogue about how different groups can learn to work with one another's value systems. And in so doing, that dialogue can also underscore what might constitute the society's most fundamental common values, a set of first principles, that can unite them and provide the basis for them to move forward.

One way to understand the need to acknowledge, remember, and reconcile the different aspects of truth that might lie in the wake of gross human rights violations can be found in research on the effects of individual-level trauma we considered in chapter 2. Hundreds of papers on this topic have documented how people can repress the memory of trauma, only to have that memory resurface years or even decades later.[28] Moreover, in a study that compared how people's recollection of benign and traumatic experiences differed, trauma expert Bessel van der Kolk and his colleagues found that when people recalled benign experiences, those stories contained a clear beginning, middle, and end, with no participants reporting periods when any of those events were forgotten. However, when people recalled traumatic experiences, those memories were far more disorganized. Some of the details were remembered all too clearly (such as the smell of the rapist or the gash in the forehead of a dead child), other vital details could not be recalled at all (such as the first person who arrived to help or how they arrived at the hospital), and the sequence of events could likewise be forgotten.[29]

This is a harmful type of forgetting. As Van der Kolk writes, even when we are not consciously aware of our trauma, due to the repression of those memories, our subconscious minds, brains, and bodies keep a record of those horrific experiences and can remind us with harmful slivers of recollection, debilitating flashes of recall, and serious psychological and physiological disorders.[30] Efforts to heal individual-level trauma have underscored the need for those traumatic memories to be integrated not merely by constructing a narrative of the experience but through active efforts to reconcile all the elements of what happened in ways that can allow victims to differentiate between what was then and what is now.

The challenge of healing from trauma at the individual level is, of course, different from the difficulties societies confront in their efforts to overcome the ravages of gross human rights violations. There aren't necessarily direct societal equivalents to all the physiological imprints individual-level trauma can leave in people's brains and bodies, for example. Nevertheless, those physiological imprints will almost certainly be evident in many people who had been affected by those atrocities. Moreover, certain symptoms of trauma, such as the repression of memories, can be magnified when they are manifested at a societal level, as perpetrators of those crimes and other members of that society engage in deliberate efforts to suppress, discount, or forget certain elements of those histories.

That is why the attempts to establish the truth of what happened and make it part of the public's awareness and historical record in Germany, Rwanda, and South Africa have been so critical. It is only by counteracting the inclination to remember more selectively (and to suppress or forget the rest); by making concerted efforts to bring the full scope of the atrocities to the surface; and by striving to find some way to reconcile all those elements into a coherent whole that people can reach a shared understanding of how the trust that is so fundamental to society has been broken. As we considered in chapters 2 and 9, if those involved cannot even agree on how trust has been violated, there is little hope it can be repaired. Perpetrators, bystanders, and victims thus have a collective responsibility to take the steps needed to resolve those differences. This may be why the South African TRC's final report stressed, "An inclusive remembering of painful truths about the past is crucial to the creation of national unity and transcending the divisions of the past."[31]

Yet despite their promise, all three forms of transitional justice we have considered, including South Africa's TRC, are now viewed to have achieved mixed results at best. As we discussed earlier, it was practically infeasible for the Nuremberg and other Allied trials to investigate and prosecute the enormous numbers of crimes that had been committed by Germany during World War II. The Nuremberg trials indicted 24 high-ranking leaders, and the other Allied trials prosecuted more than 1,500 Nazi war criminals. However, even when we include the many additional trials of Nazi criminals that have been conducted through 2005, Mary Fulbrook, a professor of German history, writes that only 6,656 have been convicted, just a tiny fraction of more than 200,000 perpetrators of Nazi-era crimes.[32]

Rwanda's grassroots Gacaca courts, in contrast, are reported to have tried approximately 1.2 million cases. Thus, many Rwandans believe the Gacaca courts helped shed light on what happened in their communities during the 1994 genocide, even if not all the truth was revealed. Those courts helped some families find the bodies of their murdered relatives and finally bury them with some dignity, and some Rwandans say that it has helped set in motion reconciliation within their communities.

However, the compromises the Gacaca court system required to traditional court procedure, particularly to the fair trial rights of the accused, also produced multiple shortcomings and failures. As Penal Reform International (PRI) reports, these problems included basic violations of the right to a fair trial and limitations on the defendants' ability to effectively defend themselves; numerous incidents of witness intimidation and corruption; and flawed decision-making due to inadequate training for lay judges, who were expected to handle complex cases.[33] It is also noteworthy that the Gacaca courts did not allow trials of crimes committed during the genocide by members of the RPF, despite multiple reports of the RPF killing civilians in numerous summary executions and massacres.[34,35] This naturally led to a one-sided account of the atrocities, a form of victor's justice similar to what was criticized about the Nuremberg trials, that significantly diminished the scope and complexity of truth needed to achieve real reconciliation.

As journalist Zahra Moloo observes, "The official narrative of the genocide, which claims that Tutsi victims were rescued from Hutu killers by the RPF, has persisted for decades, rendering the stories of one side continuously visible and subject to official commemoration while actively silencing the memories and stories of the other."[36] That narrative, which was supported by the one-sided prosecutions of the Gacaca courts, has certainly served the regime of Paul Kagame, the former commander of the RPF, quite well, as he became Rwanda's de facto leader after the genocide and assumed office as its president in April 2000.[37] Kagame has received awards, adulation, hundreds of millions of dollars in aid, and unwavering support from many prominent figures. However, for those seeking true reconciliation, as PRI observed with respect to the Gacaca courts' many shortcomings and failures even before the Gacaca process was completed, "the net result is that there is a risk that the process is perverted and the people no longer believe in it."[38]

The South African TRC managed to avoid this one-sided approach to truth. However, even there, that outcome was far from guaranteed. Once in power, the amnesty provision of the TRC created controversy among members of the ANC, who resented having their movement accused of moral violations akin in any way to the violations of the apartheid movement.[39] The premier and legal advisor to the ANC, Mathews Phosa, claimed that ANC members do not have to apply for amnesty, because the war against apartheid was just, and the TRC's report was almost refused publication. This opposition led writer Antjie Krog to ask, "When the Truth Commission says, 'The truth will set us free,' is the ANC adding, 'The truth as determined by us'?"[40] It was only after the TRC chair, Archbishop Desmond Tutu, announced that he would resign if the ANC granted itself amnesty and that he refused to be abused by a party that would not accept equal treatment before the Truth Commission, that the TRC was allowed to continue its more evenhanded approach.

Yet both the scope and success of South Africa's TRC ultimately remained limited. While some perpetrators testified to get amnesty, others remained silent. They chose to risk prosecution and punishment by the criminal courts, and they have largely won that gamble. Decades later, several hundred cases of apartheid crimes, including murder and torture, remain unprosecuted despite growing pressure to bring truth and justice to the families of those killed.[41] The TRC's mandate to investigate "gross violations of human rights" also did not include attention to the systematic dispossession of Black South Africans, who were deprived of South African citizenship and designated as citizens of "homelands," or Bantustans, to exclude them from the South African political system.[42] Nor did the TRC call into question established property rights. Thus, white South Africans who owned land that was stolen during apartheid were able to keep it.[43] Moreover, even though the TRC's final report observed that "it will be impossible to create a meaningful human rights culture without high priority being given to economic justice by the public and private sectors,"[44] its proposal for a "once-off wealth tax" as a mechanism to effect the transfer of resources was ignored.[45] Finally, the recommendations the TRC made for reparations to those who testified about their experiences never received the full support of the national government, with each being paid about $3,900 apiece, far less than what the TRC recommended.[46]

Thus, even though the work of South Africa's TRC has been celebrated outside of South Africa and emulated by many other nations, sentiments about its success within that country are much more muted. Although the commission helped avert mass violence during the country's transition from apartheid to majority rule, the TRC did not address apartheid's enduring economic and political consequences. This has led to growing income inequality and persistent corruption in the years since. As recently as 2016, for example, most Blacks still lived in shantytowns outside South Africa's prosperous cities, with a third of Cape Town's 3.7 million residents living in those settlements with limited access to basic services, such as water, electricity, and toilets.[47] It is in those crucial respects that historian Joan Wallach Scott concludes that South Africa's TRC failed to deliver the judgment of history.[48] It is also for these reasons that the late Archbishop Tutu himself noted the government left the commission's business "so scandalously unfinished."[49]

Each of the three approaches to transitional justice underscores how both the pursuit of truth and the reconciliation it might promote can be warped by power. Whether through charges of victor's justice in the Nazi trials,[50] the Rwandan Gacaca courts excluding atrocities committed by the RPF,[51] or the African National Congress' attempts to obstruct the efforts of its country's truth commission,[52,53] we can see how people try to tilt the transitional justice process in their own favor.

The experience of South Africa's TRC also illustrates how these implications of power can affect all forms of transitional justice, not just those that follow military victory, including the many truth and reconciliation commissions that have since been held in other nations. In all those efforts, people must agree on whose truth should be part of that new historical record. Yet that agreement can often prove elusive. Those involved can find themselves disputing who gets to decide who apologizes and for what. And in such cases, those with power often wind up exerting greater influence, with the likely result being ambivalence and resentment by others rather than reconciliation. All of this can impede efforts to establish a mutual understanding of what occurred and how trust might ultimately be repaired.

Consider, for example, the results of the first truth and reconciliation commission ever conducted in the United States. The city of Greensboro, North Carolina, formed this commission in 2004 to investigate the November 3, 1979, killing of five leftists by white supremacists during an anti-Klan protest in a local housing project. As journalists Peter Keating and Shaun Assael adeptly recount,[54] although the Greensboro massacre was the worst incident of violence to have occurred in the South in a decade, no one was ever convicted, and two criminal trials that ended in acquittals left troubling questions about whether the police steered the Communist protesters into a fatal ambush. The Greensboro TRC was formed to bridge the "deep divides of distrust and skepticism" that it claimed ran through the city due to this incident.

Nevertheless, after obtaining testimony from more than one hundred witnesses and compiling a 210-page report that exhaustively reconstructed the massacre, that commission found itself accused of *deepening* the divides it sought to heal, by promoting a vocal minority's demand for an apology. Whereas the Greensboro survivors believed they had created a model process for the TRC, a survey of more than 1,500 randomly sampled residents by Jeffrey Sonis, a professor of social medicine at the University of North Carolina, found that the TRC made no significant difference when it came to attitudes about reconciliation or social trust. However, this did not discourage the Greensboro survivors from returning to seek further "reconciliation" on their own terms. They subsequently compelled officials on the city's Human Rights Commission to express regret in 2008 for the way the march leading to the massacre was allowed to get out of control. Then, in 2017, after the violence at the Unite the Right rally in Charlottesville, Virginia, demands for even more contrition led to what city board member Marikay Abuzuaiter called "a blanket apology" by the city on behalf of all the city's agencies to all of Greensboro's residents to encompass "everyone who was involved that day." This was then followed by a 2019 demand for an apology from the police, rather than the entire city government, which was ultimately drafted to specify that "if the police had been on the scene, that those people would not have lost their lives. There would not have been a massacre."[55]

The net result of all these efforts has been that the Greensboro TRC only really helped the massacre survivors who created the TRC in the first place. Others, such as John Young, a longtime antiwar activist who was one of the earliest backers of the commission, felt frozen out as the TRC's efforts grew unbalanced. He said, "Sadly, it got a little one-dimensional. At the hearings, I wanted a fuller version of what happened that day [in 1979]."[56] The commission failed to offer that and ultimately did very little to achieve the kind of reconciliation it sought to promote. This outcome is consistent with the broader observations of James Gibson, a truth commission scholar at Washington University in St. Louis, who writes, "Many commissions appear to have had little, if any, impact on societal transformations."[57] This seems, at least in part, due to people using power to prioritize their own group's goals over more meaningful reconciliation.

Nevertheless, TRCs can still serve the invaluable function of revealing more truth. As American philosopher Elizabeth Kiss observed, the best TRCs strive for inclusive truth in their determination to honor multiple moral principles and to pursue profoundly nuanced moral ends.[58] That truth can provide the building blocks for awareness, evidence for trials, and as Michael Ignatieff (a Canadian author, historian, and politician) mentioned as early as 1996, "reduce the number of lies that can be circulated unchallenged in public discourse."[59] That can make it easier to reach a shared understanding of how trust has been violated and how it might be repaired. However, people's tendency to use power to prioritize their own group's goals, even in the pursuit of that reconciliation, also suggests that we should not expect to see a straight line running from increased truth to social change.

Overall, it is probably unrealistic to expect any form of transitional justice to achieve reconciliation quickly. As historian Joan Wallach Scott observed, wide acceptance of collective political responsibility for Nazi crimes did not happen until many years after Nuremberg, but those trials (along with the other tribunals the Allies held) helped make it happen by presenting irrefutable evidence of those crimes.[60] Likewise, the final report of South Africa's TRC recognized that reconciliation required more than forgiveness, by referring to the difficult history of reconciliation between Afrikaners and white English-speaking South Africans after the devastating Anglo-Boer / South African War of 1899–1902 and noting, "Despite coexistence and participation with English-speaking South Africans in the political system that followed the war, it took many decades to rebuild relationships and redistribute resources—a process that was additionally complicated by a range of urban/rural, class, and linguistic and other barriers." This points to how reconciliation requires not just individual justice but also social justice—real steps need to be taken to ensure the harms won't be repeated and that the harms that had been inflicted are repaired as much as possible. Otherwise, as Peter Keating and Shaun Assael observed, "reconciliation" becomes just another form of forced forgetting, "and then it's only a matter of time before the zombies from the past return."[61]

Yet these challenges also underscore the extraordinary nature of the ambition in these attempts—the idea that we can witness our fellow citizens intentionally brutalize and murder our friends, family, and neighbors for no other reason than because they belonged to the wrong group, or to have played some role in these atrocities ourselves, and then somehow learn not just to live alongside but also trust one another again. That ambition is so great that it is almost certain to exceed our full grasp, especially in the near term. But as with all worthy goals, that does not mean those ambitions should be abandoned. Like the long and difficult road that often needs to be traveled to heal from individual-level trauma, we need to consider these attempts at transitional justice only the first step from which the real journey to repair trust in society can begin.

HOW WE MOVE FORWARD

Now that you have made it to this point, it is time for me to make a confession. I am ultimately a pragmatist. I don't think repairing trust is always feasible or even the best option. In fact, if someone violates trust, my sense is that efforts to repair it without first addressing the causes and consequences of what happened can be a recipe for disaster. That would amount to a type of "forced forgetting," in which the harms are likely to persist or reoccur, and victims find themselves clamoring ever more stridently for recourse.

That is why, if a violator does not regret the offense, is likely to commit another, and poses a real risk of harm, it can simply make more sense to focus on making oneself less vulnerable to those possibilities by deciding *not* to trust. After all, you wouldn't expect sheep to build trust in a wolf. The same thing goes for those whose violations seem assured for a host of other reasons, such as a fundamental lack of ability that can't be corrected or a lack of conscientiousness or willingness to consider interests other than their own. They may not necessarily be bad people, but life is short, and if you have better options, it can simply make more sense to move on. There are certainly plenty of cases where it's abundantly clear that trusting someone will not pay off. And if that is evident in your situation, there is little point in becoming a martyr.

Yet it is also clear that if we don't repair trust in relationships that do warrant salvaging, then much can be lost—for the trustee, for the trustor, and for society. Moreover, the evidence reveals that we far too often make these decisions without understanding whether trust is worth repairing or not. These concerns point to a core theme in this book. If I were to ask how important trust is in your life, I have no doubt you would say it is vital. Yet time and time again, the research findings have made clear that we make these judgments quite poorly. Simple differences in wording can produce dramatic disparities in how we respond to the exact same trust-repair effort, even when the objective nature of the transgression is the same. Our reactions to those efforts can, furthermore, discourage those who wish to repair trust from doing what we are likely to want most, whether that's the offer of an apology, the acceptance of full responsibility, or a more substantive response.

These issues reveal how we can sometimes be our own worst enemy and point to our own share of accountability for what unfolds. They point to the need for us to develop a better understanding of both the nature of the transgression and the likelihood of redemption before we respond to these kinds of incidents. And this means that we should ultimately take greater responsibility for how we engage in at least three core elements of the trust-repair process—our attributions, our moral judgments, and our retributions.

OUR ATTRIBUTIONS

First, the critical role attributions have been found to play in how people respond to trust violations underscores the need to make and consider the implications of these attributions more carefully. Just as our initial willingness to trust can arise from our personal dispositions and quick cognitive cues based on group memberships and stereotypes, our inclinations to view transgressions as a matter of competence or integrity can also be influenced by a host of assumptions that can distort our understanding of why the incident might have happened. Too often, we make these attributions automatically, without real thought or reflection. Moreover, even when we take the time to engage in more deliberate thinking, that deliberation can be based more on what we are motivated to think rather than what truly happened. We may decide, for example, that a loved one's transgression must have been unintentional (i.e., a matter of competence) because we want their apology to help repair that relationship. Or we may decide that the transgression of an enemy or out-group member was intentional (i.e., a matter of integrity) so we can interpret their apology as confirmation that the person should not be trusted.

Yet if we want to become better stewards of trust and assess the trustworthiness of others more effectively, our responses to the transgressions we see in the world should begin with more thoughtful consideration of why those offenses could have arisen. In fact, there are plenty of examples of how changing our attributions for behavior, from matters of competence to integrity or the reverse, can make an enormous difference. Consider, for example, the shift in society's attitude about alcoholism from a matter of moral deficiency to a disease after the American Medical Association deemed it to be an illness in 1956.[1] Although we still haven't found a definitive remedy, there is little doubt that this change in attribution has made a positive difference for many of those afflicted, their friends and families, and their ability to contribute to society. Likewise, consider how society's attitudes about homosexuality have become more accepting over time (not only in the Americas and Western Europe but also in countries like South Africa, Kenya, India, South Korea, and Japan)[2] as public discourse has shifted from portraying it as a moral perversion to an orientation about which one does not have a choice. The prior attribution of intentional moral deviance (i.e., a matter of integrity) tore many families apart and prompted hostility, discrimination, and violence against LGBTQ people. Or think about the "tough on crime" movement in the U.S. that also sought to try more juvenile offenders as adults. Given the scientific evidence, which makes clear that there are significant developmental differences between youths and adults that affect juvenile decision-making, impulse control, and susceptibility to peer pressure,[3] my sense is that this effort to alter how juvenile offenses are viewed (by treating them as matters of integrity rather than competence) has generally made our world worse.

We, furthermore, need to recognize that the causes of trust violations may not be so simple. They can arise from a complex set of reasons, and this may require more careful consideration to determine what to do. How should we respond to transgressions that arise from the offender's lack of knowledge, for example, if they haven't bothered to learn what was needed? Or what if the offender commits a deliberate offense, in part, based on a lack of awareness of how much harm it would create? How should we respond to claims that the transgression "was an error in judgment" (an intentional act due to a lack of competence), and should our reactions depend on the power or demographic characteristics of the offender? Moreover, if we are to consider the offender less blameworthy when there are extenuating circumstances, should it matter if the violation had been at least partly driven by external forces like peer pressure, or internal forces like a serious drug habit or gambling addiction?

These considerations further complicate our ability to understand the trust-repair process, and the scientific research on such questions has yet to be done. This research field is still only in its nascent state, and efforts to fill in the blanks will take many more years. However, these issues point to the need for all of us to start giving more thought to how we make sense of these kinds of incidents if we want to improve our ability to address them.

OUR MORAL JUDGMENTS

These attributional concerns reveal how crucial it is to nurture a deeper understanding of how people make moral judgments. As we considered in chapter 9, people can prioritize the same basic set of moral principles quite differently. Furthermore, those different ways of prioritizing the same moral principles can often conflict. Thus, we can easily fall into the trap of assuming that if our moral standards are right, the moral standards of others must be wrong. We anoint ourselves the hero and regard all those who don't share our views as corrupt, based on the delusion that our own narrow conception of integrity is the only one that matters.

People can likewise make different moral judgments even when they subscribe to the same moral code. This is not only because those committing transgressions are motivated to rationalize their behavior so they can still consider themselves good people despite doing bad things (something that those observing such actions are less inclined to do) but also because people often differ in their access to information about the incident (as we considered in chapter 8). A CEO, for example, may temporarily "cook the books" to keep the company solvent and keep people employed, and thereby consider the violation justified for those reasons. Those who later discover this accounting gimmickry, however, may not be aware of the good the violation was intended to serve,[4] dismiss the violator's efforts to provide such justifications as self-serving,[5] and ultimately consider such actions unethical. This is one of the reasons why people's personal truths can so often differ, as well as why the best truth commissions around the world have ultimately sought to hear more of them.

The bottom line is that these differences in how people make moral judgments need to be reconciled in some way. This requires an effort to move beyond our own interpretive bubble that can foster overconfidence in the universal validity of one's own view. And it highlights the need for concerted dialogues that can reveal, and provide a basis for negotiating, these competing perspectives. As we considered in chapter 9, it is essential for people to confront the difficult trade-offs their own moral stances can create, to recognize the multiplicity of ethical principles, and to appreciate how different situations can shift their priorities from one principle to another. That is how we can move beyond simple questions of right and wrong to address more difficult choices between right and right, and, in so doing, attend to the more substantive challenge of how, given that complexity, we might best uphold the principles we all share.

The problem, however, is that so many trends in modern society seem to work against the conditions that this kind of resolution requires. It has become far too easy to focus on media streams whose business model is based on reinforcing what we already want to think rather than prompting us to examine the pros and cons of multiple perspectives. People naturally gravitate toward others who are like themselves in terms of wealth, race, education, and political orientation. Moreover, redistricting efforts have both allowed and forced politicians to cater to the increasingly unidimensional viewpoints of their strategically curated constituency rather than reconcile a broader diversity of opinions. Thus, the prevailing mode of interaction has become less about dialogue than about domination, about simply imposing one's moral views on others. To become better stewards of trust, we ultimately need to break this pattern to nurture more meaningful conversations about how to reconcile these differing values.

OUR RETRIBUTIONS

At its core, the repair of trust is about how we weigh matters of guilt and redemption. In some cases, redemption may not even be necessary, such as when we have been falsely accused and thus lack guilt. In other cases, redemption may be required and achievable, because perceivers will be inclined to believe the violator can change for the better (such as after competence-based violations). But in the remaining cases, redemption may be almost impossible to achieve, because those signals of redemption are likely to be discounted (such as after integrity-based violations).

These considerations ultimately raise the need for us to calibrate our retributions more carefully. We may certainly demand more repentance from a violator and punish them more severely to achieve that end. But this can do little good if the penalties are so severe and demands for restitution are so unachievable that offenders choose instead to deny culpability, find it easier to justify and rationalize their behavior, and resent us for demanding too much. Even worse, this approach can create a self-fulfilling prophecy, if the punished believe the repair of trust is beyond their reach, if they expect to be permanently stigmatized and forever precluded from a normal life, and if this leads them to conclude they have little to lose by committing other transgressions in the future.

Of course, we cannot be naive enough to infer that we should simply be more lenient. The solution is not to just let trust violations go. Punishment can be critical for deterrence, as well as clarifying our stance toward right and wrong. However, it is also clear that our justice system in the U.S. is seriously flawed. Evidence suggests that increasing some types of punishment (such as the length of prison sentences) doesn't necessarily increase deterrence[6] and that we disproportionately punish those who are poor and less privileged.[7] Our approaches to punishment can, furthermore, not only decrease the likelihood of redemption in some cases, such as when juveniles are tried as adults, but quite often also do little to rectify harm to the victims.

These considerations raise the need for a more enlightened path forward. And though this book is ultimately not about the justice system, it does highlight the need for more careful attention to be given to our systems of punishment and deterrence. The U.S. has only 5 percent of the world's population, but one-quarter of its prisoners. Our prisons house ten times as many mentally ill individuals as state hospitals.[8] They hold a far greater percentage of the country's Black population than the prisons of South Africa did under apartheid.[9] And nearly two-thirds of those released every year return to prison,[10] in part due to crippling employment discrimination that makes it extraordinarily difficult for them to find legitimate jobs. To be sure, there are certainly plenty of societal differences that may keep us from adopting justice systems like the one in Sweden, which have focused not on punishment but on rehabilitation and experience far lower incarceration and crime rates than the U.S.[11] However, it is imperative that we start exploring what's possible, because these are enormous problems, and we must find a way to turn the tide.

A TRUSTFUL LIFE

The findings in this book also provide a host of insights on how to maintain and repair trust in our personal relationships. As I mentioned at the start, that kind of advice is not something I wanted to provide on a superficial level. This was never intended to be a step-by-step guide for how to get away with doing bad things or to cater to those who are only interested in crude quick fixes. I have deliberately avoided that approach, not only because too much of what the research has uncovered is ripe for abuse but also because efforts to apply these findings without taking the time to understand their nuances can quite simply backfire.

That is why this book is intended for those who are prepared to do the hard work first. It is for those who recognize the need to understand the complexity of these problems and who are willing to approach these challenges with the sensitivity they deserve. With that said, I think those of you who have dedicated the time to stick with me through this final chapter meet those criteria. Thus, if you have made it this far and would like a bit more help with how to make use of what this book has covered in your own lives, you have earned it. So let me try to distill some of its core lessons in a way that might serve that end.

Although each successive chapter in this book has sought to broaden its scope beyond the ideas that preceded it—from interpersonal relationships to groups, cultures, and even nations—it is important to keep in mind that the broader levels of analysis add nuance to what is fundamentally about the trust of an individual. Even when we're talking about trust on a nation-wide level, it's built with individual people and is thus subject to the same odd quirks of social perception that reside in each one of us. That includes our tendencies to weigh positive information more heavily than negative information about competence; to weigh negative information more heavily than positive information about integrity; or to filter information in ways that allow us to preserve our important relationships, denigrate outsiders, polarize our opinions, and believe we are being fair and ethical even when we fall short.

Each chapter can thus be seen as identifying these kinds of quirks, demon-strating how that can affect trust maintenance and repair, and, through that process, providing insights into how one might address those challenges. For example, let's consider one of the thorniest problems in this book—how people's tendency to weigh negative information more heavily than positive information for matters of integrity can make even sincere efforts to convey remorse for a trust violation ineffective and how this ultimately gives violators an incentive to instead deny their guilt. What I have tried to reveal through this work is how each side of the equation can help address this problem.

For violators, we've seen the problems of denying guilt when one is guilty or of trying to obfuscate or ignore what happened. When there is evidence of guilt and the violation touches on people's fundamental concerns, those concerns need to be meaningfully addressed. But, as we've also seen, doing so can involve more than simply conveying greater remorse or facing harsher punishments, since those options are quite often not enough to repair trust on their own. It can also hinge on efforts to shape how the violation itself is viewed. Yet this is something violators tend to overlook or approach in such ham-fisted ways that perceivers find them unconvincing. This is where more might be done—where violators may be able to shape our understanding of what happened in ways that can help make the repair of trust possible. And though that may not always be feasible (particularly if the counterpart is un-willing to listen), I do think that if such efforts are made with honesty, sensi-tivity, and a real desire to make things right, that can often make a difference.

These considerations also underscore the critical role perceivers can play in this process. They suggest that perceivers should question the attributions they might make about those incidents; consider how much of that view is based on their motivations; question their own assumptions about how to evaluate the trustworthiness of other people; and take more serious stock of their assumptions about the meaning of integrity itself. In so doing, I hope the results encourage each one of us to become more aware of how readily we can put those like ourselves on pedestals and denigrate those who fail to meet our narrow standards. The worst kind of monster is often the one that anoints itself the hero, based on self-serving conceptions of what's right, since this makes it easy to attack others without a shred of guilt. That is why one of the most important steps perceivers can take toward the repair of trust is the one that begins with humility and grace.

FOUR GUIDING LESSONS

I have devoted my career to studying these issues not because I have found these challenges easy but because I found them so hard. Before the age of thirty, I had moved every four years or less, through different countries, both cities and suburbs, different racial and ethnic communities, and alongside the working poor, middle-class, and well-to-do. It was a crash course on the complexity of human nature that often left me surprised by people's acts of mindless insensitivity to those unlike them, the astonishing cruelty people can sometimes inflict on one another, as well as the fundamental decency that can often be found in others. But as I reflect on those experiences and all those that have occurred since those tumultuous years, based on what I have learned through this research, I would probably put the sharpest focus on four guiding lessons.

Our Desire to Be Good

First, we should start with the premise that most of us want to be good. There is a chapter in John Steinbeck's book *East of Eden* in which he writes about remembering the deaths of three men.[12] The first was one of the richest of the century, who had clawed his way to wealth "through the souls and bodies of men" and then spent his remaining years trying to buy back through great acts of service the love he had forfeited. The second used his insights to warp, bribe, threaten, and seduce others until he found himself in a position of great power and then "clothed his motives in the names of virtue." Steinbeck notes that the news of each of their deaths was received with gladness and pleasure. But when the third man, who made plenty of errors but whose life was devoted to making others brave, dignified, and good despite many ugly forces in the world, passed away, people in the streets burst into tears and felt lost without him. By reflecting on those lives, Steinbeck shared what for him was a core truth. He wrote, "I am certain that underneath their topmost layers of frailty men want to be good and want to be loved. Indeed, most of their vices are attempted short cuts to love."

The findings in this book support this conclusion. Some of my own studies we reviewed in chapter 1 found that when people are told others think they are ethical, they typically respond not by trying to exploit that perception but by wanting to prove them right.[13] Other research we considered in chapter 6 found that people may be dishonest enough to profit but not so dishonest that they would need to see themselves as dishonest people.[14] Likewise, another set of findings we reviewed in that same chapter points to how people try to account for their good and bad acts over time in an effort to remain on the positive side of the ledger and avoid becoming morally bankrupt.[15,16] Thus, the evidence suggests that, even if most of us don't strive to be saints, we at least want to be good enough to be able to look at ourselves in the mirror.

Yet the findings also point to our need to take stock of the factors that can affect what "good enough" ultimately means and how this can underlie a wide range of violations. This requires taking stock of how we may be inconsistent or hypocritical when deciding what is justified for ourselves versus others. They point to the problems that arise when we underestimate the power of the situation and assume others have more control over what happens than they really do. They also suggest, based on the studies in chapter 5 demonstrating how easily any of us can be made to do bad things, that our tendency to believe that ethical people would behave ethically regardless of the situation—and, thus, weigh negative information about integrity so much more heavily than positive information about integrity—may not even make much sense.

If we start with the premise that most of us want to be good, then at least part of the solution to the trust challenges we face is to help each other get there. We can shift our focus toward addressing the situational influences that might entice even well-meaning people in moments of weakness to do the wrong thing, such as by simply making cheating more difficult or by putting other temptations out of easy reach. We can increase their incentives for doing the right thing by highlighting the important benefits that could accrue from a trusting relationship. Likewise, to the extent that trust violations can arise from ambiguities about what is right and wrong, the more we can do to clarify our expectations in a way that others are able to comprehend (rather than add to the confusion, for example, with lengthy contracts filled with legalese that embeds little gotchas in the fine print), the likelier it is that our expectations will be fulfilled. The goal is not to treat these steps as alternatives to trust but rather as a set of basic guardrails to help nurture and support the trust that most of us deserve.

But above all, the findings point to how the relatively high levels of initial trust people have been found to exhibit in others generally make sense. We are right to trust each other. Few of us start with the goal of exploiting the trust of other people and, as chapter 1 detailed, the benefits of trusting one another have received overwhelming empirical support. We just need to work harder to keep that trust from being threatened and, when necessary, to be more thoughtful about repairing it.

The Complexity of Truth

This way of viewing the problem, as a matter of addressing the "short cuts" Steinbeck mentioned that can tempt even well-meaning people to do bad things, in turn provides the basis for the second guiding lesson. The different ways in which people can interpret what and why things might have happened highlight our need to account for the complexity of truth. This includes the need not only to obtain all the objective facts but also to consider people's different views of what and why things occurred, and to work toward building a collective understanding of these issues. As the guiding ideals of the best truth commissions have underscored, we need to exchange our stories and take the time to really listen.

This is essential because the evidence has made the alternative quite clear. What we know from this book is that people tend to form snap judgments based on their gut intuitions,[17] with only a portion of the information that might be available,[18] and with a motivation to see themselves and others in their tribe in a positive light.[19] We also know that this can create serious distortions in how one can view the exact same incident, produce major inconsistencies in how we evaluate trustworthiness, and stack the deck against those who are different.[20,21] Thus, one of our most important tasks is to turn off that kind of autopilot and strive to interpret trust violations with the same level of thoughtful and nuanced consideration that we would hope to receive from others when our own trustworthiness is on the line. Because at some point, it probably will be.

To fight against the seduction of simplistic stories when trust has been violated, our first stop is to explore the diversity of attributions people have made about what happened. We need to seek and compare the stories that might be told by others like ourselves, the alleged offenders, as well as third parties, with the goal of uncovering all the situational and motivational influences that may shed light on the ways in which the transgression could have been intentional or not. We then need to check our assumptions about what the intentional acts really tell us about the offender's moral character. This requires that we move beyond our own interpretive bubbles to consider the broader range of ethical principles we all share, explore how people can prioritize those principles differently based on their views of the situation, and take stock of the difficult trade-offs that can arise when we are confronted with the choice between right and right.

Those efforts don't require us to abandon our views. They simply represent a desire to learn more, given that the information we have is almost always incomplete. The efforts can add shades of gray to a picture that might have otherwise been black and white, help establish a shared understanding of what and why things might have happened, and thereby provide a stronger basis from which trust might ultimately be repaired.

Indeed, even if those efforts do not entirely succeed, our efforts to take the time to listen to others' views and account for that complexity of truth offer the benefit of conveying that we care and that we are doing our best to get things right, rather than simply imposing our opinions through force.

The Upside of Intent

Third, although we have largely focused on the problems that can arise when people attribute offenses to the lack of integrity in others, the other side of this coin is that it can also be easier to maintain and repair trust when others believe our intentions are good. This doesn't require that we all share the exact same moral priorities. It simply means that we make clear that we are doing our very best (despite such differences, the situational pressures we are facing, the difficult trade-offs we might confront, and our own limitations) to deserve their trust, even if we might sometimes fall short.

This is the essence of the third life story Steinbeck recounted—the man who made many errors but whose life was devoted to making others brave, dignified, and good even when ugly forces were loose in the world to exploit their fears. It is also something I have seen time and time again with others both within and outside my profession. When we make clear that we are doing our very best not just for ourselves but for others, it becomes easier for those others to view our failures as mistakes, as matters of competence, which could more readily be forgiven. Indeed, they will *want* to see those failures as mistakes when they know we are looking out for them, because this will give them a greater stake in preserving the relationship.

But we must also recognize that even if our intentions are good, this may not be as evident to others as it is to ourselves. That is why taking the time to listen, open ourselves to the differences in our stories, and recognize the complexity of truth can be so important. It is easy to assume that our own views are the only ones that matter, particularly if we are solely concerned with those exactly like us. However, if we want to maintain trust in a broader world where people's interpretations might be different, then it is essential that they see us do our best to understand those differences and integrate them in ways that each side can accept.

That is how we can make clear our intentions are good not just to our-selves but also to others. It is how we make clear that we are not taking their trust for granted and that we are doing our best to preserve it. It is how we can help shield ourselves from attributions of nefarious intent that can make the repair of trust so difficult. And it is also how we might encourage others to engage in similar efforts to convey positive intentions toward us. All these implications can ultimately help turn what might have otherwise become an intractable conflict, in which each side condemns the integrity of the other, into a more manageable problem of how best to reconcile the different perspectives and ethical priorities of well-meaning people.

The Need to Walk Through the Doors

However, this book also makes clear that the repair of trust isn't entirely up to us. That is perhaps the hardest lesson of all. Although forgiveness does not require cooperation by the offender or the offender even acknowledg-ing the harm, the repair of trust will always depend on that offender to some degree. It is not a one-sided action.

What we know from chapter 1 is that efforts to compel others to be-have as we wish (through financial penalties, legal prosecution, or threats of other sanctions) ultimately do little to improve trust. They simply allow us to act as if we trust them by reducing risk. What's more, those efforts can even backfire by encouraging us to believe that others would *not* have behaved in a trustworthy manner if they had not been compelled. We also know from chapter 10 that the use of force can lead to one-sided forms of reconciliation that are quite likely to overlook some of the underlying causes and consequences of the violation that can impede its repair. That chapter likewise considered how this can lead those involved to push back against both the reconciliation process and its remedies and how it can lay the basis for violations to erupt again in the future.

That is why we may often need to wait for the time to be ripe for real rec-onciliation to happen. As we considered in chapter 9, people are frequently unwilling to engage in constructive dialogues to address these kinds of chal-lenges until each side believes more unilateral means of getting its way are blocked and this puts them in a costly predicament. That belief is what can make them more receptive to proposals that might offer a way out of that painful stalemate, encourage them to start listening and asking questions, and prod them to move past their dogmatic stances to search for common ground and explore more substantive ways to resolve their differences.

But such moments don't happen often. They can require waiting for the counterpart to experience major losses first, much like waiting for an addict to hit rock bottom before they are ready to rehabilitate. They also require each side to care enough about repairing trust to go through the effort, and that won't always be the case. Moreover, even when each side is ready to work through their issues, the temptation to use power and force to get our way when things get difficult will always be present, as we have seen time and time again with efforts to address gross human rights violations around the world. That is something we will always need to guard against. However, those moments when each side becomes truly willing to explore a different path forward are also the most precious opportunities to make real change happen. As Father Greg, the founder of Homeboy Industries we met in chapter 6, once observed in an interview, "They have to walk through the doors. Otherwise, it doesn't work."[22]

CONCLUSION

O
ne dubious benefit of writing a book on trust is that it lends it-self to an endless stream of examples. Every day I read the news, there are a host of new incidents ranging from the peculiar to the salacious to the horrific. In the pages of this book, I have selected just a few of these cases that I thought best illuminated the key insights from the research. However, I would be remiss if, by the end, I didn't also at least touch on two of the most troubling signs of mistrust in modern times.

The first of these signs occurred when I was still completing the proposal for this book—the violent insurrection at the U.S. Capitol Building on January 6, 2021, which led to the deaths of five people. That moment put into stark focus how much trust has been lost in the U.S. (in our elections, in the media, and in our political leaders). It was a tragedy that left an indelible mark in the public's consciousness of how bad things had truly become. And that dark moment will likely find a place in the lessons we share from history with future generations.

The second of these signs occurred as the book itself was nearing completion and continues to unfold as I write to you today—Russia's full-scale military invasion of Ukraine on February 24, 2022, and the start of what appears to be a new cold war.[1] It is a harsh reminder of how, no matter how bad our crisis of trust might have seemed in the wake of the 2021 U.S. insurrection, things can always get worse. Although reports of casualties vary widely, the Office of the United Nations High Commissioner for Human Rights (OHCHR) has already verified the deaths of over three thousand civilians just a little over two months into the war.[2] More than twelve million people are believed to have fled their homes in Ukraine as refugees.[3] And by May 3, 2022, Ukraine's prosecutor general's office had opened more than 9,300 investigations into alleged war crimes in the country (including rape, torture, and summary executions), with the true number of cases estimated to be much higher.[4]

Despite their many notable differences, each event underscores how dangerously close we stand on the precipice between trust in our systems of laws, rules, and norms and the "law of the jungle," where might makes right. Each of these events was based on a flagrant lie—groundless claims that the 2020 presidential election had been stolen in the U.S.[5] and the purported goal of "de-Nazification" and preventing "genocide" in Ukraine (despite that country democratically electing a Jewish president who lost relatives in the Holocaust).[6] Those lies were each promoted by authoritarian-minded leaders seeking to put their own interests above all others. Moreover, the devastating consequences of those lies had each been fueled by long-simmering resentments, based on socioeconomic tensions and mistrust of those who are different, the likes of which seem to have also taken root in countries like France, Hungary, and other parts of the world.[7]

But we must remember that it was during each of those dark times that there have also been glimmers of hope. In the wake of the U.S. insurrection, several members of Congress chose to stand against their own party by condemning a president for inciting the rebellion. Corporations broke their typical silence to announce they would withdraw campaign funding for politicians who voted to cast doubt on the election results. Wealthy backers of politicians who had challenged the election results declared that their support had been a mistake. And technology firms took major steps to curb the former president's efforts to incite conspiracy theorists and extremists.

Likewise, in response to the war in Ukraine, over thirty countries around the world have imposed sanctions and export controls on Russia.[8] By May 5, 2022, almost one thousand companies had publicly announced that they would voluntarily curtail operations in that country.[9] European leaders have rallied in a united front in this struggle by recasting their foreign policies to send weapons to defend Ukraine.[10] A veteran Russian diplomat, Boris Bondarev, resigned as counselor at the Russian permanent mission to the United Nations in Geneva, due to the Ukraine invasion, with a public statement saying, "Never have I been so ashamed of my country."[11] And even China's staunch support for Putin's rhetoric has wavered in the wake of reports and pictures of brutal massacres of civilians, which China's Foreign Ministry spokesman Zhao Lijian acknowledged to be "very disturbing."[12]

Those steps on their own almost certainly won't be enough. It will likely take more fundamental, more comprehensive, and lasting efforts to address these problems, and we have already seen a host of efforts by different stakeholders to justify, ignore, or downplay what happened. A little more than a year after the U.S. insurrection, the Republican Party sought to diminish the attack by calling it "legitimate political discourse" and censuring both Liz Cheney and Adam Kinzinger, the only Republicans in the U.S. House of Representatives serving on the House panel investigating the incident.[13] Likewise, when the United Nations General Assembly voted on April 7, 2022, to suspend Russia from the Human Rights Council after hundreds of civilian bodies were found on the streets and in mass graves in the city of Bucha, a suburb of Ukraine's capital, Kyiv, dozens of countries abstained, including Thailand, Brazil, South Africa, Mexico, Indonesia, and Singapore.[14]

However, as the costs to society of not changing course continue to grow, it is also the case that more and more of us will join the ranks of those who seek a more enlightened path forward as we strive for more substantive and enduring ways in which trust might be repaired. It is when we lose so much that we are ultimately reminded of what can hold us together. We return to first principles—of the importance of honesty and truth, of the need to be free from tyranny and oppression, of the sanctity of human life. And it is from that basis that we will sift through the rubble, make sense of what can be salvaged, and try to mend what was broken.

As with the repair of trust in our governments, groups, and institutions; with their leaders; and in one another, the science of redemption is still at its beginning. But this is a good beginning, a solid foundation on which we can build. We have never been in more need of a serious conversation about how to repair trust. But we have also never been more capable of having it. And as our understanding continues to grow, who knows what we'll eventually accomplish together?

ACKNOWLEDGMENTS

Special thanks to all those at the Park & Fine Literary and Media agency who helped make this book possible. To Alison MacKeen, for replying so quickly to my initial inquiry, conveying such enthusiasm for this topic, encouraging me to explore how broadly it could scale, and taking the time to suggest many helpful edits with the final book proposal. To Celeste Fine, the brilliant agency partner who, in just a thirty-minute conversation, offered the essential insight that helped me frame this book. To Jaidree Braddix, for offering such extraordinary support throughout this publishing journey, from the very first draft of the proposal, through the publisher meetings and ensuing auction, as well as through all the phases of the publication process itself. To Andrea Mai, for lending her critical expertise with sales, publisher, and retail relations; as well as to Abigail Koons, for her diligent work negotiating international rights for this work. I cannot imagine having a more talented and conscientious team standing by my side.

Thanks as well to those at Flatiron Books who helped bring this book to fruition. This includes Meghan Houser, the acquiring editor who offered several indispensable suggestions for this book before leaving Flatiron, as well as Lee Oglesby, for her help with line editing after Meghan's departure. I am, furthermore, particularly grateful to Laury Frieber, who worked so diligently to complete the legal review of this book and who became such a thoughtful and delightful collaborator as we worked through those final revisions.

Last, but most significant of all, my deepest appreciation goes to my dear wife, Beth Fortune, a gifted writer and Cordon Bleu–trained chef who has dedicated her life to bringing so much beauty into the world as an interior architect and designer. For your encouragement from the very first sentences of this book, for being a much-needed sounding board throughout this process, for taking the time to provide honest feedback on both the initial proposal and final book draft, and for sacrificing so many weekend and evening hours we could have enjoyed together so I could keep writing, I owe so much of this journey to you.

NOTES

INTRODUCTION

1. L. Ranine and A. Perrin, "Key Findings About Americans' Declining Trust in Government and Each Other," Pew Research Center, July 22, 2019, https://www .pewresearch.org/fact-tank/2019/07/22/key-findings-about-americans-declining -trust-in-government-and-each-other/.

2. J. Perry, "Trust in Public Institutions: Trends and Implications for Economic Security," United Nations Department of Economic and Social Affairs, July 20, 2021, https://www.un.org/development/desa/dspd/2021/07/trust-public -institutions/.

3. R. Axelrod, *The Evolution of Cooperation* (New York: Basic Books, 1984).

4. E. Lutz, "Trump Admits Russia Helped Him Win, Denies It 20 Minutes Later," *Vanity Fair,* May 30, 2019, https://www.vanityfair.com/news/2019/05/trump -admits-russia-helped-him-win-denies-it-20-minutes-later.

5. J. Nicas, "Brazilian Leader Accused of Crimes Against Humanity in Pandemic Response," *New York Times,* October 19, 2021, https://www.nytimes.com/2021/10 /19/world/americas/bolsonaro-covid-19-brazil.html.

6. "Three MPs and One Peer to Be Charged over Expenses," BBC, February 5, 2010, http://news.bbc.co.uk/2/hi/uk_news/politics/8500885.stm.

7. "British MP Resigns After Being Caught Watching Pornography, Twice, in the House of Commons," ABC News, April 30, 2022, https://www.abc.net.au/news /2022-05-01/uk-mp-resigns-over-porn-scandal/101028768.

8. J. Guy, L. McGee, and I. Kottasová, "UK Prime Minister Boris Johnson Resigns After Mutiny in His Party," *CNN World,* July 7, 2022, https://www.cnn.com/2022 /07/07/europe/boris-johnson-resignation-intl/index.html.

9. "Fourth Quarter 2021 Social Weather Survey: 69% of Adult Filipinos Say the Problem of Fake News in Media Is Serious," Social Weather Stations, February 25, 2022, https://www.sws.org.ph/swsmain/artcldisppage/?artcsyscode=ART -20220225130129&mc_cid=368bdea2b7&mc_eid=1eeee26a57.

10. Z. Qureshi, "Trends in Income Inequality: Global, Inter-Country, and Within Countries," Brookings, https://www.brookings.edu/wp-content/uploads/2017/12 /global-inequality.pdf.

11. E. Ortiz-Ospina and M. Rosner, "Trust," Our World in Data, 2016, https:// ourworldindata.org/trust.

12. "Civic and Social Bonds Fortify Communities, but Millions of Americans Lack Connections That Could Bolster Pandemic Recovery," Associated Press–NORC Center for Public Affairs Research, June 2021, https://apnorc.org/wp-content /uploads/2021/06/APNORC_Social_Capital_report_final.pdf.

1: YOU'RE NOT AS CYNICAL AS YOU THINK

1. S. Vaknin, *Malignant Self-Love: Narcissism Revisited* (Skopje, Macedonia: Narcissus Publications, 2015).

2. O. E. Williamson, "Calculativeness, Trust, and Economic Organization," *Journal of Law and Economics* 36, no. 1 (1993): 453–486.

3. D. M. Rousseau, S. B. Sitkin, R. S. Burt, and C. Camerer, "Not So Different After All: A Cross-Discipline View of Trust," *Academy of Management Review* 23 (1998): 393–404.

4. J. M. Rangel, P. H. Sparling, C. Crowe, P. M. Griffin, and D. L. Swerdlow, "Epidemiology of *Escherichia coli* O157:H7 Outbreaks, United States, 1982–2002," *Emerging Infectious Diseases* 11, no. 4 (2005): 603–609.

5. P. H. Kim, D. L. Ferrin, C. D. Cooper, and K. T. Dirks, "Removing the Shadow of Suspicion: The Effects of Apology vs. Denial for Repairing Ability- vs. Integrity-Based Trust Violations," *Journal of Applied Psychology* 89, no. 1 (2004): 104–118.

6. M. Vultaggio, "Everyone Lies on Their Resume, Right?," Statista, March 3, 2020, https://www.statista.com/chart/21014/resume-lie-work-jobs/; V. Bolden-Barrett, "More Than a Third of People Admit to Lying on Resumes," HR Dive, January 7, 2020, https://www.hrdive.com/news/more-than-a-third-of-people-admit-to -lying-on-resumes/570565/; J. Liu, "78% of Job Seekers Lie During the Hiring Process—Here's What Happened to 4 of Them," CNBC, February 20, 2020, https://www.cnbc.com/2020/02/19/how-many-job-seekers-lie-on-their-job -application.html.

7. E. Duffin, "Average Number of People Per Family in the United States from 1960 to 2021," Statista, September 30, 2022, https://www.statista.com/statistics/183657 /average-size-of-a-family-in-the-us/.

8. D. Cox, "The State of American Friendship: Change, Challenges, and Loss," Survey Center on American Life, June 8, 2021, https://www.americansurveycenter.org /research/the-state-of-american-friendship-change-challenges-and-loss/.

9. M. Granovetter, *Getting a Job: A Study in Contacts and Careers,* 2nd ed. (Chicago: University of Chicago Press, 1995).

10. E. C. Bianchi and J. Brockner, "In the Eyes of the Beholder? The Role of Dispositional Trust in Judgments of Procedural and Interactional Fairness," *Organizational Behavior and Human Decision Processes* 118, no. 1 (2012): 46–59.

11. J. B. Rotter, "Interpersonal Trust, Trustworthiness, and Gullibility," *American Psychologist* 35, no. 1 (1980): 1–7.

12. L. B. Alloy and L. Y. Abramson, "Judgment of Contingency in Depressed and Nondepressed Students: Sadder but Wiser?," *Journal of Experimental Psychology: General* 108, no. 4 (1979): 441–485.

13. S. E. Taylor and J. D. Brown, "Positive Illusions and Well-Being Revisited: Separating Fact from Fiction," *Psychological Bulletin* 116, no. 1 (1994): 21–27.

14. D. Dunning, C. Heath, and J. M. Suls, "Flawed Self-Assessment: Implications for Health, Education, and the Workplace," *Psychological Science in the Public Interest* 5, no. 3 (2004): 69–106.

15. J. K. Butler Jr., "Toward Understanding and Measuring Conditions of Trust: Evolution of a Conditions of Trust Inventory," *Journal of Management* 17, no. 3 (1991): 643–663.

16. D. H. McKnight, L. L. Cummings, and N. L. Chervany, "Initial Trust Formation in New Organizational Relationships," *Academy of Management Review* 23, no. 3 (1998): 473–490.

17. R. E. Nisbett, *Mindware: Tools for Smart Thinking* (New York: Farrar, Straus & Giroux, 2015).

18. P. H. Kim, K. A. Diekmann, and A. E. Tenbrunsel, "Flattery May Get You Somewhere: The Strategic Implications of Providing Positive vs. Negative Feedback About Ability vs. Ethicality in Negotiation," *Organizational Behavior and Human Decision Processes* 90, no. 2 (2003): 225–243.

19. M. L. Slepian and D. R. Ames, "Internalized Impressions: The Link Between Apparent Facial Trustworthiness and Deceptive Behavior Is Mediated by Targets' Expectations of How They Will Be Judged," *Psychological Science* 27, no. 2 (2016): 282–288.

20. Q. Li, G. D. Heyman, J. Mei, and K. Lee, "Judging a Book by Its Cover: Children's Facial Trustworthiness and Peer Relationships," *Child Development* 90, no. 2 (2019): 562–575.

21. E. Ortiz-Ospina and M. Rosner, "Trust," Our World in Data, 2016. https://ourworldindata.org/trust-and-gdp.

2: WHEN TRUST IS BROKEN

1. National Domestic Violence Hotline, https://www.thehotline.org/.

2. J. Kaufman and E. Zigler, "Do Abused Children Become Abusive Parents?," *American Journal of Orthopsychiatry* 57, no. 2 (1987): 186–192.

3. B. E. Bell and E. F. Loftus, "Trivial Persuasion in the Courtroom: The Power of (a Few) Minor Details," *Journal of Personality and Social Psychology* 56, no. 5 (1989): 669–679.

4. A. Tversky and D. Kahneman, "Loss Aversion in Riskless Choice: A Reference-Dependent Model," *Quarterly Journal of Economics* 106, no. 4 (1991): 1039–1061.

5. "The U.S. Public Health Service Syphilis Study at Tuskegee," Centers for Disease Control and Prevention, https://www.cdc.gov/tuskegee/index.html.

6. K. V. Brown, "Understanding Vaccine Hesitancy Among Black Americans," Bloomberg, April 13, 2021, https://www.bloomberg.com/news/articles/2021-04-13/understanding-vaccine-hesitancy-among-black-americans.

7. P. Bacon, "Why a Big Bloc of Americans Is Wary of the COVID-19 Vaccine—Even as Experts Hope to See Widespread Immunization," *FiveThirtyEight,* December 11, 2020, https://fivethirtyeight.com/features/many-black-americans-republicans-women-arent-sure-about-taking-a-covid-19-vaccine/.

8. COVID Collaborative, UnidosUS, and NAACP, "Coronavirus Vaccine Hesitancy in Black and Latinx Communities," 2020, https://static1.squarespace.com/static

/5f85f5a156091e113f96e4d3/t/5fb72481b1eb2e6cf845457f/1605837977495
/VaccineHesitancy_BlackLatinx_Final_11.19.pdf.

9. "Risk for COVID-19 Infection, Hospitalization, and Death by Race/Ethnicity," Centers for Disease Control and Prevention, June 2, 2022, https://www.cdc.gov /coronavirus/2019-ncov/covid-data/investigations-discovery/hospitalization-death -by-race-ethnicity.html.

10. "COVID-19 Vaccine Efficacy Summary," Institute for Health Metrics and Evaluation, February 18, 2022, http://www.healthdata.org/covid/covid-19-vaccine -efficacy-summary.

11. N. Ndugga, L. Hill, S. Artiga, and S. Haldar, "Latest Data on COVID-19 Vaccinations by Race/Ethnicity," Kaiser Family Foundation, April 7, 2022, https:// www.kff.org/coronavirus-covid-19/issue-brief/latest-data-on-covid-19-vaccinations -race-ethnicity/.

12. E. Gawthorp, "The Color of Coronavirus: COVID-19 Deaths by Race and Ethnicity in the U.S.," APM Research Lab, May 10, 2022, https://www .apmresearchlab.org/covid/deaths-by-race.

13. H. Recht and L. Weber, "Black Americans Are Getting Vaccinated at Lower Rates Than White Americans," Kaiser Family Foundation, January 17, 2021, https://khn .org/news/article/black-americans-are-getting-vaccinated-at-lower-rates-than-white -americans/.

14. O. J. Kim and L. N. Magner, *A History of Medicine* (London: Taylor & Francis, 2018).

15. C. Elliott, "Tuskegee Truth Teller," *American Scholar,* December 4, 2017, https:// theamericanscholar.org/tuskegee-truth-teller/.

16. M. Newsome, "We Learned the Wrong Lessons from the Tuskegee 'Experiment,'" *Scientific American,* March 31, 2021, https://www.scientificamerican.com/article/we -learned-the-wrong-lessons-from-the-tuskegee-experiment/.

17. B. van der Kolk, *The Body Keeps the Score: Brain, Mind, and Body in the Healing of Trauma* (New York: Penguin, 2015).

18. A. C. Boudewyn and J. H. Liem, "Childhood Sexual Abuse as a Precursor to Depression and Self-Destructive Behavior in Adulthood," *Journal of Traumatic Stress* 8, no. 3 (1995): 445–459.

19. W. B. Swann Jr., *Resilient Identities: Self, Relationships, and the Construction of Social Reality* (New York: Basic Books, 1999).

20. L. Raine, S. Keeter, and A. Perrin, "Trust and Distrust in America," Pew Research Center, July 22, 2019, https://www.pewresearch.org/politics/2019/07/22/trust-and -distrust-in-america/.

21. U. Gneezy and A. Rustichini, "A Fine Is a Price," *Journal of Legal Studies* 29, no. 1 (2000): 1–17.

22. S. L. Murray, "Motivated Cognition in Romantic Relationships," *Psychological Inquiry* 10, no. 1 (1999): 23–34.

23. S. L. Murray and J. G. Holmes, "Seeing Virtues in Faults: Negativity and the Transformation of Interpersonal Narratives in Close Relationships," *Journal of Personality and Social Psychology* 65, no. 4 (1993): 707–722.

24. J. Stromberg, "B. F. Skinner's Pigeon-Guided Rocket," *Smithsonian,* August 18, 2011, https://www.smithsonianmag.com/smithsonian-institution/bf-skinners -pigeon-guided-rocket-53443995/.

25. L. L. Toussaint, E. Worthington, and D. R. Williams, *Forgiveness and Health: Scientific Evidence and Theories Relating Forgiveness to Better Health* (Dordrecht, Netherlands: Springer, 2015).

26. D. Malhotra and J. K. Murnighan, "The Effects of Contracts on Interpersonal," *Administrative Science Quarterly* 47 (2002): 534–559.

3: THE PROBLEM WITH APOLOGIES

1. J. Mooney and M. O'Toole, *Black Operations: The Secret War Against the Real IRA* (Dunboyne, Ireland: Maverick House, 2003), 156.

2. A. Mullan, "Mackey Slams Provos as RIRA Vows Resumption of Violence," *Ulster Herald,* February 7, 2008, https://web.archive.org/web/20080213223602/http:// www.nwipp-newspapers.com/UH/free/349259728115496.php.

3. J. Latson, "How Poisoned Tylenol Became a Crisis-Management Teaching Model," *Time,* September 29, 2014, https://time.com/3423136/tylenol-deaths-1982/.

4. "Crisis Communication Strategies," University of Oklahoma, https://www.ou.edu /deptcomm/dodjcc/groups/02C2/Johnson%20&%20Johnson.htm.

5. R. Donnelly, "Apology a 'Cynical Insult,'" *Irish Times,* August 19, 1998, https:// www.irishtimes.com/news/apology-a-cynical-insult-1.184391.

6. R. J. Lewicki, B. Polin, and R. B. Lount Jr., "An Exploration of the Structure of Effective Apologies," *Negotiation and Conflict Management Research* 9, no. 2 (2016): 177–196.

7. Latson, "How Poisoned Tylenol Became a Crisis-Management Teaching Model."

8. J. K. Butler Jr. and R. S. Cantrell, "A Behavioral Decision Theory Approach to Modeling Dyadic Trust in Superiors and Subordinates," *Psychological Reports* 55 (1984): 19–28. P. L. Schindler and C. C. Thomas, "The structure of interpersonal trust in the workplace," *Psychological Reports, 73* (1993): 563–573.

9. G. D. Reeder and M. B. Brewer, "A Schematic Model of Dispositional Attribution in Interpersonal Perception," *Psychological Review* 86, no. 1 (1979): 61–79.

10. P. H. Kim, D. L. Ferrin, C. D. Cooper, and K. T. Dirks, "Removing the Shadow of Suspicion: The Effects of Apology vs. Denial for Repairing Ability- vs. Integrity-Based Trust Violations," *Journal of Applied Psychology* 89, no. 1 (2004): 104–118.

11. D. H. Harmon, P. H. Kim, and K. J. Mayer, "Breaking the Letter Versus Spirit of the Law: How the Interpretation of Contract Violations Affects Trust and the Management of Relationships," *Strategic Management Journal* 36 (2015): 497–517.

12. M. D. Dubber, *Criminal Law: Model Penal Code* (New York: Foundation Press, 2002).

13. "Theranos, CEO Holmes, and Former President Balwani Charged with Massive Fraud," U.S. Securities and Exchange Commission, March 14, 2018, https://www .sec.gov/news/press release/2018 41.

14. C. Y. Johnson, "Elizabeth Holmes, Founder of Blood-Testing Company Theranos, Indicted on Wire Fraud Charges," *Washington Post,* June 15, 2018, https://www

.washingtonpost.com/business/economy/elizabeth-holmes-founder-of-blood-testing
-company-theranos-indicted-on-wire-fraud-federal-authorities-announce/2018/06
/15/8779f538-70df-11e8-bd50-b80389a4e569_story.html.

15. E. Griffith, "Elizabeth Holmes Found Guilty of Four Charges of Fraud," *New York Times,* January 3, 2022, https://www.nytimes.com/live/2022/01/03/technology /elizabeth-holmes-trial-verdict.

16. E. Griffith, "No. 2 Theranos Executive Found Guilty of 12 Counts of Fraud," *New York Times,* July 7, 2022, https://www.nytimes.com/2022/07/07/technology /ramesh-balwani-theranos-fraud.html.

17. J. Godoy, "'Failure Is Not a Crime,' Defense Says in Trial of Theranos Founder Holmes," Reuters, September 9, 2021, https://www.reuters.com/business/healthcare -pharmaceuticals/fraud-trial-theranos-founder-elizabeth-holmes-set-begin-2021-09-08/.

18. W. Isaacson, *Steve Jobs: The Exclusive Biography* (Boston: Little, Brown, 2011).

19. E. Berger, *Liftoff: Elon Musk and the Desperate Early Days That Launched SpaceX* (New York: William Morrow, 2021).

20. Scott Kupor (@skupor), Twitter, September 2, 2001, 12:23 p.m., https://twitter .com/skupor/status/1433465491603918855.

21. Godoy, "'Failure Is Not a Crime.'"

4: SOWING THE SEEDS OF OUR FRUSTRATION

1. "Central Park Five: The True Story Behind *When They See Us,*" BBC, June 12, 2019, https://www.bbc.com/news/newsbeat-48609693.

2. A. Wilkinson, "A Changing America Finally Demands That the Central Park Five Prosecutors Face Consequences," *Vox,* July 8, 2019, https://www.vox.com/the -highlight/2019/6/27/18715785/linda-fairstein-central-park-five-when-they-see-us -netflix.

3. L. Fairstein, "Netflix's False Story of the Central Park Five," *Wall Street Journal,* June 10, 2019, https://www.wsj.com/articles/netflixs-false-story-of-the-central-park-five -11560207823.

4. "*When They See Us*: History vs. Hollywood," *History vs Hollywood,* 2019, https:// www.historyvshollywood.com/reelfaces/when-they-see-us/.

5. E. Harris and J. Jacobs, "Linda Fairstein, Once Cheered, Faces Storm After 'When They See Us,'" *New York Times,* June 6, 2019, https://www.nytimes.com/2019/06 /06/arts/television/linda-fairstein-when-they-see-us.html.

6. C. Dwyer, "Linda Fairstein, Former 'Central Park 5' Prosecutor, Dropped by Her Publisher," NPR, June 7, 2019, https://www.npr.org/2019/06/07/730764565/linda -fairstein-former-central-park-5-prosecutor-dropped-by-her-publisher.

7. Wilkinson, "A Changing America."

8. J. Stempel, "Netflix Must Face Ex-Prosecutor's Defamation Lawsuit over Central Park Five Series," Reuters, August 10, 2021, https://www.reuters.com/lifestyle /netflix-must-face-ex-prosecutors-defamation-lawsuit-over-central-park-five-case -2021-08-09/.

9. Ibid.

10. "Backlash Against D&G Intensifies as Apology Fails to Appease Anger," *Global Times,* November 28, 2018, https://www.globaltimes.cn/page/201811/1129445 .shtml.

11. "Dolce&Gabbana Apologizes," YouTube video, 1:25, posted by Dolce & Gabbana, November 23, 2018, https://www.youtube.com/watch?v=7Ih62lTKicg.

12. "Backlash Against D&G Intensifies."

13. M. C. Hills, "Three Years After Ad Controversy, D&G Is Still Struggling to Win Back China," CNN, June 17, 2021, https://www.cnn.com/style/article/dolce -gabbana-karen-mok-china/index.html.

14. A. Shahani, "In Apology, Zuckerberg Promises to Protect Facebook Community," NPR, March 22, 2018, https://www.npr.org/2018/03/22/595967403/in-apology -zuckerberg-promises-to-protect-facebook-community.

15. R. Mac and S. Frenkel, "No More Apologies: Inside Facebook's Push to Defend Its Image," *New York Times,* September 21, 2021, https://www.nytimes.com/2021 /09/21/technology/zuckerberg-facebook-project-amplify.html?referringSource =articleShare.

16. J. Horowitz, "The Facebook Files," *Wall Street Journal,* https://www.wsj.com/articles /the-facebook-files-11631713039.

17. N. Clegg, "What the Wall Street Journal Got Wrong," Meta, September 18, 2021, https://about.fb.com/news/2021/09/what-the-wall-street-journal-got-wrong/.

18. B. Carey, "Denial Makes the World Go Round," *New York Times,* November 20, 2007, https://www.nytimes.com/2007/11/20/health/research/20deni.html.

19. "Ask Amy: How Do I Make Someone Apologize?," NPR, *Talk of the Nation,* October 28, 2010, https://www.npr.org/templates/story/story.php?storyId =130890844.

20. B. Engel, "Why We Need to Apologize," *Psychology Today,* June 12, 2020, https:// www.psychologytoday.com/us/blog/the-compassion-chronicles/202006/why-we -need-apologize.

21. P. H. Kim, D. L. Ferrin, C. D. Cooper, and K. T. Dirks, "Removing the Shadow of Suspicion: The Effects of Apology vs. Denial for Repairing Ability- vs. Integrity-Based Trust Violations," *Journal of Applied Psychology* 89, no. 1 (2004): 104–118.

22. M. Mays, "Complex Behavioral Trauma, Part 3: Emotional and Psychological Trauma," PartnerHope, https://partnerhope.com/complex-betrayal-trauma-part-3 -emotional-and-psychological-trauma/.

23. E. E. Levine and M. E. Schweitzer, "Prosocial Lies: When Deception Breeds Trust," *Organizational Behavior and Human Decision Process* 126 (2015): 88–106.

24. P. H. Kim, K. T. Dirks, C. D. Cooper, and D. L. Ferrin, "When More Blame Is Better Than Less: The Implications of Internal vs. External Attributions for the Repair of Trust After a Competence- vs. Integrity-Based Trust Violation," *Organizational Behavior and Human Decision Processes* 99 (2006): 49–65.

25. D. L. Ferrin, P. H. Kim, C. D. Cooper, and K. T. Dirks, "Silence Speaks Volumes: The Effectiveness of Reticence in Comparison to Apology and Denial for Responding to Integrity- and Competence-Based Trust Violations," *Journal of Applied Psychology* 92, no. 4 (2007): 893–908.

26. D. L. Roth, *Crazy from the Heat* (London: Ebury, 2000).

27. I. Shatz, "The Brown M&M's Principle: How Small Details Can Help Discover Big Issues," Effectivology, https://effectiviology.com/brown-mms/.

28. J. Zeveloff, "There's a Brilliant Reason Why Van Halen Asked for a Bowl of M&Ms with All the Brown Candies Removed Before Every Show," *Insider,* September 6, 2016, https://www.insider.com/van-halen-brown-m-ms-contract-2016-9.

29. D. H. Harmon, P. H. Kim, and K. J. Mayer, "Breaking the Letter Versus Spirit of the Law: How the Interpretation of Contract Violations Affects Trust and the Management of Relationships," *Strategic Management Journal* 36 (2015): 497–517.

5: THE SEDUCTION OF SIMPLISTIC STORIES

1. "Top 10 Apologies," *Time,* http://content.time.com/time/specials/packages/article/0,28804,1913028_1913030_1913103,00.html.

2. "Schwarzenegger Apologizes for Behavior Toward Women," CNN, October 3, 2003, https://www.cnn.com/2003/ALLPOLITICS/10/03/schwarzenegger.women/index.html.

3. S. Vedantam, "Apologies Accepted? It Depends on the Offense," *Washington Post,* September 25, 2006, https://www.washingtonpost.com/wp-dyn/content/article/2006/09/24/AR2006092400765.html.

4. O. Darcy, "Fox News Says It 'Mistakenly' Cropped Trump out of Photo Featuring Jeffrey Epstein and Ghislaine Maxwell," CNN Business, July 6, 2020, https://www.cnn.com/2020/07/06/media/fox-news-trump-crop-epstein-maxwell/index.html.

5. D. Folkenflik, "You Literally Can't Believe the Facts Tucker Carlson Tells You. So Say Fox's Lawyers," NPR, September 29, 2020, https://www.npr.org/2020/09/29/917747123/you-literally-cant-believe-the-facts-tucker-carlson-tells-you-so-say-fox-s-lawye.

6. M. C. Hills, "Three Years After Ad Controversy, D&G Is Still Struggling to Win Back China," CNN, June 17, 2021, https://www.cnn.com/style/article/dolce-gabbana-karen-mok-china/index.html.

7. "Backlash Against D&G Intensifies as Apology Fails to Appease Anger," *Global Times,* November 28, 2018, https://www.globaltimes.cn/page/201811/1129445.shtml.

8. D. Campbell, "Schwarzenegger Admits Behaving Badly After Groping Claims," *Guardian,* October 3, 2003, https://www.theguardian.com/world/2003/oct/03/usa.filmnews.

9. G. Cohn, C. Hall, and R. Welkos, "Women Say Schwarzenegger Groped, Humiliated Them," *Los Angeles Times,* October 2, 2003, https://www.latimes.com/local/la-me-archive-schwarzenegger-women-story.html.

10. "Maria Shriver Defends Husband Schwarzenegger," CNN, October 3, 2003, https://www.cnn.com/2003/ALLPOLITICS/10/03/shriver/.

11. Y. Yu, Y. Yang, and F. Jing, "The Role of the Third Party in Trust Repair Process," *Journal of Business Research* 78 (2017): 233–241.

12. "Gray Davis Recall, Governor of California (2003)," Ballotpedia, https://ballotpedia.org/Gray_Davis_recall,_Governor_of_California_(2003).

13. P. H. Kim, R. L. Pinkley, and A. R. Fragale, "Power Dynamics in Negotiation," *Academy of Management Review* 30, no. 4 (2005): 799–822.

14. "Total Recall: California's Political Circus," CNN Audio, https://www.cnn.com/audio/podcasts/total-recall?episodeguid=6d9a75c5-8f38-4b53-9b57-adb100efb55b.

15. J. West, "Melania Trump Breaks Silence about Her Husband's Sexual Assault Boast," *Mother Jones,* October 8, 2016, https://www.motherjones.com/politics/2016/10/melania-trump-reaction-trump-tape-boast-grope/.

16. T. Liddy, "Donald Trump Says 'I Was Wrong' After Groping Comments, Takes Aim at Bill Clinton," ABC News, October 8, 2016, https://abcnews.go.com/US/donald-trump-wrong-groping-comments/story?id=42660651.

17. B. Witz, "A Cog in the College Admissions Scandal Speaks Out," *New York Times,* September 27, 2021, https://www.nytimes.com/2021/09/27/sports/stanford-varsity-blues-college-admission.html.

18. Ibid.

19. J. Coleman, "Surviving Betrayal," *Greater Good Magazine,* September 1, 2008, https://greatergood.berkeley.edu/article/item/surviving_betrayal.

20. B. Brown, *Daring Greatly: How the Courage to Be Vulnerable Transforms the Way We Live, Love, Parent, and Lead* (New York: Avery, 2012).

21. S. Milgram, "Behavioral Study of Obedience," *Journal of Abnormal and Social Psychology* 67, no. 4 (1963): 371–378.

22. J. M. Darley and C. D. Batson, "'From Jerusalem to Jericho': A Study of Situational and Dispositional Variables in Helping Behavior," *Journal of Personality and Social Psychology* 27, no. 1 (1973): 100–108.

23. L. Ross, "The Intuitive Scientist and His Shortcomings," in *Advances in Experimental Social Psychology,* vol. 10, ed. L. Berkowitz (Cambridge, MA: Academic Press, 1977), 174–220.

24. Mark Zuckerberg, Facebook, October 6, 2021, https://www.facebook.com/zuck/posts/10113961365418581.

25. A. Mak, "What Mark Zuckerberg Knew and When He Knew It," *Slate*, October 6, 2021, https://slate.com/technology/2021/10/facebook-scandal-zuckerberg-what-he-knew.html.

26. J. Horowitz, "The Facebook Files," *Wall Street Journal,* https://www.wsj.com/articles/the-facebook-files-11631713039.

27. D. L. Ferrin, P. H. Kim, C. D. Cooper, and K. T. Dirks, "Silence Speaks Volumes: The Effectiveness of Reticence in Comparison to Apology and Denial for Responding to Integrity- and Competence-Based Trust Violations," *Journal of Applied Psychology* 92, no. 4 (2007): 893–908.

28. C. O'Kane, "South Korean Broadcaster Apologizes After Using Stereotypical and

Offensive Images to Represent Countries During Olympics Opening Ceremony," CBS News, July 26, 2021, https://www.cbsnews.com/news/olympics-mbc-korean -broadcast-company-apologize-offensive-images/.

29. O'Kane, "South Korean Broadcaster Apologizes."

30. S.-J. Lee, "[Newsmaker] MBC Apologizes for Tokyo Olympics Opening Ceremony Broadcast Fiasco," *Korea Herald,* July 25, 2021, http://www.koreaherald.com/view .php?ud=20210725000165.

31. H.-R. Lee, "MBC Given Slap on the Wrist for Discriminatory Olympics Broadcasts," *Korea Times,* September 10, 2021, https://www.koreatimes.co.kr/www /sports/2021/09/663_315367.html.

32. P. H. Kim, A. Mislin, E. Tuncel, R. Fehr, A. Cheshin, and G. A. Van Kleef, "Power as an Emotional Liability: Implications for Perceived Authenticity and Trust After a Transgression," *Journal of Experimental Psychology: General* 146, no. 10 (2017): 1379–1401.

33. "Backlash Against D&G Intensifies as Apology Fails to Appease Anger."

34. B. Springsteen, *Born to Run* (New York: Simon & Schuster, 2016).

6: YOUR BALANCE SHEET IS BROKEN

1. Homeboy Industries, https://homeboyindustries.org/.

2. "Criminal Justice Facts," Sentencing Project, https://www.sentencingproject.org /criminal-justice-facts/#:~:text=The%20United%20States%20is%20the,over%20 the%20last%2040%20years.

3. P. H. Kim and D. H. Harmon, "Justifying One's Transgressions: How Rationalizations Based on Equity, Equality, and Need Affect Trust After Its Violation," *Journal of Experimental Psychology: Applied* 20, no. 4 (2014): 365–379.

4. I. Kant, "The Science of Right," trans. W. Hastie, in *Great Books of the Western World,* ed. R. Hutchins (Edinburgh: T&T Clark, 1952), 397–446.

5. J. Bentham, "Principles of Penal Law," in *The Works of Jeremy Bentham,* ed. J. Bowring (Edinburgh: W. Tait, 1962), 396.

6. C. L. Ten, "Crime and Punishment," in *A Companion to Ethics,* ed. P. Singer (Oxford: Blackwell Publishers, 1993).

7. K. M. Carlsmith, "The Roles of Retribution and Utility in Determining Punishment," *Journal of Experimental Social Psychology* 42 (2006): 437–451.

8. K. M. Carlsmith and J. M. Darley, "Psychological Aspects of Retributive Justice," in *Advances in Experimental Social Psychology,* vol. 40, ed. M. P. Zanna (Cambridge, MA: Elsevier Academic Press, 2008), 193–236.

9. D. Kahneman, *Thinking, Fast and Slow* (New York: Farrar, Straus & Giroux, 2011).

10. J. D. Greene, L. E. Nystrom, A. D. Engell, J. M. Darley, and J. D. Cohen, "The Neural Bases of Cognitive Conflict and Control in Moral Judgement," *Neuron* 44 (2004): 389–400.

11. J. D. Greene, R. B. Summerville, L. E. Nystrom, J. M. Darley, and J. D. Cohen, "An fMRI Investigation of Emotional Engagement in Moral Judgment," *Science* 293 (2001): 2105–2108.

12. Carlsmith and Darley, "Psychological Aspects of Retributive Justice."

13. "Crime Survivors Speak," Alliance for Safety and Justice, https://allianceforsafetyandjustice.org/crimesurvivorsspeak/.

14. "Public Opinion on Sentencing and Corrections Policy in America," Public Opinion Strategies and the Mellman Group, March 2012, https://www.pewtrusts.org/~/media/assets/2012/03/30/pew_nationalsurveyresearchpaper_final.pdf.

15. A. Eglash, "Creative Restitution: Its Roots in Psychiatry, Religion and Law," *British Journal of Delinquency* 10, no. 2 (1959): 114–119.

16. P. Keating and S. Assael, "The USA Needs a Reckoning. Does 'Truth and Reconciliation' Actually Work?," *Mother Jones,* March 5, 2021, https://www.motherjones.com/politics/2021/03/greensboro-massacre-does-truth-and-reconciliation-actually-work/.

17. J. Latimer, C. Dowden, and D. Muise, "The Effectiveness of Restorative Justice Practices: A Meta-Analysis," *Prison Journal* 85, no. 2 (2005): 127–144.

18. L. Stack, "Light Sentence for Brock Turner in Stanford Rape Case Draws Outrage," *New York Times,* June 6, 2016, https://www.nytimes.com/2016/06/07/us/outrage-in-stanford-rape-case-over-dueling-statements-of-victim-and-attackers-father.html.

19. M. Astor, "California Voters Remove Judge Aaron Persky, Who Gave a 6-Month Sentence for Sexual Assault," *New York Times,* June 6, 2018, https://www.nytimes.com/2018/06/06/us/politics/judge-persky-brock-turner-recall.html.

20. M. Nisan, "Moral Balance: A Model of How People Arrive at Moral Decisions," in *The Moral Domain: Essays in the Ongoing Discussion Between Philosophy and the Social Sciences,* ed. T. E. Wren (Cambridge, MA: MIT Press, 1990), 283–314.

21. F. LeCraw, D. Montanera, J. Jackson, J. Keys, D. Hetzler, and T. Mroz, "Changes in Liability Claims, Costs, and Resolution Times Following the Introduction of a Communication-and-Resolution Program in Tennessee," *Journal of Patient Safety and Risk Management* 23, no. 1 (2018): 13–18, https://journals.sagepub.com/doi/full/10.1177/1356262217751808.

22. T. Fredricks, "Efficacy of a Physician's Words of Empathy: An Overview of State Apology Laws," *Journal of the American Osteopathic Association* 112, no. 7 (2012): 405–406, https://jaoa.org/article.aspx?articleid=2094307.

23. T. Molloy, "Weiner Resigns in Humiliation: 'Bye-Bye, Pervert!,'" *Wrap,* June 16, 2011, https://www.thewrap.com/weiner-resigns-congressman-out-online-sex-scandal-28292/.

24. K. T. Dirks, P. H. Kim, D. L. Ferrin, and C. D. Cooper, "Understanding the Effects of Substantive Responses on Trust Following a Transgression," *Organizational Behavior and Human Decision Processes* 114 (2011): 87–103.

25. E. Wong, "Under Fire for Perks, Chief Quits American Airlines," *New York Times,* April 25, 2003, https://www.nytimes.com/2003/04/25/business/under-fire-for -perks-chief-quits-american-airlines.html.

26. B. Monin and D. T. Miller, "Moral Credentials and the Expression of Prejudice," *Journal of Personality and Social Psychology* 81, no. 1 (2001): 33–43.

27. N. Mažar, O. Amir, and D. Ariely, "The Dishonesty of Honest People: A Theory of Self-Concept Maintenance," *Journal of Marketing Research* 45, no. 6 (2008): 633–644.

28. P. H. Kim, J. Han, A. A. Mislin, and E. Tuncel, "The Retrospective Imputation of Nefarious Intent," *Academy of Management Proceedings* 1 (2019): 16137.

29. W. Isaacson, *Steve Jobs* (New York: Simon & Schuster, 2011).

30. A. Tapalaga, "Steve Jobs' Dark Past," *Medium,* October 3, 2020, https://medium .com/history-of-yesterday/steve-jobss-dark-past-55a98044f3b4.

31. R. Reynolds, "Why Couples Fail After an Affair: Part 2—Not Getting It," Affair Recovery, https://www.affairrecovery.com/newsletter/founder/infidelity-unfaithful -spouse-needs-to-show-empathy.

32. B. Stevenson, *Just Mercy: A Story of Justice and Redemption* (London: One World, 2014).

7: THE POTENTATE'S CURSE

1. P. Radden Keefe, "The Sackler Family's Plan to Keep Its Billions," *New Yorker,* October 4, 2020, https://www.newyorker.com/news/news-desk/the-sackler-familys -plan-to-keep-its-billions.

2. M. Holcombe and M. Schuman, "Multiple States Say the Opioid Crisis Cost American Economy over $2 Trillion," CNN, August 18, 2020, https://www .cnn.com/2020/08/18/us/opioid-crisis-cost-united-state-2-trillion-dollars/index .html.

3. D. Knauth and T. Hals, "Purdue Pharma Judge Overrules DOJ to Approve $6 Bln Opioid Settlement," Reuters, March 9, 2022, https://www.reuters.com/legal /transactional/purdue-seeks-approval-6-billion-opioid-settlement-over-state-doj -objections-2022-03-09/.

4. E. Crankshaw, *Maria Theresa* (New York: Viking, 1970).

5. L. Morrow, "A Reckoning with Martin Luther King," *Wall Street Journal,* June 17, 2019, https://www.wsj.com/articles/a-reckoning-with-martin-luther-king -11560813491.

6. P. H. Kim, R. L. Pinkley, and A. R. Fragale, "Power Dynamics in Negotiation," *Academy of Management Review* 30, no. 4 (2005): 799–822.

7. P. H. Kim and A. R. Fragale, "Choosing the Path to Bargaining Power: An Empirical Comparison of BATNAs and Contributions in Negotiation," *Journal of Applied Psychology* 90, no. 2 (2005): 373–381.

8. M. Jurkowitz and A. Mitchell, "An Oasis of Bipartisanship: Republicans and Democrats Distrust Social Media Sites for Political and Election News," Pew

Research Center, January 29, 2020, https://www.pewresearch.org/journalism/2020/01/29/an-oasis-of-bipartisanship-republicans-and-democrats-distrust-social-media-sites-for-political-and-election-news/.

9. B. Auxier and M. Anderson, "Social Media Use in 2021," Pew Research Center, April 7, 2021, https://www.pewresearch.org/internet/2021/04/07/social-media-use-in-2021/.

10. B. Hart, "Two MLK Scholars Discuss Explosive, Disputed FBI Files on the Civil-Rights Icon," *New York,* June 30, 2019, https://nymag.com/intelligencer/2019/06/martin-luther-king-fbi-files.html.

11. J. R. Meindl, S. B. Ehrlich, and J. M. Dukerich, "The Romance of Leadership," *Administrative Science Quarterly* 30 (1985): 78–102.

12. J. R. Overbeck, L. Z. Tiedens, and S. Brion, "The Powerful Want To, the Powerless Have To: Perceived Constraint Moderates Causal Attributions," *European Journal of Social Psychology* 36 (2006): 479–496.

13. C. Friedersdorf, "The Fight Against Words That Sound Like, but Are Not, Slurs," *Atlantic,* September 21, 2020, https://www.theatlantic.com/ideas/archive/2020/09/fight-against-words-sound-like-are-not-slurs/616404/.

14. P. H. Kim, A. Mislin, E. Tuncel, R. Fehr, A. Cheshin, and G. A. Van Kleef, "Power as an Emotional Liability: Implications for Perceived Authenticity and Trust After a Transgression," *Journal of Experimental Psychology: General* 146, no. 10 (2017): 1379–1401.

15. P. Reilly, "No Laughter Among Thieves: Authenticity and the Enforcement of Community Norms in Stand-Up Comedy," *American Sociological Review* 83, no. 5 (2018): 933–958.

16. D. McAdams, "The Mind of Donald Trump," *Atlantic,* June 2016, https://www.theatlantic.com/magazine/archive/2016/06/the-mind-of-donald-trump/480771/.

17. E. Lutz, "Trump Admits Russia Helped Him Win, Denies It 20 Minutes Later," *Vanity Fair,* May 30, 2019, https://www.vanityfair.com/news/2019/05/trump-admits-russia-helped-him-win-denies-it-20-minutes-later.

18. J. M. George, "Emotions and Leadership: The Role of Emotional Intelligence," *Human Relations* 53, no. 8 (2000): 1027–1055.

19. M. W. Kraus, S. Chen, and D. Keltner, "The Power to Be Me: Power Elevates Self-Concept Consistency and Authenticity," *Journal of Experimental Social Psychology* 47 (2011): 974–980.

20. R. Ransby, "A Black Feminist's Response to Attacks on Martin Luther King Jr.'s Legacy," *New York Times,* June 3, 2019, https://www.nytimes.com/2019/06/03/opinion/martin-luther-king-fbi.html.

21. M. V. Thompson, *The Only Unavoidable Subject of Regret: George Washington, Slavery, and the Enslaved Community at Mount Vernon* (Charlottesville: University of Virginia Press, 2019).

22. "America's Gandhi: Rev. Martin Luther King Jr.," *Time,* January 3, 1964, http://content.time.com/time/subscriber/article/0,33009,940759-3,00.html.

23. R. D. Abernathy, *And the Walls Came Tumbling Down: An Autobiography* (New York: Harper & Row, 1989).

24. W. K. Krueger, *Northwest Angle* (New York: Atria Books, 2011).

8: BEWARE THE HIVE MIND

1. J. Heim, "Recounting a Day of Rage, Hate, Violence and Death," *Washington Post*, August 12, 2017, https://www.washingtonpost.com/graphics/2017/local/charlottesville-timeline/.

2. "Social Judgment Theory Experiment," Explorable, June 10, 2010, https://explorable.com/social-judgment-theory-experiment.

3. "Group Perception: Hastorf and Cantril," Age of the Sage, https://www.age-of-the-sage.org/psychology/social/hastorf_cantril_saw_game.html.

4. N. Hajari, *Midnight's Furies: The Deadly Legacy of India's Partition* (New York: Penguin, 2016).

5. W. Dalrymple, "The Great Divide," *New Yorker*, June 22, 2015, https://www.newyorker.com/magazine/2015/06/29/the-great-divide-books-dalrymple.

6. A. Muldoon, *Empire, Politics and the Creation of the 1935 India Act: Last Act of the Raj* (London: Ashgate, 2013).

7. F. Robinson, "The British Empire and Muslim identity in South Asia," *Transactions of the Royal Historical Society* 8 (1998): 271–289.

8. A. J. Christopher, "'Divide and Rule': The Impress of British Separation Policies," *Area* 20, no. 3 (1988): 233–240.

9. P. D. Joshi, N. J. Fast, and P. H. Kim, "The Curse of Loyalty: Cultural Interdependence and Support for Pro-Organizational Corruption," paper presented at the virtual Annual Meeting of the Academy of Management, August 7–11, 2020.

10. "Police Union Head Says Race Didn't Play a Role in Breonna Taylor Shooting, Believes Investigation Was 'Thorough,'" CBS News, October 29, 2020, https://www.cbsnews.com/news/breonna-taylor-police-union-ryan-nichols/.

11. A. Forliti, "Prosecutors: Officer Was on Floyd's Neck for About 9 Minutes," AP News, March 4, 2021, https://apnews.com/article/trials-derek-chauvin-minneapolis-racial-injustice-060f6e9e8b7079505a1b096a68311c2b.

12. M. Nesterak, "'I Didn't See Race in George Floyd.' Police Union Speaks for First Time Since Killing," *Minnesota Reformer*, June 23, 2020, https://minnesotareformer.com/2020/06/23/i-didnt-see-race-in-george-floyd-police-union-speaks-for-first-time-since-killing/.

13. J. Campbell and J. Jones, "Four Weeks After George Floyd's Death, an Embattled Police Union Finally Speaks Out," CNN, June 23, 2020, https://www.cnn.com/2020/06/23/us/minneapolis-police-union-intvu/index.html.

14. B. Park and M. Rothbart, "Perception of Out-Group Similarity and Level of Social Categorization," *Journal of Personality and Social Psychology* 42, no. 6 (1982): 1051–1068.

15. J. McGahan, "How USC Became the Most Scandal-Plagued Campus in America,"

Los Angeles Magazine, April 24, 2019, https://www.lamag.com/citythinkblog/usc -scandals-cover/.

16. Los Angeles Times Investigative Team, "An Overdose, a Young Companion, Drug-Fueled Parties: The Secret Life of a USC Med School Dean," *Los Angeles Times,* July 17, 2017, https://www.latimes.com/local/california/la-me-usc-doctor-20170717 -htmlstory.html.

17. D. Rapaport, "What We Know About Each School Implicated in the FBI's College Basketball Investigation," *Sports Illustrated,* November 17, 2017, https://www.si .com/college/2017/11/17/what-we-know-about-each-school-fbi-investigation.

18. H. Ryan, M. Hamilton, and P. Pringle, "A USC Doctor Was Accused of Bad Behavior with Young Women for Years. The University Let Him Continue Treating Students," *Los Angeles Times,* May 16, 2018, https://www.latimes.com/local /california/la-me-usc-doctor-misconduct-complaints-20180515-story.html.

19. McGahan, "How USC Became the Most Scandal-Plagued Campus."

20. C. Weber, "USC Ex-Dean, LA Politician Charged with Bribery Scheme," AP News, October 13, 2021, https://apnews.com/article/university-of-southern -california-los-angeles-california-scholarships-education-0533487b999544cbf79ec f0da535c5a2.

21. A. Gross, "As a USC Professor, I Can't Stay Quiet About the Administration's Toxic Culture," *Los Angeles Times,* November 3, 2021, https://www.latimes.com/opinion /story/2021-11-03/uscs-administrative-culture-is-still-rotten-from-the-top-we -faculty-wont-keep-quiet.

22. "Commitment to Change," University of Southern California, https://change.usc .edu/.

23. "We Are SC," University of Southern California, https://we-are.usc.edu/.

24. M. Forsythe and W. Bogdanich, "McKinsey Settles for Nearly $600 Million over Role in Opioid Crisis," *New York Times,* February 3, 2021, https://www.nytimes .com/2021/02/03/business/mckinsey-opioids-settlement.html.

25. I. MacDougall, "How McKinsey Helped the Trump Administration Carry Out Its Immigration Policies," *New York Times,* December 9, 2019, https://www.nytimes .com/2019/12/03/us/mckinsey-ICE-immigration.html.

26. S. Hwang and R. Silverman, "McKinsey's Close Relationship with Enron Raises Question of Consultancy's Liability," *Wall Street Journal,* January 17, 2002, https:// www.wsj.com/articles/SB1011226439418112600/.

27. P. H. Kim, S. S. Wiltermuth, and D. T. Newman, "A Theory of Ethical Accounting and Its Implications for Hypocrisy in Organizations," *Academy of Management Review* 48, no. 1 (2021): 172–191.

28. C. R. Sustein and R. Hastie, *Wiser: Getting Beyond Groupthink to Make Groups Smarter* (Boston: Harvard Business Review Press, 2014).

29. G. Aisch, J. Huang, and C. Kang, "Dissecting the #PizzaGate Conspiracy Theories," *New York Times,* December 10, 2016, https://www.nytimes.com /interactive/2016/12/10/business/media/pizzagate.html.

30. P. H. Kim, C. D. Cooper, K. T. Dirks, and D. L. Ferrin, "Repairing Trust with

Individuals vs. Groups," *Organizational Behavior and Human Decision Processes* 120, no. 1 (2013): 1–14.

31. E. McMorris-Santoro and Y. Pomrenze, "A Small-Town Mom Wanted to Help Her Community. and Then the Community Took Aim at Her Child," CNN, November 29, 2021, https://www.cnn.com/2021/11/28/us/minnesota-school -board-transgender-hate/index.html.

32. K. Waits, "Building Community, Together," *Hastings Journal,* August 11, 2021, https://www.thepaperboy.news/2021/08/11/building-community-together -20210811154958/?destination=hastings-journal.

33. "Drowning of a Witch," National Archives, https://www.nationalarchives.gov.uk /education/resources/early-modern-witch-trials/drowning-of-a-witch/.

34. D. H. Gruenfeld, M. Thomas-Hunt, and P. H. Kim, "Divergent Thinking, Accountability, and Integrative Complexity: Public Versus Private Reactions to Majority and Minority Status," *Journal of Experimental Social Psychology* 34 (1998): 202–226.

35. P. H. Kim, "When What You Know Can Hurt You: A Study of Experiential Effects on Group Discussion and Performance," *Organizational Behavior and Human Decision Processes* 69, no. 2 (1997): 165–177.

9: PLAYING THE WRONG RULES OF THE GAME

1. H. French, "The Pretenders," *New York Times Magazine,* December 3, 2000, https:// archive.nytimes.com/www.nytimes.com/library/magazine/home/20001203mag -french.html.

2. Associated Press, "Debt and Suicide: Japan's Culture of Shame," *Deseret News,* March 7, 2003, https://www.deseret.com/2003/3/7/19708183/debt-and-suicide -japan-s-culture-of-shame.

3. V. Giang and A. Horowitz, "19 Successful People Who Have Been Fired," *Business Insider,* October 19, 2013, https://www.businessinsider.com/people-who-were-fired -before-they-became-rich-and-famous-2013-10?op=1#madonna-lost-her-job-at -dunkin-donuts-for-squirting-jelly-filling-all-over-customers-8.

4. E. Trex, "7 Wildly Successful People Who Survived Bankruptcy," *Mental Floss,* November 5, 2015, https://www.mentalfloss.com/article/20169/7-wildly-successful -people-who-survived-bankruptcy.

5. D. Kelly, "The Untold Truth of Hershey," *Mashed,* October 18, 2021, https://www .mashed.com/112889/untold-truth-hershey/.

6. N. Martin, "The Role of History and Culture in Developing Bankruptcy and Insolvency Systems: The Perils of Legal Transplantation," *Boston College International and Comparative Law Review* 28, no. 2 (2005), https://www.bc.edu/content/dam /files/schools/law/lawreviews/journals/bciclr/28_1/01_TXT.htm.

7. Y. Kin, "Western Japan Mayor Under Fire for Personal Bankruptcy Filing," *Mainichi,* August 7, 2020, https://mainichi.jp/english/articles/20200807/p2a/00m /0na/028000c.

8. S. Liu, M. W. Morris, T. Talhelm, and Q. Yang, "Ingroup Vigilance in Collectivistic

Culture," *Proceedings of the National Academy of Sciences* 116, no. 29 (2019): 14538–14546, https://doi.org/10.1073/pnas.1817588116.

9. M. Gelfand, *Rule Makers, Rule Breakers: How Tight and Loose Cultures Wire Our World* (New York: Simon & Schuster, 2018).

10. T. Menon, M. W. Morris, C.-Y. Chiu, and Y.-Y. Hong, "Culture and the Construal of Agency: Attribution to Individual Versus Group Dispositions," *Journal of Personality and Social Psychology* 76, no. 5 (1999): 701–717, https://doi.org/10.1037/0022-3514.76.5.701.

11. I. Choi, R. Dalal, C. Kim-Prieto, and H. Park, "Culture and Judgement of Causal Relevance," *Journal of Personality and Social Psychology* 84, no. 1 (2003): 46–59, https://doi.org/10.1037/0022-3514.84.1.46.

12. E. Flitter, "The Price of Wells Fargo's Fake Account Scandal Grows by $3 Billion," *New York Times,* February 21, 2020, https://www.nytimes.com/2020/02/21/business/wells-fargo-settlement.html.

13. T. Yamagishi and M. Yamagishi, "Trust and Commitment in the United States and Japan," *Motivation and Emotion* 18, no. 2 (1994): 129–166.

14. C. Haberman, "The Apology in Japan: Mea Culpa Spoken Here," *New York Times,* October 4, 1986, https://www.nytimes.com/1986/10/04/world/the-apology-in-japan-mea-culpa-spoken-here.html.

15. W. W. Maddux, P. H. Kim, T. Okumura, and J. Brett, "Cultural Differences in the Function and Meaning of Apology," *International Negotiation* 16 (2011): 405–425.

16. J. Graham, B. A. Nosek, J. Haidt, R. Iyer, S. Koleva, and P. H. Ditto, "Mapping the Moral Domain," *Journal of Personality and Social Psychology* 101, no. 2 (2011): 366–385.

17. J. Graham, J. Haidt, and B. A. Nosek, "Liberals and Conservatives Rely on Different Sets of Moral Foundations," *Journal of Personality and Social Psychology* 96, no. 5 (2009): 1029–1046.

18. D. L. Sayers, *Gaudy Night* (New York: Harper & Row, 1986).

19. P. Buchanan, "Culture War Speech. Address to the Republican National Convention," Voices of Democracy, August 17, 1992, https://voicesofdemocracy.umd.edu/Buchanan-culture-war-speech-speech-text/.

20. J. D. Hunter, *Culture Wars: The Struggle to Define America* (New York: Basic Books, 1991).

21. J. Haidt, "The Emotional Dog and Its Rational Tail: A Social Intuitionist Approach to Moral Judgment," *Psychological Review* 108, no. 4 (2001): 814–834.

22. P. E. Tetlock, "Thinking the Unthinkable: Sacred Values and Taboo Cognitions," *Trends in Cognitive Sciences* 7, no. 7 (2003): 320–324.

23. Associated Press, "Cheney at Odds with Bush on Gay Marriage," NBC News, August 25, 2004, https://www.nbcnews.com/id/wbna5817720.

24. J. Hohmann and K. Glueck, "Dick Cheney Takes Liz's Side," *Politico,* November 18, 2013, https://www.politico.com/story/2013/11/dick-cheney-liz-cheney-gay-marriage-099999.

25. L. Stahl, "Liz Cheney on Being a Republican While Opposing Donald Trump," *60*

Minutes, September 26, 2021, https://www.cbsnews.com/news/liz-cheney-donald
-trump-wyoming-60-minutes-2021-09-26/.

26. I. W. Zartman, "The Timing of Peace Initiatives: Hurting Stalemates and Ripe
Moments," *Global Review of Ethnopolitics* 1, no. 1 (2001): 8–18.

10: BEYOND THE RAVAGES OF HISTORY

1. "The Nine Lives of Rwanda Genocide Survivor Albertine," France 24, January 27,
2021, https://www.france24.com/en/live-news/20210127-the-nine-lives-of-rwanda
-genocide-survivor-albertine.

2. "Rwanda Genocide: 100 Days of Slaughter," BBC, April 4, 2019, https://www.bbc
.com/news/world-africa-26875506.

3. T. Bamford, "The Nuremberg Trial and Its Legacy," National WWII Museum,
November 17, 2020, https://www.nationalww2museum.org/war/articles/the
-nuremberg-trial-and-its-legacy.

4. Ibid.

5. N. Frei, *Adenauer's Germany and the Nazi Past,* trans. J. Gold (New York: Columbia
University Press, 2002).

6. J. W. Scott, *On the Judgment of History* (New York: Columbia University Press,
2002).

7. Bamford, "The Nuremberg Trial and Its Legacy."

8. Scott, *On the Judgment of History.*

9. Frei, *Adenauer's Germany and the Nazi Past.*

10. Scott, *On the Judgment of History.*

11. "Report of the Chilean National Commission on Truth and Reconciliation," United
States Institute of Peace, posted by the USIP Library on October 4, 2002, https:
//www.usip.org/sites/default/files/resources/collections/truth_commissions/Chile90
-Report/Chile90-Report.pdf.

12. "Truth and Reconciliation Commission," Department of Justice and Constitutional
Development, https://www.justice.gov.za/trc/.

13. D. W. Shriver Jr., "Truth Commissions and Judicial Trials: Complementary or
Antagonistic Servants of Public Justice?," *Journal of Law and Religion* 16, no. 1
(2001): 1–33.

14. National University of Rwanda—Centre for Geographic Information System and
Remote Sensing, "Justice Compromised: The Legacy of Rwanda's Community-Based
Gacaca Courts," Human Rights Watch, May 31, 2011, https://www.hrw.org/report
/2011/05/31/justice-compromised/legacy-rwandas-community-based-gacaca-courts#.

15. "The ICTR in Brief," United Nations International Residual Mechanism for
Criminal Tribunals, https://unictr.irmct.org/en/tribunal.

16. National University of Rwanda, "Justice Compromised."

17. "What Is Transitional Justice?," International Center for Transitional Justice, https://
www.ictj.org/about/transitional-justice.

18. T. Ryback, "Evidence of Evil," *New Yorker,* November 7, 1993, https://www
.newyorker.com/magazine/1993/11/15/evidence-of-evil.

19. G. York, "At Least 1,200 Are Also Missing or Murdered in South Africa," *Globe and Mail,* April 1, 2016, https://www.theglobeandmail.com/news/world/south-african -families-seek-closure-for-loved-ones-abducted-during-apartheid/article29504241/.

20. "Rwanda," International Commission on Missing Persons, https://www.icmp.int /the-missing/where-are-the-missing/rwanda/.

21. *Truth and Reconciliation Commission of South Africa Report: Volume One,* Department of Justice and Constitutional Development, October 29, 1988, https:// www.justice.gov.za/trc/report/finalreport/Volume%201.pdf.

22. A. Krog, *Country of My Skull: Guilt, Sorrow, and the Limits of Forgiveness in the New South Africa* (New York: Crown, 1999).

23. Shriver, "Truth Commissions and Judicial Trials."

24. "Treaty of Versailles," Holocaust Encyclopedia, https://encyclopedia.ushmm.org /content/en/article/treaty-of-versailles.

25. M. J. Osiel, *Obeying Orders: Atrocity, Military Discipline, and the Law of War* (Piscataway, NJ: Transaction Publishers, 1999).

26. S. Daley, "Apartheid Torturer Testifies, as Evil Shows Its Banal Face," *New York Times,* November 9, 1997, https://www.nytimes.com/1997/11/09/world/apartheid -torturer-testifies-as-evil-shows-its-banal-face.html.

27. Shriver, "Truth Commissions and Judicial Trials."

28. K. S. Pope and L. S. Brown, *Recovered Memories of Abuse: Assessment, Therapy, Forensics* (Washington, DC: American Psychological Association, 1996).

29. B. A. van der Kolk and R. Fisler, "Dissociation and the Fragmentary Nature of Memories: Overview and Exploratory Study," *Journal of Traumatic Stress* 8 (1995): 505–525.

30. B. van der Kolk, *The Body Keeps the Score: Brain, Mind, and Body in the Healing of Trauma* (New York: Penguin, 2015).

31. *Truth and Reconciliation Commission of South Africa Report: Volume One.*

32. M. Fulbrook, *Reckonings: Legacies of Nazi Persecution and the Quest for Justice* (New York: Oxford University Press, 2018).

33. *Monitoring and Research Report on the Gacaca: Testimonies and Evidence in the Gacaca Courts* (London: Penal Reform International, 2008), https://cdn.penalreform.org/wp -content/uploads/2013/05/Gacaca-Report-11-testimony-and-evidence-1.pdf.

34. "The Rwandan Patriotic Front," Human Rights Watch, https://www.hrw.org/legacy /reports/1999/rwanda/Geno15-8-03.htm.

35. J. Rever, *In Praise of Blood: The Crimes of the Rwandan Patriotic Front* (Toronto: Random House Canada, 2018).

36. Z. Moloo, "The Crimes of the Rwandan Patriotic Front," Africa Is a Country, April 10, 2019, https://africasacountry.com/2019/04/the-crimes-of-the-rwanda -patriotic-front.

37. A. Chakravarty, *Investing in Authoritarian Rule: Punishment and Patronage in Rwanda's Gacaca Courts for Genocide Crimes* (New York: Cambridge University Press, 2015).

38. *Monitoring and Research Report on the Gacaca.*

39. A. Boraine, *A Country Unmasked: Inside South Africa's Truth and Reconciliation Commission* (New York: Oxford University Press, 2001).

40. Krog, *Country of My Skull.*

41. G. York, "Apartheid's Victims Bring the Crimes of South Africa's Past into Court at Last," *Globe and Mail,* April 16, 2019, https://www.theglobeandmail.com/world /article-apartheids-victims-bring-the-crimes-of-south-africas-past-into-court/.

42. Scott, *On the Judgment of History.*

43. Ibid.

44. *Truth and Reconciliation Commission of South Africa Report: Volume Five,* Department of Justice and Constitutional Development, https://www.justice.gov.za /trc/report/finalreport/Volume5.pdf.

45. "Tutu: 'Unfinished Business' of the TRC's Healing," *Mail & Guardian,* April 24, 2014, https://mg.co.za/article/2014-04-24-unfinished-business-of-the-trc-healing/.

46. P. Keating and S. Assael, "The USA Needs a Reckoning. Does 'Truth and Reconciliation' Actually Work?," *Mother Jones,* March 5, 2021, https://www .motherjones.com/politics/2021/03/greensboro-massacre-does-truth-and -reconciliation-actually-work/.

47. N. Milne, "The Tale of Two Slums in South Africa as Residents Seek to Upgrade Lives," Reuters, December 14, 2016, https://www.reuters.com/article/us-safrica -slums-upgrading/the-tale-of-two-slums-in-south-africa-as-residents-seek-to -upgrade-lives-idUSKBN1431PO.

48. Scott, *On the Judgment of History.*

49. "Tutu: 'Unfinished Business.'"

50. Frei, *Adenauer's Germany and the Nazi Past.*

51. National University of Rwanda, "Justice Compromised."

52. Boraine, *A Country Unmasked.*

53. "Tutu: 'Unfinished business.'"

54. Keating and Assael, "The USA Needs a Reckoning."

55. Ibid.

56. Ibid.

57. J. L. Gibson, "On Legitimacy Theory and the Effectiveness of Truth Commissions," *Law and Contemporary Problems* 72, no. 2 (2009): 123–141.

58. E. Kiss, "Moral Ambition Within and Beyond Political Constraints: Reflections on Restorative Justice," in *Truth v. Justice,* ed. R. I. Rotberg and D. Thompson (Princeton, NJ: Princeton University Press, 2010), 68–98.

59. M. Ignatieff, "Articles of Faith," NiZA, http://archive.niza.nl/uk/publications/001 /ignatieff.htm.

60. Scott, *On the Judgment of History.*

61. Keating and Assael, "The USA Needs a Reckoning."

11: HOW WE MOVE FORWARD

1. "Reports of Officers," *Journal of the American Medical Association* 162, no. 8 (1956): 748–819, https://doi.org/10.1001/jama.1956.02970250048013.

2. J. Poushter and N. Kent, "The Global Divide on Homosexuality Persists," Pew Research Center, June 25, 2020, https://www.pewresearch.org/global/2020/06/25/global-divide-on-homosexuality-persists/.

3. P. Kambam and C. Thompson, "The Development of Decision-Making Capabilities in Children and Adolescents: Psychological and Neurological Perspectives and Their Implications for Juvenile Defendants," *Behavioral Sciences and the Law* 27 (2009): 173–190.

4. P. H. Kim, S. S. Wiltermuth, and D. Newman, "A Theory of Ethical Accounting and Its Implications for Hypocrisy in Organizations," *Academy of Management Review* 46, no. 1 (2021): 172–191.

5. P. H. Kim and D. J. Harmon, "Justifying One's Transgressions: How Rationalizations Based on Equity, Equality, and Need Affect Trust After Its Violation," *Journal of Experimental Psychology: Applied* 20, no. 4 (2014): 365–379.

6. S. N. Durlauf and D. S. Nagin, "Imprisonment and Crime: Can Both Be Reduced?," *Criminology & Public Policy* 10, no. 1 (2011): 13–54, https://doi.org/10.1111/j.1745-9133.2010.00680.x.

7. J. Mathews II and F. Curiel, "Criminal Justice Debt Problems," *American Bar Association: Human Rights Magazine* 44, no. 3 (2019), https://www.americanbar.org/groups/crsj/publications/human_rights_magazine_home/economic-justice/criminal-justice-debt-problems/.

8. A. AbuDagga, S. Wolfe, M. Carome, A. Phatdouang, and E. Fuller Torrey, *Individuals with Serious Mental Illnesses in County Jails: A Survey of Jail Staff's Perspectives,* Public Citizen's Health Research Group and the Treatment Advocacy Center, July 14, 2016, https://www.treatmentadvocacycenter.org/storage/documents/jail-survey-report-2016.pdf.

9. "Section IV: Global Comparisons," Prison Policy Initiative, *The Prison Index: Taking the Pulse of the Crime Control Industry,* https://www.prisonpolicy.org/prisonindex/us_southafrica.html.

10. "Recidivism and Reentry," Bureau of Justice Statistics, https://www.bjs.gov/content/reentry/recidivism.cfm.

11. E. James, "Interview: 'Prison Is Not for Punishment in Sweden. We Get People into Better Shape,'" *Guardian,* November 26, 2014, https://www.theguardian.com/society/2014/nov/26/prison-sweden-not-punishment-nils-oberg.

12. J. Steinbeck, *East of Eden* (New York: Penguin, 2002).

13. P. H. Kim, K. A. Diekmann, and A. E. Tenbrunsel, "Flattery May Get You Somewhere: The Strategic Implications of Providing Positive vs. Negative Feedback About Ability vs. Ethicality in Negotiation," *Organizational Behavior and Human Decision Processes* 90, no. 2 (2003): 225–243.

14. N. Mažar, O. Amir, and D. Ariely, "The Dishonesty of Honest People: A Theory of Self-Concept Maintenance," *Journal of Marketing Research* 45, no. 6 (2008): 633–644.

15. B. Monin and D. T. Miller, "Moral Credentials and the Expression of Prejudice," *Journal of Personality and Social Psychology* 81, no. 1 (2001): 33–43.

16. P. H. Kim, A. J. Han, A. A. Mislin, and E. Tuncel, "The Retrospective Imputation of Nefarious Intent," *Academy of Management Proceedings* 1 (2019): 16137.

17. D. L. Ferrin, P. H. Kim, C. D. Cooper, and K. T. Dirks, "Silence Speaks Volumes: The Effectiveness of Reticence in Comparison to Apology and Denial for Responding to Integrity- and Competence-Based Trust Violations," *Journal of Applied Psychology* 92, no. 4 (2007): 893–908.

18. Kim, Wiltermuth, and Newman, "A Theory of Ethical Accounting."

19. S. L. Murray and J. G. Holmes, "Seeing Virtues in Faults: Negativity and the Transformation of Interpersonal Narratives in Close Relationships," *Journal of Personality and Social Psychology* 65, no. 4 (1993): 707–722.

20. P. H. Kim, D. L. Ferrin, C. D. Cooper, and K. T. Dirks, "Removing the Shadow of Suspicion: The Effects of Apology vs. Denial for Repairing Ability- vs. Integrity-Based Trust Violations," *Journal of Applied Psychology* 89, no. 1 (2004): 104–118.

21. J. Graham, J. Haidt, and B. A. Nosek, "Liberals and Conservatives Rely on Different Sets of Moral Foundations," *Journal of Personality and Social Psychology* 96, no. 5 (2009): 1029–1046.

22. "The Power of Extravagant Tenderness with Father Gregory Boyle," *Impact Podcast with John Shegerian,* December 22, 2021, https://impactpodcast.com/episode/2021/12/the-power-of-extravagant-tenderness-with-father-gregory-boyle/.

CONCLUSION

1. E. Wong, "Bond Between China and Russia Alarms U.S. and Europe amid Ukraine Crisis," *New York Times,* February 20, 2022, https://www.nytimes.com/2022/02/20/us/politics/russia-china-ukraine-biden.html.

2. "Ukraine: Civilian Casualty Update," United Nations Office of the High Commissioner for Human Rights, May 2, 2022, https://www.ohchr.org/en/news/2022/05/ukraine-civilian-casualty-update-2-may-2022.

3. "How Many Ukrainians Have Fled Their Homes and Where Have They Gone?," BBC, June 6, 2022, https://www.bbc.com/news/world-60555472.

4. F. Ordoñez, "The Complex Effort to Hold Vladimir Putin Accountable for War Crimes," NPR, May 3, 2022, https://www.npr.org/2022/05/03/1096094936/Ukraine-russia-war-crimes-investigations.

5. "Exhaustive Fact Check Finds Little Evidence of Voter Fraud, but 2020's 'Big Lie' Lives On," *PBS NewsHour,* December 17, 2021, https://www.pbs.org/newshour/show/exhaustive-fact-check-finds-little-evidence-of-voter-fraud-but-2020s-big-lie-lives-on.

6. R. Treisman, "Putin's Claim of Fighting Against Ukraine 'Neo-Nazis' Distorts History, Scholars Say," NPR, March 1, 2022, https://www.npr.org/2022/03/01/1083677765/putin-denazify-ukraine-russia-history.

7. S. Collinson, "Trump-Style Populism Rises in US and Europe as Putin Assaults World Order," CNN, April 12, 2022, https://www.cnn.com/2022/04/12/politics/rise-of-extremism-us-and-europe/index.html.

8. "Fact Sheet: United States, European Union, and G7 to Announce Further

Economic Costs on Russia," White House, March 11, 2022, https://www
.whitehouse.gov/briefing-room/statements-releases/2022/03/11/fact-sheet-united
-states-european-union-and-g7-to-announce-further-economic-costs-on-russia/.

9. "Almost 1,000 Companies Have Curtailed Operations in Russia—but Some
Remain," Yale School of Management, Chief Executive Leadership Institute, June
12, 2022, https://som.yale.edu/story/2022/almost-1000-companies-have-curtailed
-operations-russia-some-remain.

10. D. De Luce, "A New Cold War Without Rules: U.S. Braces for a Long-Term
Confrontation with Russia," NBC News, March 6, 2022, https://www.nbcnews
.com/news/investigations/new-cold-war-rules-us-braces-long-term-confrontation
-russia-rcna18554.

11. A. Roth, "'Warmongering, Lies and Hatred': Russian Diplomat in Geneva Resigns
over Ukraine Invasion," *Guardian,* May 23, 2022, https://www.theguardian.com
/world/2022/may/23/warmongering-lies-and-hatred-russian-diplomat-in-geneva
-resigns-over-ukraine-invasion?CMP=oth_b-aplnews_d-1.

12. B. Klein, "This Isn't a New Cold War. It's Worse," *Barron's,* April 7, 2022, https:
//www.barrons.com/articles/this-isnt-a-new-cold-war-its-worse-51649359292.

13. M. Pengelly, "Republican Party Calls January 6 Attach 'Legitimate Political
Discourse,'" *Guardian,* February 4, 2022, https://www.theguardian.com/us-news
/2022/feb/04/republicans-capitol-attack-legitimate-political-discourse-cheney
-kinzinger-pence.

14. H. Beech, A. L. Dahir, and O. Lopez, "With Us or with Them? In a New Cold
War, How About Neither," *New York Times,* April 24, 2022, https://www.nytimes
.com/2022/04/24/world/asia/cold-war-ukraine.html.

ABOUT THE AUTHOR

DR. PETER H. KIM is a professor of management and organization at the University of Southern California's Marshall School of Business. His research has been published in numerous scholarly journals, received ten national and international awards, and been featured by *The New York Times, The Washington Post,* and National Public Radio.